By the same author

THE SILVER SALVER

The Story of the Guinness Family

THE SILVER SALVER

The Story of the Guinness Family

Frederic Mullally

GRANADA
London Toronto Sydney New York

Granada Publishing Limited
Frogmore, St Albans, Herts AL2 2NF
and
36 Golden Square, London W1R 4AH
866 United Nations Plaza, New York, NY 10017, USA
117 York Street, Sydney, NSW 2000, Australia
100 Skyway Avenue, Rexdale, Ontario M9W 3A6, Canada
61 Beach Road, Auckland, New Zealand

Published by Granada Publishing 1981

ISBN 0 246 11271 9

Printed in Great Britain
by Mackays of Chatham Ltd

Granada ®
Granada Publishing ®

Contents

For Lauren

The Guinness Family Genealogical Charts

TABLE 1
THE SENIOR BRANCH (1) FROM RICHARD OF CELBRIDGE

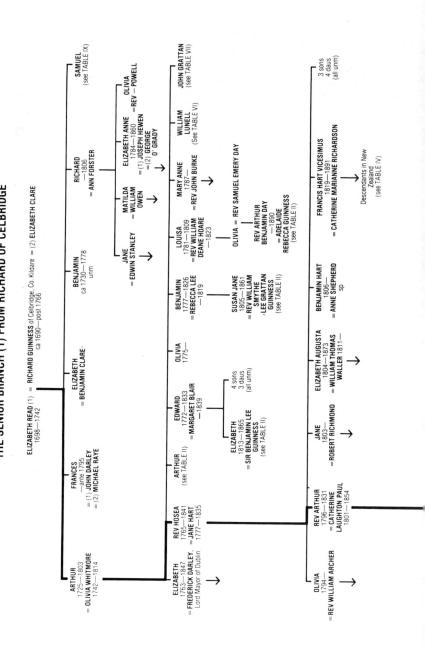

ELIZABETH READ (1) = RICHARD GUINNESS of Celbridge, Co. Kildare = (2) ELIZABETH CLARE
1698—1742   ca 1690—post 1766

ARTHUR
1725—1803
= OLIVIA WHITMORE
1742—1814

FRANCES
—ante 1795
= (1) JOHN DARLEY
= (2) MICHAEL RAYE

ELIZABETH
= BENJAMIN CLARE·

BENJAMIN
ca 1730—1778
unm

RICHARD
—1806
= ANN FORSTER

SAMUEL
(see TABLE IX)

JANE
= EDWIN STANLEY
→

MATILDA
= WILLIAM
OWEN

ELIZABETH ANNE
1784—1860
= (1) JOSEPH HEWEN
—1806
= (2) GEORGE
O' GRADY

OLIVIA
= REV — POWELL

ELIZABETH
1763—1847
= FREDERICK DARLEY,
Lord Mayor of Dublin

REV HOSEA
1765—1841
= JANE HART
1777—1835

ARTHUR
(see TABLE II)

EDWARD
1772—1833
—1839
= MARGARET BLAIR

OLIVIA
1775—

BENJAMIN
1777—1826
= REBECCA LEE
—1819

LOUISA
1781—1809
= REV WILLIAM
DEANE HOARE
—1823

MARY ANNE
1787—
= REV JOHN BURKE

WILLIAM
LUNELL
(See TABLE VI)

JOHN GRATTAN
(see TABLE VII)

4 sons
3 daus
(all unm)

ELIZABETH
1813—1865
= SIR BENJAMIN LEE
GUINNESS
(see TABLE II)

SUSAN JANE
1805—1861
= REV WILLIAM
SMYTHE
-LEE GRATTAN
GUINNESS
(see TABLE II)

OLIVIA = REV SAMUEL EMERY DAY

REV ARTHUR
BENJAMIN DAY
—1890
= ADELAIDE
REBECCA GUINNESS
(see TABLE II)

OLIVIA
1794—
= REV WILLIAM ARCHER
→

REV ARTHUR
1796—1831
= CATHERINE
LAUGHTON PAUL
1801—1854

JANE
1803—
= ROBERT RICHMOND
→

ELIZABETH AUGUSTA
1804—1873
= WILLIAM THOMAS
WALLER 1811—
→

BENJAMIN HART
1806—
= ANNE SHEPHERD
sp

FRANCIS HART VICESIMUS
1819—1891
= CATHERINE MARIANNE RICHARDSON

3 sons
4 daus
(all unm)

Descendants in New
Zealand
(see TABLE IV)
→

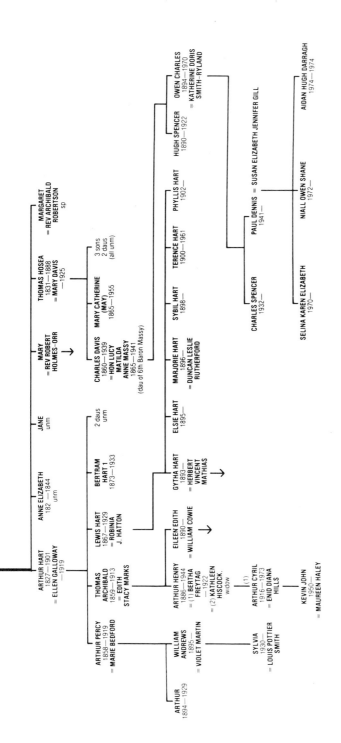

TABLE II
THE "LEE" (BREWERY) GUINNESSES (1)

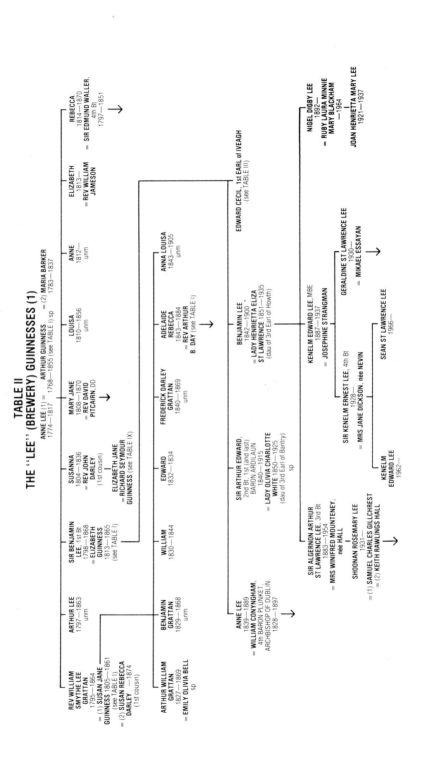

ANNE LEE (1) = ARTHUR GUINNESS = (2) MARIA BARKER
1774—1817   1768—1855 (see TABLE I) sp   1783—1837

REV WILLIAM SMYTHE LEE GRATTAN 1795—1864
= (1) SUSAN JANE GUINNESS 1805—1861 (see TABLE I)
= (2) SUSAN REBECCA DARLEY —1874 (1st cousin)

ARTHUR LEE 1797—1863 unm

SIR BENJAMIN LEE, 1st Bt 1798—1868
= ELIZABETH GUINNESS 1813—1865 (see TABLE I)

SUSANNA 1804—1836
= REV JOHN DARLEY (1st cousin)
ELIZABETH JANE = RICHARD SEYMOUR GUINNESS (see TABLE IX)

MARY JANE 1808—1870
= REV DAVID PITCAIRN, DD →

LOUISA 1810—1856 unm

ANNE 1812— unm

ELIZABETH 1813—
= REV WILLIAM JAMESON

REBECCA 1814—1870
= SIR EDMUND WALLER, 4th Bt 1797—1851 →

ARTHUR WILLIAM GRATTAN 1827—1869
= EMILY OLIVIA BELL sp

BENJAMIN GRATTAN 1829—1868 unm

WILLIAM 1830—1844

EDWARD 1832—1834

FREDERICK DARLEY GRATTAN 1840—1869 unm

ADELAIDE REBECCA 1843—1884
= REV ARTHUR B. DAY (see TABLE I) →

ANNA LOUISA 1843—1905 unm

EDWARD CECIL, 1st EARL of IVEAGH (see TABLE III)

ANNE LEE 1839—1889
= WILLIAM CONYNGHAM, 4th BARON PLUNKET, ARCHBISHOP OF DUBLIN. 1828—1897

SIR ARTHUR EDWARD, 2nd Bt. 1st (and last) BARON ARDILAUN 1840—1915
= LADY OLIVIA CHARLOTTE WHITE 1850—1925 (dau of 3rd Earl of Bantry) sp

BENJAMIN LEE 1842—1900 -
= LADY HENRIETTA ELIZA ST LAWRENCE 1851—1935 (dau of 3rd Earl of Howth)

SIR ALGERNON ARTHUR ST LAWRENCE LEE, 3rd Bt 1883—1954
= MRS WINIFRED MOUNTENEY, née HALL

SHOONAN ROSEMARY LEE 1931—
= (1) SAMUEL CHARLES GILLCHREST
= (2) KEITH RAWLINGS HALL →

KENELM EDWARD LEE, MBE 1887—1937
= JOSEPHINE STRANGMAN

SIR KENELM ERNEST LEE, 4th Bt 1928—
= MRS JANE DICKSON, née NEVIN

KENELM EDWARD LEE 1962—

SEAN ST LAWRENCE LEE 1966—

GERALDINE ST LAWRENCE LEE 1930—
= MIKAEL ESSAYAN →

NIGEL DIGBY LEE 1892—
= RUBY LAURA MINNIE MARY BLACKHAM —1964

JOAN HENRIETTA MARY LEE 1921—1937

TABLE III
THE "LEE" (BREWERY) GUINNESSES (2)

EDWARD CECIL GUINNESS, 1st EARL of IVEAGH, KP, GCVO = ADELAIDE MARIA GUINNESS
1847—1927 (see TABLE II)   1844—1916 (see TABLE X)

RUPERT EDWARD CECIL LEE, = LADY GWENDOLEN ONSLOW, CBE
2nd EARL of IVEAGH, KG, CB,   1881—1966
CMG   (dau of 4th Earl of Onslow)
1874—1967

HON ARTHUR ERNEST
1876—1949
= MARIE CLOTILDE RUSSELL
(CLOE)
(dau of Sir George Russell 4th Bt)

WALTER EDWARD, 1st BARON MOYNE
(see TABLE V)

RICHARD
1906—1906

AILEEN SIBELL MARY
1904—
= (1) HON BRINSLEY SHERIDAN
BUSHE PLUNKET 1903—1941
(2nd son of 5th Baron Plunket)
= (2) VALERIAN STUX-RYBAR

MAUREEN CONSTANCE
1907—
= (1) 4th MARQUESS OF DUFFERIN
AND AVA 1909—1945
= (2) HARRY ALEXANDER DESMOND
BUCHANAN
= (3) JUDGE JOHN CYRIL MAUDE

OONAGH
1910—
= (1) HON PHILIP LEYLAND
KINDERSLEY (yst
son of 1st Baron
Kindersley)
= (2) 4th BARON ORANMORE
AND BROWNE
= (3) MIGUEL FERRERAS

LADY HONOR DOROTHY MARY
1909—1976
= (1) HENRY (later SIR HENRY)
CHANNON MP
= (2) FRANTISEK VACLAV
SVEJDAR

ARTHUR ONSLOW EDWARD
VISCOUNT ELVEDEN
1912—1945
= LADY ELIZABETH CECILIA
HARE (dau of 4th Earl
of Listowel)

LADY PATRICIA FLORENCE SUSAN
1918—
= 1st VISCOUNT BOYD OF
MERTON, PC, CH

LADY BRIGID
KATHARINE RACHEL
1920—
= (1) HRH PRINCE
FRIEDRICH GEORG
WILHELM CHRISTOPH
OF PRUSSIA
1911—1966
= (2) ANTHONY
PATRICK NESS

ARTHUR FRANCIS BENJAMIN,
3rd EARL OF IVEAGH
1937—
= MIRANDA DAPHNE
JANE SMILEY
1940—

LADY ELIZABETH MARIA
1939—
= DAVID HUGH LAVALLIN
NUGENT 1935—
(yr son of Sir Hugh Charles
Nugent 6th Bt)

LADY HENRIETTA
1942—1978
= LUIGI MARINORI

LADY LOUISA JANE
1967—

ARTHUR EDWARD RORY,
VISCOUNT ELVEDEN
1969—

HON RORY MICHAEL
BENJAMIN
1974—

LADY EMMA LAVINIA
1963—

TABLE IV
THE SENIOR BRANCH (2): NEW ZEALAND

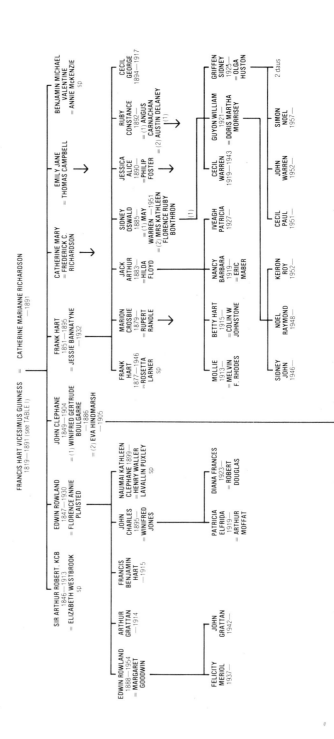

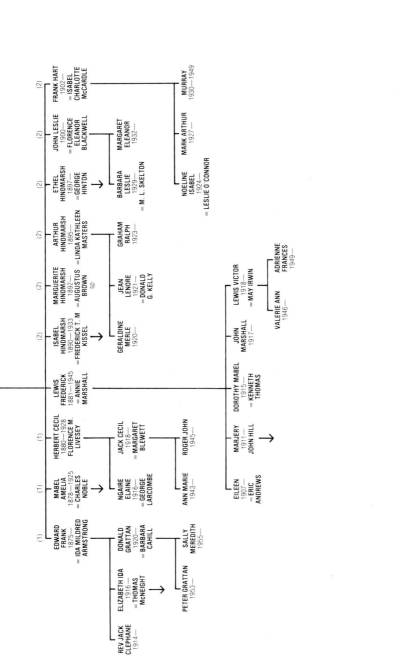

TABLE V
THE MOYNE SUCCESSION

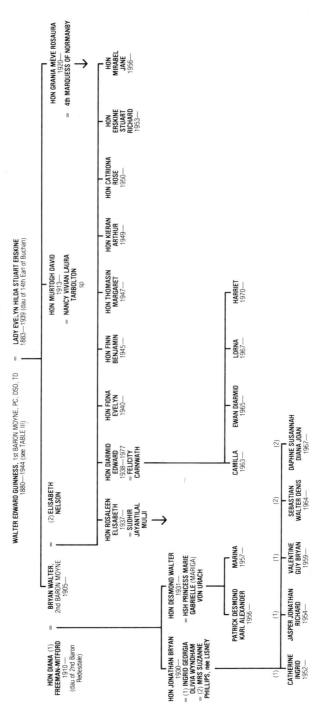

TABLE VI
THE "LUNELL" GUINNESSES

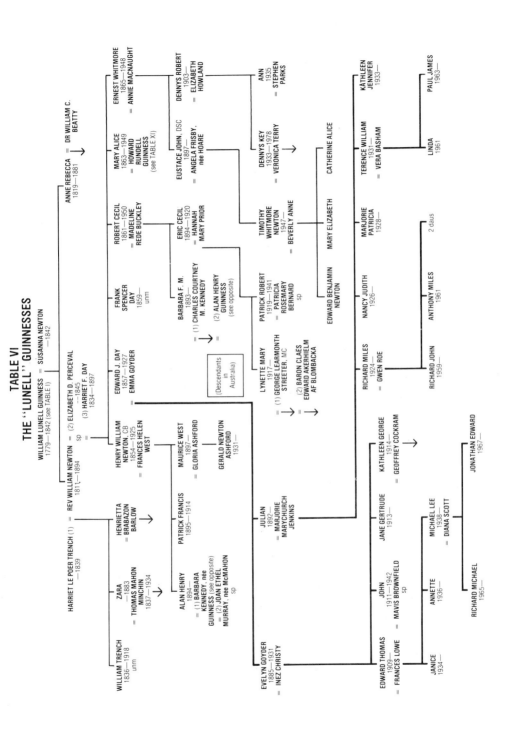

TABLE VII
THE MISSIONARY GUINNESSES (1)

SUSANNA HUTTON (1) = JOHN GRATTAN GUINNESS = (2) MRS JANE MARY LUCRETIA D'ESTERRE, née CRAMER
—1826   1783—1850 (see TABLE I)

ARTHUR GRATTAN, MD
1813—1897
= AMELIA HENRIETTA
D'ESTERRE (his stepsister)

ANNE
= DR. NELSON
SIREE
sp

REBECCA
= REV J.
LOCKWOOD
sp

SUSAN
OLIVIA
—1866
unm

LUCY
unm

REV FREDERICK WILLIAM
1839—1885
unm

REV HENRY GRATTAN
1835—1910
= (1) FANNY E.
FITZGERALD —1898
= (2) GRACE ALEXANDRA
HURDITCH

REV ROBERT WYNDHAM
1837—1919
= DORA SARAH
BOXWELL

WYNDHAM MALAN
1873—1920
= ELEANOR G.
CHASE
sp

REV PERCY
WYNDHAM, DSO, MC
1875—1948
= FRIEDA K.
THOMPSON
sp

FLORA
LUCRETIA
HENRIETTA
1877—1949

JOHN GRATTAN
—1870
= SARAH CAROLINE
LAMPREY

ARTHUR LEE
1841—

ALBERT GRATTAN
STOCK
1843—

JANE A. G.
1845—
= J. P. SYDENHAM →

ARTHUR D'ESTERRE
1849—1893
= _____
sp

CECELIA
LEE
= C. P. McCARTHY →

ALFRED GRATTAN
1858—1866

AMELIA
JANE
NELSON
MASON
sp

BENJAMIN G.
HARRISON
1836—18?

HENRY CRAMER
1838—1902
= EMILY
GORE ORMSBY

ELIZABETH
SMYTH, RA
1841—1927

LUCY
AUGUSTA
1843—1937
= WENTWORTH
AUSTIN
sp

MABEL
1885—

REV PAUL GRATTAN
1908—
= JEAN ELLIOT

AMY ORMSBY
1876—
= REV P.
PIRRIE CONERNY

EVA
1878—1916
= ALFRED
SPENCER CHURCHILL
sp

NORA
1880—1944

LILY
1882—1928
= THOMAS GREY

JOHN CHRISTOPHER
1906—1979
= GERALDINE KARIS
MACKENZIE
(see TABLE VIII)

AGNES
OCTAVIA
1871—1878

REV PETER GRATTAN
1949—
= MICHELE

HENRY GRATTAN, MD
1861—1915
(see TABLE VIII)

(1)
(MARY)
GERALDINE
1863—1949
= H. HOWARD
TAYLOR
sp

(1)
LUCY
EVANGELINE
1865—1906
= DR KARL KUMM
1862—1946

(1)
HENRIETTA
MATILDA
1867—1868

GERSHOLM WHITFIELD, MD
1869—1927
= JANE AF SANDEBERG

PHOEBE
CANFIELD
1870—1878

JOHN ELLIOT
1941—
= CHRISTIANE

JOEL GRATTAN
1977—

ISABEL GORDON
1906—

HENRY WHITFIELD
1908—
= MARY TAYLOR

MARY GERALDINE
1910—1919

LINDIS CHLOE
(FIONA)
1938—

CHLOE FAITH
1942—
= WILLIAM WADSWORTH

ANTHEA
1948—

MARGARET
GERALDINE
1937—

OLIVER
1973—

ARTHUR GERALD
1940—1942

IAN OSWALD
1941—
= JENNIE
MACDONALD

BRIAN REGINALD
1943—1944

PATRICK
1971—

TABLE VIII
THE MISSIONARY GUINNESSES (2)

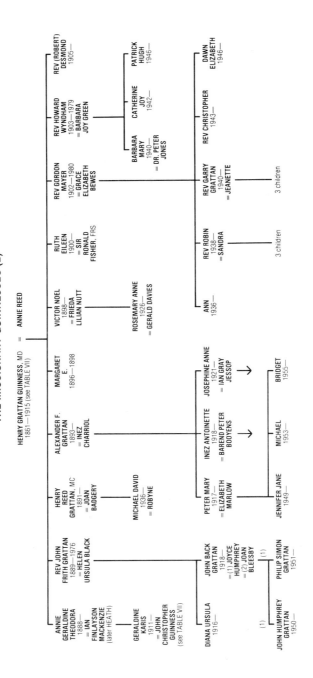

HENRY GRATTAN GUINNESS, MD = ANNIE REED
1861—1915 (see TABLE VII)

TABLE IX
THE "RUNDELL" (BANKER) GUINNESSES (1)

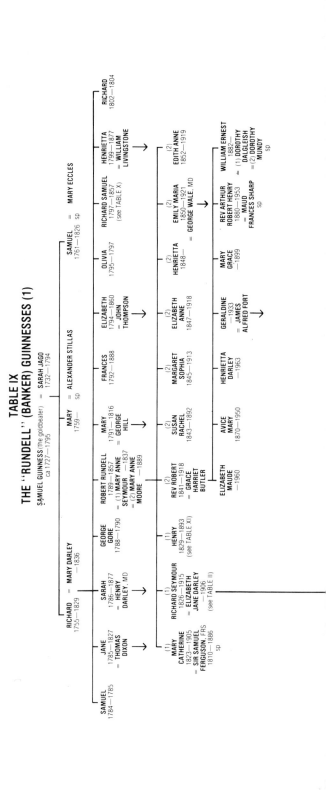

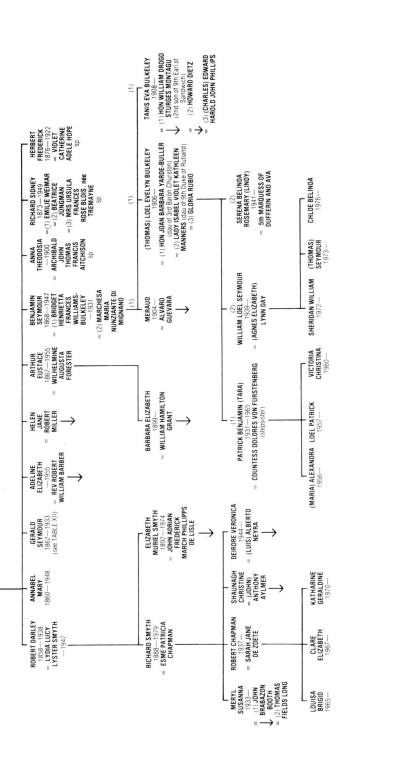

ROBERT DARLEY 1858—1938 = LYDIA LUCY LYSTER SMYTH —1947

ANNABEL MARY 1860—1948

GERALD SEYMOUR 1862—1933 (see TABLE XII)

ADELINE ELIZABETH —1955 = REV ROBERT WILLIAM BARBER →

HELEN JANE 1899— = ROBERT MILLER →

ARTHUR EUSTACE 1867—1955 = WILHELMINE AUGUSTA FORESTER

BENJAMIN SEYMOUR 1868—1947 = (1) BRIDGET HENRIETTA FRANCES WILLIAMS-BULKELEY —1931 = (2) MARCHESA MARIA NUNZIANTE DI MIGNANO

ANNA THEODOSIA —1900 = ARCHIBALD JOHN THOMAS FRANCIS AITCHISON sp

RICHARD SIDNEY 1873—1949 = (1) EMILIE WEIMAR = (2) BEATRICE JUNGMAN = (3) MRS URSULA FRANCES ROSE BLOIS, nee TREMAYNE sp

HERBERT FREDERICK 1876—1922 = VIOLET CATHERINE ADELE HOPE sp

(1) TANIS EVA BULKELEY 1908— = (1) HON WILLIAM DROGO STURGES MONTAGU (2nd son of 9th Earl of Sandwich) = (2) HOWARD DIETZ = (3) (CHARLES) EDWARD HAROLD JOHN PHILLIPS

(1) (THOMAS) LOEL EVELYN BULKELEY 1906— = (1) HON JOAN BARBARA YARDE-BULLER (dau of 3rd Baron Churston) = (2) LADY ISABEL VIOLET KATHLEEN MANNERS (dau of 9th Duke of Rutland) = (3) GLORIA RUBIO

(1) MERAUD 1904— = ALVARO GUEVARA →

ELIZABETH MURIEL SMYTH 1892—1974 = JOHN ADRIAN FREDERICK MARCH PHILLIPS DE LISLE

RICHARD SMYTH 1888—1979 = ESME PATRICIA CHAPMAN

BARBARA ELIZABETH 1899— = WILLIAM HAMILTON GRANT →

(1) PATRICK BENJAMIN (TARA) 1931—1965 = COUNTESS DOLORES VON FURSTENBERG (stepsister)

(2) WILLIAM LOEL SEYMOUR 1939— = (AGNES ELIZABETH) LYNN DAY

(2) SERENA BELINDA ROSEMARY (LINDY) 1941— = 5th MARQUESS OF DUFFERIN AND AVA

(MARIA) ALEXANDRA LOEL PATRICK 1956—

VICTORIA CHRISTINA 1960—

SHERIDAN WILLIAM 1972—

(THOMAS) SEYMOUR 1973—

CHLOE BELINDA 1976—

DEIRDRE VERONICA 1944— = (LUIS) ALBERTO NEYRA →

ROBERT CHAPMAN 1937— = SARAH JANE DE ZOETE

SHAUNAGH CHRISTINE = (JOHN) ANTHONY AYLMER →

MERYL SUSANNA 1933— = (1) JOHN BRABAZON BOOTH = (2) THOMAS FIELDS LONG

LOUISA BRIGID 1965—

CLARE ELIZABETH 1967—

KATHARINE GERALDINE 1970—

TABLE X
THE "RUNDELL" (BANKER) GUINNESSES (2)

RICHARD SAMUEL GUINNESS = KATHERINE FRANCES JENKINSON
1797—1857 (see TABLE IX) | (dau of Sir Charles Jenkinson, 10th Bt)
1808—1881

MILDRED
1835—
unm

EDITH FRANCES SHERIDAN
1837—1899
= (1) ROBERT CHARLES
sp   THOMAS PEARSE
= (2) CHRISTOPHER
CAMPBELL OLDFIELD
→

GERALDINE HENRIETTA
1838—
= (1) GEORGE
KINGSTON OLLIVER
= (2) REV BEAUCHAMP
KERR-PEARSE
→

CHARLES WOLFRAN, CB
1839—1894

ARTHUR CECIL
COPE JENKINSON
1841—1897
= (1) MARION
JANE FORLONGS
= (2) AGNES MARY
GILCHRIST

SIR REGINALD
ROBERT BRUCE
1842—1909
= THOMASINA
ANNE BLOOMFIELD
STUDDERT

ADELAIDE MARIA
1844—1916
= 1st EARL OF
IVEAGH
(see TABLE III)

CLAUDE HUME
CAMPBELL
1852—1895
= (1) GLADYS HELEN
LOUISA ROWLEY
= (2) BARONESS ZOE
VIRGINIE NUGENT

MABEL CONSTANCE
= WALTER LANG
(1)

KATHERINE
JOHN BRENNAND

JOHN CECIL COPE JENKINSON
1890—1970
= BETTY KNOWLES DAVIES
(2)

AGNES MILDRED
1893—1975
= ERIC McEVOY
sp   GUNNING
(2)

JANE AGNES MAUD
1867—1953
= (1) HENRY ANSTRUTHER
KINLOCH 1859—1903
= (2) WALTER TRAVERSARI
sp   LEGGE 1874—1949

MARJORIE GLADYS
1888—1949
= HON ALEXANDER
VICTOR FREDERICK
VILLIERS RUSSELL,
CMG, MVO (yst son
of 1st Baron Ampthill)
(1)
→

GRACE ZOE
1893—
= 2nd VISCOUNT
DAVENTRY
(2)
→

(CECIL) EDWARD
1924—
= ELIZABETH THOMPSON

ROBIN ARTHUR
1925—
= JUDITH ANNE HARE

(IVEAGH) PERRY
1927—
= (1) HEATHER ROBINSON
= (2) DAPHNE POLLARD

MARY CAROL
1928—
= PIETER ROBERT
GEOFFREY GRAHAM

RICHARD IVEAGH
1938—

3 daus

ANDREW
ARTHUR
CLIFFORD
1961—

ALINA DOONE
1963—

RUPERT
1962—
(2)

TABLE XI
THE "RUNDELL" (BANKER) GUINNESSES (3)

HENRY GUINNESS = EMELINA BROWN
1829–1893   1829–1906
(see TABLE IX)

HENRY SEYMOUR 1858–1945 = MARY MIDDLETON BAINBRIDGE

EUSTACE, DSO 1860–1901 = ISABEL GERTRUDE BELL

ETHEL MARY 1861–1940 = CHARLES FREDERIC HILL →

HOWARD RUNDELL 1863–1937 = MARY ALICE GUINNESS (see TABLE VI)

GEOFFREY GWYNNE 1864–1923 = SEVERINE MARCELLE CURNTCHET →

AMY HENRIETTA —1923 = EDWARD WILLS SANDFORD-WILLS →

MARY KATHERINE —1923 = JOHN ALEXANDER WRIGHT FALLS →

EVA FRANCES umm

LUCY MADELEINE 1870–1950 = PHILIP ALEXIUS LOMBOS, LASZLO DE MVO, FRS, PRA, HRBA, RSPP →

(RICHARD) NOEL 1870–1960 = MARY STOKES →

BEATRICE GRACE —1944 = JOHN CHRISTOPHER PETER DU TOIT →

CONSTANCE ELLEN 1876–1964 = ERNEST CRAIG-BROWN, DSO

HENRY EUSTACE 1897–1972 = BEATRICE MAUD HILL BOOTHBY

JOHN HENRY 1935— = MARY JENNIFER HOLLWEY

EUSTACE FRANCIS 1900—

HUMPHREY PATRICK 1902— = MRS GLADYS ELLEN DENISON, nee GATACRE →

MOIRA EMELINE 1902— = ARTHUR LAFONE FRANK HILLS →

RACHEL URSULA ISOLDE 1906— = PRINCE JOHN BRYANT DIGBY DE MAHE →

PATRICIA 1909— = FREDERICK CHARLES LEOPOLD ULLSTEIN →

HEATHER SEYMOUR 1910–1952 = (1) CLIFTON PENN-HUGHES = (2) JOHN HENNING (1) (2) →

VICTOR EDWARD GWYNNE 1890— = STELLA HOWSIN →

ANN SEVERINE 1939— = RICHARD HENRY SALTER →

ROBERT CELESTIN 1893–1970 = MRS DOROTHY HILDA HYEM, nee BINGHAM →

DAVID ROBERT MANCKNOIS 1948— = CAROL HUMPHREYS

MARGARET AIDEEN 1895–1973

(ANTHONY) PETER BOOTHBY 1925— = (1) RISSA PARKER = (2) SUSAN PETRONELLA CARBUTT

ANTHONY JACK 1949— = BARBARA CAROLINE MULDOWNEY (1)

CHRISTOPHER JENS 1957— (2)

LUCINDA CLAIRE 1959— (2)

IAN RICHARD 1961—

GILLIAN SARAH 1962—

TANIA CAROLINE 1966—

(HENRY) SAMUEL HOWARD 1888–1975 = ALFHILD HOLTER

GEORGE FRANCIS HOWARD 1915–1930

HELGA MARY 1916— = (1) HUGH CARLETON GREENE (later Sir Hugh) = (2) (HENRY) STUART CONNELLY →

MARIT VICTORIA 1919— = CARL NILS GUNNAR ASCHAN →

INGRID LOUISE 1922— = WINSTON ALISON WILLIAMS = →

EDWARD DOUGLAS, CBE 1895— = (1) MRS MARTHA LETIERE GOSS, nee SHELDON = (2) MRS JEANNE AMY THOMPSON

HOWARD CHRISTIAN SHELDON 1932— = EVADNE JANE GIBBS (1)

JOHN RALPH SYDNEY 1935— = VALERIE SUSAN NORTH (1)

SIR ARTHUR RUNDELL, KCMG 1895–1951 = FRANCES PATIENCE WRIGHT

JAMES EDWARD ALEXANDER RUNDELL 1924— = PAULINE VIVIEN MANDER

PAMELA PATIENCE 1925— = MICHAEL BEAUCHAMP ST JOHN, DSC

IVAN DOUGLAS RUNDELL 1927–1956 = MAIREAD FITZGERALD →

FREDERICK ROBERTS (BOBS) 1900–1979 = EMMA NORA SHELTON

HOWARD MICHAEL SHELTON 1929— = JACQUELINE BRINK

JEREMY 1931— = HEATHER MACPHIE

BRIAN CECIL 1903— = CATHERINE CORDELIA OLDERSHAW

GEOFFREY NEIL 1938— = JILLIAN RUTH POWELL

LUCIAN FRANCIS 1940— = ELIZABETH COSGRAVE

CHRISTOPHER EDWARD HOWARD 1963—

LUCY ARABELLA 1970—

RUPERT EDWARD ROGER 1971—

PETER JOHN CHARLES 1974— 1978

HUGO ARTHUR RUNDELL 1959— TWINS

JULIA ALINE 1959— = MICHAEL SAMUEL

KEVIN MICHAEL RUNDELL 1953—

TIMOTHY ROBERTS 1956—

CHRISTOPHER 1960—

CAROLINE ALICE 1954—

PETER BRIAN 1957—

ANTONIA SOPHIA 1963—

FREYA CAROLINE 1966—

DOMINIC ALEXANDER 1969—

PAUL ROHIO 1969—

RICHARD MACKAY 1970—

LUCY FRANCES 1973—

ANNABEL EVADNE 1959—

DOMINIC EVAN MARK 1966—

MIRANDA VIVIEN 1955—

SABRINA JANE 1955— TWINS

ANITA PATIENCE 1957— = AMSCHEL ROTHSCHILD

TABLE XII
THE "RUNDELL" (BANKER) GUINNESSES (4)

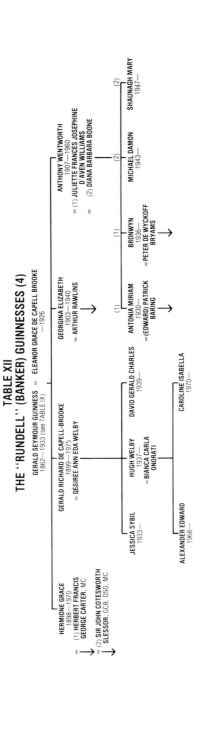

From a suburban 'two-up-and-two-down' to the 28,000-acre estate of Elveden Hall, Suffolk, is a measure of the gulf that has widened over the generations between the senior line of Guinnesses and the brewery branch started by Hosea's father, the First Arthur. Second in importance, in material terms, is the line of merchant bankers whose common ancestor was Samuel Guinness, youngest brother of the First Arthur, and a Dublin goldbeater by trade. Founded in Dublin in 1836 as Guinness, Mahon & Co., the interests of this multi-national company, developed by a succession of Guinness brothers and cousins, are now incorporated in the parent Guinness Peat Group whose deputy chairman, James E. A. R. Guinness, holds the largest directorship slice of the capital but who looks to the present Earl of Iveagh, chairman of the brewery, as the head of the clan.

There remain, to complete the pedigree, the lines of Guinnesses from the two younger brothers of the Second Arthur, William Lunell and John Grattan. In compensation, no doubt, for being unblessed by either brewing or banking wealth the descendants of these two brothers sometimes refer to themselves, light-heartedly, as 'the gentlemen Guinnesses', uncorrupted by trade and including in their numbers a band of remarkable evangelists, scholars and educationalists plus, for professional balance, a one-time bare-breasted Las Vegas showgirl, both of whose parents were Guinnesses by birth. The spiritual achievements of the 'Grattan' line, while earning it no material rewards comparable with the bounty heaped upon the brewers and bankers, deserve a separate chapter in this history and put a halo, as it were, over the composite Guinness brow.

The halo is, however, overshadowed by a coronet, for no family in British history, of origins such as those of the Guinnesses, better exemplifies the power of wealth brought to bear against the ramparts of the entrenched aristocracy. Of the 90-odd descendants of the Second Arthur's line, male and female, alive at the time of writing, no less than 41 boast titles ranging from Honourable to Earl and Marquess. For the most part these titled Guinnesses have a common ancestor in the 1st Earl of Iveagh, grandson of the Second Arthur, who on his death in 1927 was described as the second wealthiest man in England and whose personal estate was ultimately valued at £13,500,000, or the rough equivalent today of £192,000,000.

If it is true that Edward Cecil Guinness literally bought his earldom with a lifetime of benefactions, he is to be honoured for the way he employed his spare funds. It was an open secret in those days that businessmen yearning for the monarch's accolade could buy their titles with appropriate payments into the ruling political party's treasury. A knighthood could be had for £10,000, a hereditary baronetcy for £30,000 and a peerage for up to £100,000. Lloyd George—perhaps the most cynical manipulator of the titles market—justified the practice by observing that 'it is a far cleaner method of filling the party chest than the methods used in the United States', but it would have been more to the credit of this Liberal Prime Minister had he encouraged the title-seekers to follow the example of Edward Cecil who, apart from political contributions, put £250,000 into working-class housing projects and the same amount to an institution of preventive medicine.

Be that as it may, a line of Guinness earldoms was created within three generations of the founding of the Dublin brewery, and with its creation the Guinness family completed its ascent from the cobbled streets of James's Gate, Dublin, to the pinnacles of British society. The ever-loosened pursestrings of Edward Cecil put the ladder firmly in place. And the wealth earmarked for his sons, Rupert Edward and Walter Edward, provided golden rungs that would lead them to matrimonial alliances with the daughters of two belted earls—a Guinness 'double' effected within the space of four months in 1903. This further empurpled a pedigree already ennobled by their aunt Anne's marriage, 40 years earlier, to Baron Plunket and by the union of their two uncles, Arthur and Benjamin, with daughters of the Earls of Bantry and Howth.

It would be naïve to suppose that the fortunes already in trust for Iveagh's three granddaughters, Aileen, Maureen and Oonagh, were irrelevant to their own marriages to a trio of peers; but at least as seductive as their fortunes, in a society well peopled with unmarried heiresses, were the physical beauty and panache of these celebrated Guinness sisters. With or without a family earldom in the bag, a notable number of Guinness girls through the generations had, and still have, what it takes to dazzle a duke and, as we shall see in later chapters, even loftier orders than that.

The story of the Guinness family confronts the writer with genealogical data embracing nine generations, covering a period of about 280 years and comprising altogether more than 500 descendants from Richard Guinness through the family's male and female lines. Happily for the sanity of the author (and reader) this number can be substantially reduced by the elimination of daughters who married outside the clan, excepting those whose marriages are noteworthy in the context of the family's social and political ascendancy. Similarly, only passing reference need be made to those male and female descendants whose marriages produced no issue. To the formidable residue, some selectivity has to be applied, not only to keep this history to one volume but to structure its narrative around those Guinnesses most pertinent to themes of the book.

As a book it therefore falls somewhere between a work of biographical history and a more or less fleshed-out pedigree of the whole of this vast and variegated clan.

An effort was made by the author to enlist to this task the co-operation of the present head of the family, the 3rd Earl of Iveagh. It was as unsuccessful as had been all previous approaches by writers tempted to tackle a history of this remarkable family.

In the most courteous of correspondence, both Iveagh and his cousin, the 2nd Lord Moyne, pointed out that an authorized history, *Guinness's Brewery in the Irish Economy, 1759–1876*,[1] had already been published, 'and there exists in manuscript form a continuation of this history up to modern times, which could possibly be published at a future date'. But these scholarly works, invaluable as source material relevant to an industrial history of the brewery, fail by their very terms of reference to take in the broad panoramic sweep of the Guinness story, embracing descendants of the First Arthur through *all* his sons. And, as we shall see, the romance of this family does not begin and end at James's Gate.

Lord Iveagh's decision is better understood as an expression of his family's distaste for personal publicity which, in the case of the Guinnesses, immediately evokes the image of King Canute, commanding the tide to go back. The family has provided over the years more than a footnote to the social, economic and political history of England and Ireland. It bears a surname as familiar and identifiable to the people of those two nations as Ford is to the American public. Lord Moyne put his position in terms all of us can understand when he reminded the present author that 'in answering anything about a family it is very difficult to avoid treading on someone's toes and giving offence, even though the corns may be only trivial sensitivities'.

The project might have ended there had I not discovered, by personal contact with living members of all branches of the family, that in fact many of them were ready to welcome this, the first ever history of the Guinnesses, and to cooperate to that end by fully and generously responding to questions and by sharing with me their memories, their anecdotes and their insights. It would be invidious to list their names; in some cases it would be a breach of confidence.

And the same applies, with at least as much force, to the many close friends of the family who have steered this narrative around the pitfalls and out of the blind alleys that inevitably attend routine research through the published records.

One member of the family–the Rev. Paul Grattan Guinness–shall be named, for without him, and the generosity that moved him to make available to me his own authoritative study of the 'Grattan' Guinnesses, this particular chapter in the history of the Guinness family would have been so much the poorer and less colourful.

Frederic Mullally

1

A River of Gold

1

The luxury of being able to speak one's mind bluntly and publicly, in defiance of personal consequences, is a prerogative of the
dispossessed and of the immensely powerful.

When Rupert Edward Cecil Lee Guinness, the 2nd Earl of Iveagh,
visited Canada during the post-World War II regime of Britain's
Labour Government, he was asked by reporters in Vancouver, 'How
is England going?'

His retort, 'It's going to the devil', prompted one of his entourage,
concerned about political repercussions back home, to suggest to the
reporters that this was not quite what his lordship meant.

'Of course I meant it,' Iveagh cut in. 'I believe it; why shouldn't I
say it?'

'What if the British press throws it up to you when you get back?'
his adviser ventured.

'I hope they do,' Iveagh grunted, 'so I can say it again.'

Iveagh was then in his seventies and the head of an industrial
empire substantially based in England. A great new Guinness brewery had been in operation at Park Royal, on the outskirts of London,
since 1936 and the very levels of its productive output were dictated,
at the time of his visit to Canada, by a Government that had been
swept to power in a landslide election, following a campaign to
which the Guinness family had contributed neither a penny nor an
iota of good will. (Rumours that the Guinnesses intended to pull out
of Dublin completely had to be allayed by Iveagh right up to the start
of World War II. They had been spread in the thirties by, among
others, no less powerful an Irishman than Brendan Bracken, Winston Churchill's closest companion and chairman of the *Banker*, the
Investors Chronicle and the *Financial News*. His Irish stepfather had
written to ask him if he could use his influence with Iveagh or his

brother, Lord Moyne, to get Bracken's 16-year-old half-sister, Maeva, a clerkship in the Dublin brewery. Bracken wrote back: 'About Guinness, the only communication I have had with the noble lords you mention is when we attacked the British Government for not making the brewery pay more taxation. The Guinness crowd were livid and so they would hardly give a nomination to anyone who was recommended by me ... I think Maeva would be ill-advised to go to that firm. It is only too clear that as the years go on they will transfer most of their business to London. They deny that they have any policy of that kind but the denial is merely a method of forestalling criticism or action from your government or people, and so there will be little security for clerical workers.'[1])

Iveagh was no more beholden to Bracken than he was to the Prime Minister, Clement Attlee. Both were, to him, political *parvenus* and the Labour Government a mere footnote to the 300-year-old history of a family business that had survived and flourished through the Napoleonic Wars, the Crimean War, the Boer War, the Irish civil wars and two world wars. The Guinnesses had dealt with Governments all the way back to the powerful Whig and Tory administrations of the 18th and 19th centuries. They had seen eight successive monarchs seated on the throne of Great Britain and had been favoured, one way or the other, by all of them. At his Ashford and Elveden estates or in his London mansion, Iveagh himself had broken bread and swopped confidences with the then reigning monarch, George VI, and his three predecessors, and given house room to Prime Ministers Baldwin, Chamberlain and Churchill, not to mention the Premier of the first Labour Government in Britain's history, Ramsay MacDonald. At the time of his exchange with the Vancouver reporters, the Guinness group was poised for massive expansion overseas and Iveagh was counted as one of the ten richest men in the world.

Like his father, he had channelled much of the investable Guinness fortune abroad, where the trusts set up for his family would be exempt, by law, from the crushing British inheritance taxes, and among the family's Canadian assets at that time was the outright ownership of the Lion's Gate toll bridge (popularly known as 'The Guinness Bridge') which he had built in 1938, the Marine Building and the British Properties luxury suburb in West Vancouver, in the reporters' own city. His 'constituency'—in a supportive sense more enduring than votes cast in ballot boxes—encompassed every bar and household in the United Kingdom where Guinness stout was deemed to be 'good for you'. He was under no compulsion to be a good-will ambassador abroad for a Government he disliked. He could enjoy the luxury of speaking his mind.

The incident, trivial in itself, serves to sharpen our focus upon an institution–the Guinnesses–that had evolved over only five generations from a prospering family of brewers to an élitist clan whose name was now a synonym for wealth, glamour, social distinction and political power. Edward Cecil Guinness, the 1st Earl of Iveagh, had bequeathed an immense fortune to his three sons and their children. Other immovable properties abroad, owned outright, included a Manhattan office building, an hotel in San Francisco, a Canadian oilfield, an African mine, a sheep farm in New Zealand. In Britain and Ireland the Guinness wealth supported a network of town houses and country estates second only, in terms of splendour and variety, to those of the British royal family.

Facing the western wall of the Buckingham Palace gardens stood the three great mansions owned, after Edward Cecil's death, by Rupert Edward, by his younger brother the Honourable (Arthur) Ernest and by the youngest, the Honourable Walter Edward. Together, they constituted an *hôtel* (in the French usage) as sumptuous and commodious as the royal palace itself and preferred, as guest accommodation, by more than one royal and foreign cousin of the British 'royals' on visits to the capital. Here in these mansions, throughout the 1920s and 1930s, the three brothers entertained the rich, the noble and the powerful of the land and launched their celebrated daughters onto a social scene that at times must have seemed to them to have been structured for their own convenience.

In 1903, Ernest had married Cloe (Marie Clothilde) Russell, the only daughter of the 4th baronet, Sir Charles Russell. Through her mother, Constance Lennox, a granddaughter of the 5th Duke of Richmond, Cloe was descended from Charles II and his most enduring mistress, Louise de Keroualle. Cloe's maternal grandfather, Lord Arthur Lennox, had a sister, Lady Cecilia Catherine, whose great-grandson, the 8th Earl of Spencer, is the father of Diana, Princess of Wales. Thus, Ernest Guinness's three daughters–Aileen, Maureen and Oonagh–can claim cousinship with Diana. Cloe could also claim descent, via the Dukes of Argyll, from Elizabeth, youngest of the two celebrated Gunning sisters whose beauty took Dublin and London by storm in the mid-18th century. Some of the Gunning magic was certainly there, for Cloe outshone her sisters-in-law as a hostess of wit and gaiety, whether at 17 Grosvenor Place for the London season, at either of Ernest's English country houses–Thornhill, at Cowes, and Holmbury House, Sussex–or at his Glenmaroon estate in co. Dublin.

Walter had also married in 1903, taking as his wife the daughter of the 14th Earl of Buchan, Lady Evelyn Erskine. A consummate parliamentarian and diplomat, Walter made his house at 10 Grosvenor Place into an imposing private 'annexe' of the Carlton Club, where the king's (Tory) ministers could discuss affairs of State across one of the best boards in London, within a fast few minutes' drive from the division lobbies.[2] Between Parliamentary sessions and his world travels he would relax with his family on his co. Dublin estate, Knockmaroon, or at Biddesden House in Hampshire.

Rupert had followed Walter into the House of Commons five years after marrying Lady Gwendolen, eldest daughter of the 4th Earl of Onslow. As the eldest son and heir of the 1st Earl of Iveagh, Rupert had inherited the great Elveden, Farmleigh and Ashford estates and a fourth one, Phibblestown, at Clonsilla in co. Dublin. For town residences there was a mansion on St Stephen's Green, Dublin, and, in London, 4 & 5 Grosvenor Place and 11 & 12 St James's Square. He had also–years before his father's death–acquired Pyrford Court, near Woking, Surrey, with its 1,100 acres of farm and parkland, and to these residential properties he added during his lifetime the imposing town house of Gloucester Lodge in Regent's Park.

By the time of his encounter with the Canadian newsmen all three of Rupert's daughters were married, as were the three daughters of his brother, Ernest, and an invitation to stay with a Guinness 'of Founder's kin' might take one, in addition to the above, to Kelvedon Hall in Essex, Ince Castle in Cornwall, Patmore Hall in Hertfordshire or, across in Ireland, to the splendid estates of Luttrellstown Castle, the 3,000-acre Clandeboye or the romantic 12,000-acre Luggala. All in all, the Guinnesses' private homes offered a choice of properties approachable in variety and style by few other landed families in the British Isles.

And it all came out of the sale of a dark brown beer.

2

The colourful myths that have arisen over the years to explain the 'secret' of the First Arthur Guinness's success as a brewer persist to the present day, though neither he nor his successors have ever lent credence to them. One legend has it that his father, Richard, accidentally burned the malting barley while making beer for his employer, the Archbishop of Cashel, resulting in a dark, bitter but palatable brew, the 'secret' of which he passed on to his son. Another has it that Arthur stole the recipe for his stout from some monks who had stumbled upon a method of beefing up their home-made beer, with salutary effects upon the output of the Irish workmen in their employ. Yet another argues that the secret lies in the unique properties of the River Liffey, running through Dublin. And of course there is always the hoary legend—attached worldwide to other libations of strong character—about the finding of a rat, or a horse, or a human corpse in one of the fermenting tuns or storage vats and the discovery, on sampling the fluid contents, that something new and potent had been added. (This particular legend stops short of explaining how the improvement in 'body' was maintained thereafter.)

The Liffey legend still survives despite the fact that Guinness stout is now brewed in Australia, Canada, Nigeria, Kenya, Malaysia, Trinidad and ten other widely scattered nations unblessed by the miraculous properties of Dublin's turgid stream. There are Irishmen who, on sampling the local product in foreign parts, will wrinkle their noses and declare: 'It's not the same.' But if there is any variation internationally it owes itself to national tastes rather than to a shortage of ocean-going tankers in Dublin Bay.

The original porter stout—a stronger, darker version of ale—was made by adding hops to malted barley, boiling and straining the mixture and fermenting it with yeast. It was being brewed and drunk in England a hundred years before the First Arthur entered the business, and the very name owes its origin to the fact that this extra strong beer was especially favoured by the porters working in London's wholesale food markets.

Arthur's first brewery was not in Dublin but just across the boundary of co. Kildare, at Leixlip. He was able to lease the small establishment in 1756 thanks to a legacy of £100 left to him by Dr Arthur Price, the Archbishop of Cashel, whose seat was at Celbridge. Three years later, leaving his brother Richard to take care of the Leixlip enterprise, he acquired a neglected brewery on a derelict acre at James's Gate, Dublin. The property included a dwelling house, a fish pond, two malt houses and a copper brewing vessel that had seen its best years. The rent was £45 per annum and the lease was for 9,000 years. Until about 1796, Arthur's brewery produced no porter, only ale and table beer—and not a great deal of that, compared with the output of about twenty of the many rival Dublin breweries in business at that time. But in 1761 he married a Dublin heiress, Olivia Whitmore, and two years later he was able to buy a country house at Beaumont, co. Dublin, appropriate to his new status as Warden of the Dublin Corporation of Brewers. By the age of 64 he had extended the brewery, invested about £8,000 in Kilmainham flour mills and had fathered no less than 21 children, of whom only ten survived.

His health was excellent, his energy prodigious and in an age when the heat of religious and economic oppression kept Dublin politics simmering and periodically boiling over he had held a nice balance between loyalty to the Irish Protestant Establishment and sympathy for the legitimate aspirations of the Catholic majority, provided they went about it 'the right way', i.e. stage by stage and without violence. He himself was not however above violence when his brewery's interests came into conflict with the public authority.

The River Liffey was the main source of fresh water for the burgeoning city of Dublin and under the original lease acquired by Arthur Guinness he was entitled to draw free supplies from a section of the watercourse adjoining the brewery, limited only by the dimensions of the existing pipes. In 1773 an investigating committee of the city's Corporation found that Mr Guinness was not playing fair. Without authority, he had increased the size of the pipes and made breaches in the walls of the watercourse—the property of the city—thereby tapping a substantially greater supply of free fresh water than he was entitled to. When the Corporation's officers arrived at James's Gate to give notice to the brewer that 'within a reasonable time' he must surrender to Caesar what was in fact Caesar's, he sent back as answer that the water was his and that he 'would defend it by force of arms'. Enter, in due course, the city sheriff with a body of men under instruction to fill in the breaches in the watercourse. They were met by Arthur's stout employees who were about to give way, under threat of committal to prison, when the master brewer himself arrived on the scene, grabbed a pickaxe from one of his men and 'with very much improper language [declared] that they should not proceed . . . that if they filled [the watercourse] up from end to end, he would immediately re-open it.'[3]

At this stage in his career, the eminent businessman had been elected Master of the influential Corporation of Brewers and appointed official brewer to the all-powerful Dublin Castle, seat of the British Parliament's puppet executives. The sheriff wavered and finally retreated after securing a promise from Mr Guinness that he would submit his title to the water to the Pipe Water Committee. In the event, his title turned out to be no more than 'ancient custom' but he was able to frustrate Caesar a few more years by obtaining an injunction and dragging out the resultant legal procedures. When the Corporation's officers decided it was again time to inspect the state of the watercourse adjoining the brewery they were confronted by a stone-and-brick wall erected by Arthur on the city's ground, across a passage giving access to the course. This minor Battle of the Liffey was resolved when the brewer made a deal, to the relief of the Corporation, under which he became their tenant and was ensured an adequate water supply for an annual payment of £10.

By now Arthur was 54 and was to live another quarter of a century, gradually yielding control of his affairs to his sons Arthur, Benjamin and William and seeing his derelict little brewery grow into Ireland's single biggest business enterprise and the largest porter brewery in the world. He had married Olivia Whitmore when she was 19 and he 37. He had made financial provisions for her in his lifetime and his personal estate, valued for probate at around £23,000, went to his children.

He was the First Arthur Guinness. There would be others in a direct male line from the doughty wielder of pickaxes, all the way down to the present Arthur (or 'Ben', as he is known in the family), born in 1937 to the inherited title of Viscount Elveden. And during the 134 years between the death of the one Arthur and the birth of the other the River Liffey would become for the Guinnesses a river of gold.

2

The Quest for Ancestors

Hosea Guinness, eldest son of the First Arthur Guinness, was a scholar and a churchman. Born in 1765 into a family already comfortably off, Hosea went to Winchester College and Oxford, took his BA and LLD at Trinity College, Dublin, and was rector of the parish of St Werburgh in that city until his death in 1841. He inherited Beaumont in his father's will in place of a major monetary settlement, 'not being in any line of life', as his father drily observed, 'whereby he is likely by Industry to enlarge his Property'.

The Ireland in which the Rev. Hosea was born and lived for most of his adult life was a country dominated politically and economically by Britain through its vassals in the all-Protestant Irish Parliament and their executive nabobs in Dublin Castle. These were the Anglo-Irish colonists installed first by Mary Tudor, and subsequently reinforced and aggrandized by Oliver Cromwell. An entrenched minority, imposing its will on the overwhelmingly Catholic population of the country, the Anglo-Irish owed their power and therefore their allegiance to Westminster and to the established Anglican Church of Ireland which served as a political instrument for the English rulers in Dublin Castle.

Hosea was a distinguished and moderately liberal minister of that church and, as a man of God, must surely have welcomed the initiatives of the Prime Minister, William Pitt the Younger, aimed at lessening the Protestant tyranny of the Irish Parliament and ending the bloody revolts of the peasants by opening the way to a degree of Catholic emancipation. Hosea would live to see the passage of the Roman Catholic Relief Bill, giving Irish Catholics the right to sit in their own Parliament, and the abolition, later, of the hateful tithes system whereby Catholics were compelled to pay for the maintenance of the Anglican Church in Ireland. This last monstrosity was removed only 12 years before Hosea's death and by then, having seen which way the wind of change was blowing, the Rev. Hosea, as the senior member of the Guinness family, had taken steps formally to establish a noble and ancient Irish pedigree.

There is evidence that as early as 1781 the First Arthur and his brothers were using without authority the armorial bearings (coat of arms) of the Magennis family of co. Down, one of the oldest and once one of the most powerful clans in Ireland. These arms feature a *dexter* hand *couped* (cut off) at the wrist on a *chief ermine* (black 'tails' on a white background), and a lion rampant *or* (gold). On the occasion of his marriage to Olivia Whitmore, Arthur was presented with a two-handled silver cup engraved on one side with the Magennis arms impaling (adjacent to) those of Whitmore. On the other side was engraved the Magennis crest—a boar *passant quarterly or* and *gules* (red). Further evidence is provided by two original leases drawn up in 1795 between Arthur's nephews, Richard and Samuel Guinness, and his solicitor son, Edward: the deeds carried seals impressed with the same Magennis arms and crest.

By the law of arms, it is not possible to acquire a legal title to armorial bearings other than by inheritance or by a grant or confirmation of arms by the duly constituted authorities. And in order to bear arms by inheritance it must be proved to the satisfaction of the Officers of Arms that there is legitimate male descent from whoever was originally given the right to bear those arms.

In 1814 Hosea made application to Sir William Bethan, deputy Ulster King of Arms and principal Herald of all Ireland, for the granting and assignment to him, and to the other descendants of his grandfather, Richard, the right to use and bear these Magennis arms. Sir William's handling of the application was cautious, to say the least. He noted that while Hosea and other descendants of his grandfather Richard 'have been accustomed to bear and use these Armorial Ensigns', they did not 'upon examination . . . appear to have been recorded in Ulster's Office of Arms'. And he took caution even further. The original manuscript petition prayed him 'to confirm the said Armorial ensigns' to Hosea and the other descendants of Richard. This he declined to do, electing instead to strike out the plea for *confirmation* in favour of a new grant of arms, which remained, however, those of the Magennis family, with a minor change in the tinctures of the shield and a new motto.

The chief significance of all this lies in the fact that one Sir Arthur Magennis, being raised to the peerage in 1623 by James I, had taken as his hereditary title 'Viscount of Iveagh', a title chosen by the '1st'

Lord Iveagh, Edward Cecil Guinness, 268 years later, on being created Baron Iveagh of co. Down. To the Magennis arms were impaled, by the Second Arthur, those purporting to be of his wife, Anne Lee: on a bar, between three black crescents, a gold shamrock. The Iveagh arms today are an impalement of 'Guinness' and 'Lee', the Guinness section being described in Debrett's *Illustrated Peerage* as 'a lion rampant, or; on a chief ermine a dexter hand couped at the wrist'. The crest is 'a boar passant, quarterly or and gules'.

Since there is no evidence of Edward Cecil's ever having had roots in co. Down, we have to assume that he chose the title 'Iveagh' in the belief that the arms granted to his grandfather Hosea 'and the descendants' established to his own satisfaction at least that his ancestors were Magennises. Certainly it would appear that he had done nothing to discourage this fiction as perpetuated by contemporary 'experts' in genealogy.

A discussion of the evidence against the Magennis–Guinness link appears in the Appendix to this book.

The First Arthur either honestly believed he was a descendant of the Magennises or else accepted the silver cup bearing that family's arms in a spirit of 'What you don't know can't hurt you'. The Rev. Hosea took a more decisive step towards establishing the connection. And Arthur's grandson, Edward Cecil, not only perpetuated but crystallized the legend.

All this, of course, merely reflects the ambivalence of an Anglo-Irish family towards the country in which their fortunes were founded. The pendulum swings. Under the Tudor monarchs from 1494 to 1603 any assertion of native Irish origin placed a family, in terms of influence, 'beyond the Pale'. Under Charles I the Catholic Irish won back some of their rights and property, but from 1649, when Cromwell first landed in Dublin, until the accession of James II in 1685, the Protestant Anglo-Irish were back in control and in ownership of the greater part of the land. The pendulum swung again during the Catholic James's brief reign and his subsequent leadership in exile of the Irish against his usurper, William of Orange, during the 'Glorious Revolution'. Anglo-Irish supporters of William were stripped of their titles and driven from the lands and castles they had grabbed under the Tudor monarchs and Cromwell. But the defeat of James set the pendulum swinging violently back, and that is where it stayed through the lifetimes of Richard Guinness of Celbridge and his son Arthur.

During these lifetimes the Catholic Irish and their native lords smouldered under penal laws imposed by their Protestant rulers in Westminster and Dublin–laws that in some respects were no less punitive than those imposed in 1933–9 by Adolf Hitler in his persecution of the Jews. And it must be remembered that these oppressors of the Irish Catholic majority were not Brownshirt louts but highly 'civilized' English and Anglo-Irish gentlemen, many of noble birth. Irish industries were ruthlessly crushed by forbidding the export to England of cattle, milk, butter and cheese, and the export of woollens to *any* country. Until 1774 no Catholic could take a lease of land in his own native country. In that year, on the threshold of the American colonists' revolt against the autocratic George III, it was decreed that a Catholic could hold one lease not exceeding 50 square perches (275 square yards) in a city or market town, or 50 acres in the countryside, but only after taking the oath of allegiance to the English king. The Bill giving effect to this concession was entitled 'A Bill for the better encouragement of persons professing the Popish religion to become Protestants, and for the further improvement of the Kingdom'. And this with reason, since it was further decreed that on the death of the leaseholding 'Papist' the largest share of the lease would go to whomsoever of his family converted to Protestantism. Freeholds of land were entirely restricted to Protestants.

The American Revolution of 1775–83, and the sympathy it aroused among Irish nationalists, had a catalytic effect on Irish politics inasmuch as it united the Presbyterians of Ulster–who were also disqualified from holding civic or political office–with the Catholics in a common crusade for emancipation. Parliament responded nominally with the Relief Act of 1778 but it took another historic revolution, that of the French against their own absolutist monarch, followed by the peasant revolt in co. Wexford nine years later, to persuade William Pitt that something more than palliatives was called for. His solution was an Act of Union between England and Ireland, proclaimed when the First Arthur was in his 76th year. During the years leading up to the union, such was the stiffening of Irish nationalism that while it would have been wise for a Protestant businessman to sit on the fence politically it would have been no serious disadvantage to lay private claim to native Irish ancestry. This was the course the First Arthur chose to take.

By 1868, when the 20-year-old Edward Cecil and his brother Arthur inherited the world's largest porter brewery, the violent agitation against Union and for Home Rule had brought the trappings at least of victory and the battle from then on would be for Independence. The Second Arthur had scrupulously avoided

involving himself in Dublin politics, 'where party and sectarian strife
so signally abound and more especially if [a political office be] filled
by one engaged in our line of business, is fraught with difficulty and
danger'.[1] His son Benjamin followed this sound advice until he
reached his 67th year by which time (1865) the Guinness brewery
was firmly established as Dublin's principal industry and he could
take the risk, such as it was, of wearing the Tory Unionist colours as
an elected Member of Parliament for Dublin City.

In contrast, Benjamin's son Edward Cecil, though a confirmed
Unionist and pillar of the (Protestant) Church of Ireland, rejected
all invitations to stand for Parliament in the Tory interest and
devoted himself to the affairs of the business and to strengthening the
family's roots in Ireland by princely benefactions to the Irish people,
by creating the family seat of Farmleigh and by assuming the ancient
Irish title of Iveagh in 1897, three years before the founding of the Sinn
Fein, the political party that would win independence for Ireland.

A famous Guinness advertising poster depicts a smiling labourer
balancing a gigantic steel girder upon his head as he strolls past an
astonished fellow-worker. Label the girder 'Irish Politics' and it
might serve, *faute de mieux*, as an unofficial armorial symbol for the
Guinnesses of Dublin.

We have looked in vain for revealing insights into the characters of
the First and Second Arthur Guinnesses, of the kind that come down
to biographers through diaries, the memoirs of literate contemporaries or in intimate letters passing between members of the
family. The dearth of such material is not surprising. For one thing,
neither of the two Arthurs sought, or would have been comfortable in
the company of, the Dublin intelligentsia of their time. There is no
record, for example, of the First Arthur's ever having been invited to
the 'Society of Granby Row' where Lord Charlemont presided over
the artists and literati of the 1770s; nor, one can safely assume, would
Arthur have found the time or inclination to dally amongst the witty
and sophisticated Anglo-Irishmen of the period. True, he was
already living in the style of a gentleman at his Beaumont country
house and, also true, the brewers of Dublin were among the most
respected of tradesmen; but neither by birth nor education would he
have felt at ease in such Augustan society. His energies were apportioned amongst the brewery, the mills and his large family, in that
order, and his milieu was that of the rising merchant class, a class not
conspicuous for its *belles lettres*. His wife Olivia was related on her
mother's side to the Grattans of political lustre, whose most famous

son, Henry (1746–1820), would serve both Arthurs well as their political mouthpiece in the Irish Parliament. But there is no mention of the Guinnesses in the five volumes of *Memoirs of the Life and Times of the Right Hon. Henry Grattan*, published by his son in 1849, and it is more likely that the Guinnesses' best dinner plate was brought out for such other of Olivia's family connections as the Darleys, the Smyths and the La Touches, respectively merchants, speculative builders and Huguenot bankers. As to sources within the family, later generations of Guinnesses would include, here and there, a writer to favour us with perceptions of his or her kinsfolk, but the period preceding the 20th century remains barren of such material.

There is marginally more data bearing upon the character of the Second Arthur than upon his father's. He had four younger brothers, Edward, Benjamin, William and John Grattan, born 4, 9, 11 and 15 years after his own birth in 1768. All five brothers started as apprentices in the brewery but only Arthur, Benjamin and William justified their father's faith and it is from Arthur that the long line of Guinness brewery chiefs comes down to the present day.

A portrait of Arthur in the Guinness Collection, painted when he was 77, shows he had inherited the long pallid face, receding brow and prominent nose of his father, to which in old age were added the hooded, wary gaze and judicious mouth of the patriarch in tune, if not totally with man, then certainly with himself and his God.[2] He had already lived through the disruptive Napoleonic Wars and would live on through the terrible five years (1845–50) of the Great Famine when the failure of the potato crops reduced the population of Ireland, by starvation or emigration, from eight to six million. But as Patrick Lynch and John Vaisey point out in their invaluable industrial history of the period, sales of Guinness stout increased more than six-fold during the Napoleonic Wars. And the later horrors of the famine—mostly spread over the rural west and south of Ireland—far from damaging the essentially maritime economy of Dublin, proved an eventual boon to the merchant class and even to the surviving rural population. Fortunes were made from the importation of corn; mass emigration left fewer farmers with more land to work and more efficiently, and the labourers' standard of living rose with the reduction of unemployment and the increased import of cheap consumer goods. The diversion of grain from the legal and illegal whiskey distilleries to the baking ovens accelerated the drinking of porter—by now the mainstay of the Guinness brewery—and opened up a nationwide market where, previously, trade had been virtually limited to the Dublin area.

In the meantime Arthur and his energetic brother Benjamin had succeeded in opening up the market in England via the ports of Bristol and Liverpool, with an ever-improving quality of porter to compete with the English brewers and with the advantage, from 1824 onwards, of being able to transport their barrels by steamer service instead of by the sailing vessels that could take up to two weeks to cross the Irish Sea. By 1840 more Guinness was being sold in England than in Ireland, where the Second Arthur and his brothers were having to cope with outbreaks of hostility peculiar to the religious and political climate of the period.

Despite their careful and sympathetic posture, in public, towards Catholic emancipation, the brothers found themselves unjustly buffeted between Protestant and Catholic fanatics during the heated campaign—spearheaded by 'The Liberator', Daniel O'Connell—for the admission of Catholics into Parliament. A forged Guinness signature put to a petition against Catholic emancipation by the lunatic anti-Papist fringe brought a violent reaction from its counterparts at the other extreme of the spectrum. Protestant porter, they thundered, was going to be the price they must pay for representation. Through the medium of the devil's brew, poisonous doctrines 'totally subversive of the Catholic faith' were being forced upon the faithful. A contemporary satirist reported that 'the learned Dr Brennan' had analysed the anti-popery porter and found it produced 'a disposition to bowels particularly lax, an inclination to pravity and to singing praises of the Lord through the nose'.[3] Over the years, the Guinnesses had mashed up 136,000 tons of Protestant Bibles and 501,000 cartloads of Protestant catechisms and Methodist hymn books, 'thus impregnating in the act of fermentation the volatile parts of the porter with the pure ethereal essence of heresy'.[4]

Happily, the faithful's attachment to Protestant porter shortly overcame their fears of a Catholic hell's fire and the brewery survived. As Arthur put it in a letter to his brother Benjamin, '... the continued good account of our Business calls for much thankfulness to Almighty God while we humbly ask for the infinitely higher blessings of His Grace in the Lord Jesus Christ.'[5]

Personal relations between the Second Arthur and Daniel O'Connell had remained friendly during the 1826–9 campaign for emancipation. But the brewer and the patriot fell out later when the former, now 67, opposed O'Connell in his campaign for the repeal of the Union. Over-zealous supporters of repeal instigated violent attacks on the brewery's property and its customers, sledgehammering barrels of porter *en route* from the Dublin brewery and holding up carriers at pistol-point. O'Connell, despite his disappointment in 'that miserable old apostate Arthur Guinness', condemned the violence, but most of his rank-and-file supporters turned a blind eye to it. *The Times*, reporting on 8 September 1837 'Another Outrage' against Guinness, described the tipping of barrels of porter into the Royal Canal Harbour by a gang of 10 or 12 men, observed by various boatmen 'who preferred to stay out of the way'.

In that same year, the fiery friar Father Mathew launched a vigorous crusade against the evils of drink, initially directed at the consumption of spirits but broadening out to embrace malt liquor. His campaign over the succeeding years was undoubtedly responsible for the decline in the overall Irish brewery trade from more than a million barrels in 1837 to just over half that number in 1843, but the drop in Guinness sales was almost wholly in exports, as a consequence of the trade depression in England, and it is arguable that the specific blow dealt to spirit drinking boosted the later recovery in Guinness sales to a new record figure in 1846, though the greatly improved quality of the Guinness porter played its own part. Such was the antipathy towards spirits from the temperance crusaders that the Bishop of Kildare and Leighlin at one stage pleaded with the Government to support the brewers of strong ale in order to 'get rid of drunkenness'. But there is absolutely no evidence that this discriminating temperance campaigner was privately financed by the Guinness brothers.

The Second Arthur married Anne Lee, eldest daughter of a Dubliner. Eleven years later his brother Benjamin married Anne's youngest sister, Rebecca, thereby doubly enshrining the middle name 'Lee' in the baptismal certificates of later generations of Guinnesses as an identifying label of the brewery branch of the family. In addition to a legacy of £1,500 from his father's will, the Second Arthur was bequeathed the silver salver that had been presented to his father by the Corporation of Brewers of the City of Dublin. This symbolic gesture by the old man meant, in effect, that the Second Arthur assumed the mantle of head of the brewery and therefore of the family, although the senior line derived—and still does—from the Rev. Hosea. As decreed by the First Arthur, the salver has been passed on down through the generations 'to the Eldest Male Branch of my Family . . . who shall be in the Brewing Trade' and is today owned by Arthur Francis Benjamin Guinness, the 3rd Earl of Iveagh.

In fact, the Second Arthur had been made a full partner in the brewery at the age of 30, five years before his father's death, by which time his wife Anne had given him three sons: William Smythe Lee Grattan, Arthur Lee and Benjamin Lee. There would be six more children—all daughters—born to the marriage before Anne's death at the age of 43. Four years later Arthur took as his second wife the 38-year-old Maria Barker of Dublin, who died 16 years later leaving no issue to the 69-year-old widower.

Five years after the death of his father, Arthur became a director of the Bank of Ireland and subsequently its Governor, so that when George IV made a state visit to Ireland in 1821 it was Arthur who received the monarch on his visit to the bank, and a beginning was made in what was to be a developing social relationship between the Guinnesses and the British royal family.

About the time Arthur was showing the king around the bank, the brewery trade in Ireland was suffering a recession and Arthur found himself to be not only the nominal banker to Ireland but banker and troubleshooter to certain members of his immediate family whose financial acumen, not to say probity, fell short of his own high standards both as a businessman and an evangelical Christian.

This cross had been laid upon him first when his younger brother Edward, having left the brewery to set up an ironworks at Palmerston and Lucan, went bankrupt in 1811. The collapse took with it, also, the savings of the youngest brother, John Grattan, who had also left the brewery to take up a commission in the East India Company's armed forces. Faced with imprisonment for debt, Edward took off to the debtors' haven, the Isle of Man, from whence he bombarded Arthur with letters soliciting help. Arthur responded over the years with a generosity not untinged with irritation, and in 1815 the brewery bought Edward out of bankruptcy with a final settlement of £5,900. Ten years later Arthur put John Grattan into a partnership with the Liverpool agency handling imports of Guinness. A year later the agency decided it could get along better without him.

It was Arthur's fond wish that his brothers' and sisters' male children should carry on the tradition as brewers. But he was poorly served in this respect. John Grattan's son, John Grattan junior, was sacked from the brewery for 'mixing with degraded company' and exiled to Bristol where a brewery, bought for him by the Guinness agent in that city, went into bankruptcy a few years later. Two nephews died young; one went into the army, another went mad, and a further two became alcoholics. As Lynch and Vaisey soberly observe: 'these occurrences show how extraordinarily difficult it was to ensure a succession of adequate managers'.[6]

*

As we have seen, the year 1839 was a troubled one in the Guinness story. Father Mathew had launched his temperance campaign at a time when a general recession was already afflicting the brewery trade. And there had been problems of capital shortage caused by increased costs, notably in the price of hops. Against this, however, a good start had been made in securing a British market for Dublin porter. A combination of factors was responsible for this, some praiseworthy, others less so. On the good side, from the point of view of the English beer drinker, was the great improvement in the flavour of Dublin porter brought about by advanced methods of brewing and the introduction of Patent Brown Malt. A contemporary British expert, W. L. Tizard, had castigated the output of certain of his nation's breweries as 'a black, sulky beverage, on the taste of which the stranger experienced a shake, as sudden and electrical as that which seized a spaniel when quitting the water.'[7] In contrast, the best of the Irish porter—and this would certainly have applied to Guinness—was 'a mild, soft and agreeable potation of established soundness and permanently good quality'. Patent Brown Malt, which by 1828 had replaced the more lightly roasted brown malt hitherto used to give colour to the ale, produced, through controlled caramelization, a porter of consistent strength and darkness and less wasteful of the raw material. It was not a monopoly of the James's Gate brewery but it is probable that Arthur and his brothers used it with more efficiency than did most of their rivals.

On the less virtuous side there was the fact, well documented at the time, that the Irish brewers were a great deal more adept than their English competitors in the evasion of excise duty on malt purchases in Ireland. This meant that, even after shipping costs, the Irish were able to undersell the English country brewers of porter in their own market.

Arthur's brother Benjamin had died at the age of 49 and by 1839 his other brother, William, had retired from the business. Arthur was 71 and had transferred much of the burden of day-to-day administration to his sons Arthur Lee and Benjamin Lee and to John Purser junior of the family of London master brewers who had worked with the Guinnesses for three generations. All three were partners with the Second Arthur. Benjamin Lee, who was to become one of the most distinguished of the brewery Guinnesses, was then 41 and married to his wastrel uncle Edward's daughter, Elizabeth. The 42-year-old Arthur Lee...well, he was something else.

A bachelor who wrote lyrical verse in praise of Nature and sealed his letters with designs of a young Greek god, Arthur Lee's full-length portrait in the Guinness Collection is that of a slim and pretty aesthete with a carefully disarranged forelock. The problem with his life-style, as it impacted upon his father, was that it had led Arthur Lee into the issuing of promissory notes above and beyond his capacity to pay. To his credit, Arthur Lee insisted on giving up his shares and his partnership in the business after his debts had been paid, together with a golden handshake of £12,000. But his withdrawal produced a crisis over the reallocation of his shares between the remaining partners (with John Purser pressing for a bigger dip into the gravy), a crisis that at one stage threatened a dissolution of the partnership. It took all the moral fibre and strength of character of the ageing patriarch to steer the Guinness ship out of these troubled waters, and from then on he surrendered the helm to Benjamin Lee and John Purser.

The Second Arthur died in 1855. Family trust funds–the early basis of a complicated structure that would both enrich and bedevil future generations–had already been established in his father's lifetime and his own, and he was still able to leave a personal estate of £150,000–the approximate equivalent today in purchasing power of £3,000,000. (An idea of the extent of the family trust funds up to this point–as distinct from the probated wills–can be gained from the fact that within a year of Arthur's death his son Benjamin had already spent £150,000 of his own fortune on the restoration of Dublin's crumbling 600-year-old Protestant cathedral, St Patrick's.)

The brewery founded at James's Gate by the First Arthur had an initial output of about 10,500 gallons per annum. Within two years of his death the annual output stood at 350,000 gallons, the greater part of which was sold to the Dublin trade. Under the Second Arthur's administration the rest of Ireland was opened up to Guinness and, well within his lifetime, output had reached 3,200,000 gallons, of which exports to England and Scotland represented about 60 per cent in value. By 1837, the year Victoria became Queen, Guinness porter was already established in London as a quality drink. A newly elected young Member of Parliament testified to this in a letter to his sister:

So after all, there was a division on the Address in Queen Victoria's first Parliament–509 to 20. The division took an hour. I then left the House at ten o'clock, none of us scarcely having dined. The tumult and excitement unprecedented. I dined or rather supped at the Carlton with a large part of the flower of our side off oysters, Guinness and broiled bones, and got to bed at half past 12. Thus ended the most remarkable day hitherto of my life.

The writer was Benjamin Disraeli.[8]

Even more remarkable–and evidence of Guinness's early penetration of the European market–is an extract from the diary of a British cavalry officer, severely wounded in the Battle of Waterloo. The entry, dated June 1815, reads:

When I was sufficiently recovered to be able to take some nourishment, I felt the most extraordinary desire for a glass of Guinness, which I knew could be obtained in Belgium without difficulty. Upon expressing my wish to the doctor, he told me I might take a small glass... It was not long before I sent for the Guinness and I shall never forget how much I enjoyed it. I thought I had never tasted anything so delightful... I am confident that it contributed more than anything else to the renewal of my strength.[9]

The morale of the British troops sent to Europe to do battle with another dictator in 1939 was doubtless stiffened by the Christmas gift of 150,000 bottles of Guinness–roughly the equivalent of the brewery's total production in its first years. But the effect of this secret weapon against the Third Reich was, alas, diluted over the ensuing months, culminating in Dunkirk, and there appear to be no diary entries by members of the British Expeditionary Force comparable to the one quoted above.

3

Enter: the First Guinness Baronet

The assumption of Arthur's mantle by his successor Benjamin Lee was brief in years—1855–68. But these were years that would witness the rise of the Guinness family out of the milieu of respected tradesmen and towards the headier realms of national politics, civic honours and social ascendancy via marriages into the aristocracy.

The youngest son of the Second Arthur, Benjamin had started working in the brewery at the age of 16, had become a full partner six years later and was 57 at the time of his father's death in 1855. It had been Arthur's wish that control of the brewery and of the burgeoning family fortune should not be fragmented by 'unsatisfactory' marriages, and it was Benjamin's generation, more than any subsequent one, that underpinned this objective. Only three of the Second Arthur's nine children—Mary, Elizabeth and Rebecca—married outside the family. Louisa and Anne died unmarried, as did the 'black sheep', Arthur Lee. The eldest son, the Rev. William Smythe Lee Grattan was married twice, in both cases to first cousins.

None of William's five sons had children. His fifth son, Frederick Darley, died at 29 'from poison taken by mistake', making him the first of the Guinness family to die by his or her own hand, either accidentally or deliberately. Thus ended this particular line of male Guinnesses.

However, a strain of 'twice-over-Guinnesses'—or 'double-G. ale', as it has been labelled—had begun. Benjamin Lee had, as we have seen, married his Uncle Edward's daughter and would sire four 'twice-over' children. There were 'twice-over' daughters by the unions of William Smythe and Susanna with their cousins. And Benjamin Lee's own son, Edward Cecil, as we shall see, would also marry a Guinness cousin.

In 1851 Benjamin Lee was elected Lord Mayor of Dublin. His

ageing father had relinquished to him and to John Purser junior the control of the brewery, and the family business was on the threshold of an era in which production would not only equal the combined output of its ten competitors in Dublin but would be exceeded by only four major breweries operating in the hugely greater market of the United Kingdom. By the year of his death the annual output of Guinness would have reached 11,250,000 gallons.

Reporting his inauguration as Lord Mayor, the Dublin correspondent of *The Times* wrote on 3 January that 'it was conducted with more than ordinary civic pomp. The municipal procession altogether eclipsed anything that had been seen since the palmy days of the old "Orange" corporation and the day, so far as business was affected, was to all intents observed as a holiday'. The civic banquet given by the new Lord Mayor 20 days later came second only 'in the profusion and splendour of its arrangements' to the one given 30 years earlier on the occasion of George IV's visit to Ireland. 'His Excellency the Lord-Lieutenant, and all the leading officials, nobility and gentry at present in Dublin were among the guests,' reported *The Times* of 23 January. There was no mention of what Benjamin Lee's guests were given to wash their meal down with.

From this position of mercantile power and affluence he set out to broaden and elevate the base of what could by now truly be conceived as a dynasty invested with the promise of a brilliant succession. He already owned a country house and estate—St Anne's—on the outskirts of Dublin and a town house in Thomas Street, alongside the brewery. But he was looking for something more appropriate to his rank as head of Ireland's greatest industrial concern and he found it in the palladian town mansion built more than a century earlier for the rich Protestant Bishop of Clogher, Dr Robert Clayton, on the south side of St Stephen's Green, one of the largest city squares in Europe. In this three-storey *palazzo* with its four-columned projecting portico (the first to grace a Dublin house) the bishop and his wife Catherine, whose own wealth was exceeded only by the immensity of her ugliness, had held court until his death in 1758. Further owners were the Earls of Mountcashel; two successive Masters of the King's Roll; a Justice of the King's Bench, Charles Burton, and his son-in-law Robert Beatty West. West died in debt and Benjamin Lee was able to buy the mansion from the Commissioners of Encumbered Estates at the bargain price of £2,500.[1] He subsequently bought the adjoining house, No. 81, and dismantled it to merge its shell into the one great mansion, with its unified façade of Portland stone, that sets it off today from its neighbours.

Some idea of the splendour of what came to be known as Iveagh House is conveyed by the fact that when its contents were put up for auction in 1939 the sale catalogue listed 23 principal bedrooms and 11 bachelors' bedrooms, plus accommodation for a living-in staff of 20 servants. Here, when in residence, Benjamin and his cousin—wife Elizabeth—but more especially his heir, the 1st Earl of Iveagh—revived the stylish hospitality for which the house had been made famous, a century and a half earlier, by Dr and Mrs Clayton. These, the first titled Guinnesses in their own right, were of course pillars of the (Low) Protestant Church and there is a story, passed down to the proprietor of the bookshop on the opposite side of the Green, that illuminates—however apocryphally—the religious tightrope-walking of those days.

It happened that the Guinnesses were out of Dublin on the day when the Catholic faithful passed in pious procession through St Stephen's Green on their 'Seven-Churches' pilgrimage. On observing the phenomenon of a white crucifix displayed at one of the upper windows of the Guinness mansion, the pilgrims gathered in the street below, beads in hand, staring up at the holy object in awed disbelief. A Protestant caretaker in the neighbouring house, discomfited by the scene, let himself into the mansion by the servants' entrance and to his horror discovered one of the Catholic housemaids kneeling in the upper room behind the crucifix, reciting the rosary. Seizing the beads from the wench's hands he flung them down into the street and removed the crucifix from view. The shocked pilgrims redoubled their prayers as they went on their way, but whether by divine intervention or Guinness diplomacy the white cross reappeared in the window when the family resumed residence and it stayed there until the mansion was presented to the nation and became the headquarters of the Department of Foreign Affairs.

From the statue erected to Benjamin Lee in the precincts of St Patrick's Cathedral, and from portraits painted in his middle years, one gains the impression of a man in whose features all the mercantile wariness of his father and grandfather has been replaced by an expression of unassuming benevolence and a quality almost of *noblesse*. The strong prototypic Guinness jaw remains, as does the commanding nose, but the demeanour is that of a merchant prince, born to the role, rather than an aspirant to that status.

It could be said, then, that Benjamin Lee personified the elevation of the brewery Founder's kin from Dublin tradesmen into the seignorial class, and certainly all his endeavours from the year of his father's death seem to have been directed to that end. He bought the magnificent Ashford estate in co. Galway and shortly afterwards adopted as the Guinness emblem the harp of the Irish king, Brian Boru, who overthrew the pillaging Norsemen in 1014 at the Battle of Clontarf, site of Benjamin's St Anne's estate. By then he had already undertaken the restoration of St Patrick's, which he saved from collapse–as already noted–at a cost to his personal fortune of some £150,000. And before the work was completed he witnessed the marriage of his only daughter, Anne Lee, to the Hon. and Rev. William Conyngham, treasurer of the Cathedral and later Archbishop of Dublin.

This was a union that would bring the first title into the brewery line of the family, for William, who was 11 years younger than Anne, would become the 4th Baron Plunket upon the death of his father. It was also a union that would mingle (and remingle, two generations later), the blood of Guinnesses with that of an Anglo-Norman family bound by genetic flow to the British monarchy.[2] (Plunket's kinsman, the 1st Marquess of Conyngham, had married Elizabeth Denison who subsequently became the mistress of the Prince Regent–later George IV–who fathered her third son, Lord Albert Conyngham, born in 1805.)

Benjamin had been the first of the brewery chiefs to take a public stand alongside the political establishment, then under a double threat from the Liberal British chancellor, William Gladstone, who sought the disestablishment of the Anglican Church of Ireland, and from the emerging Sinn Fein movement whose aim was nothing less than full independence of the Irish nation from Britain. In 1865, when a Dublin newspaper praised 'the restorer of our National Cathedral as not the man to be found advocating or justifying, with Mr Gladstone, the destruction of the Establishment of this country',[3] Benjamin Lee was elected Conservative and Unionist Member for Dublin City, and in 1867 a grateful Establishment rewarded him with a baronetcy.

His wife, long afflicted by poor health, had died two years earlier and he followed her in 1868 at the age of 70. A report of his funeral in *The Times* of 29 May described it as 'One of the most impressive demonstrations of public feeling ever seen in this city' and goes on:

It was the desire of the family that it should be private, but the general sympathy was too great to permit their intention to be strictly carried out. The procession left St Anne's, Clontarf...at 10 o'clock and arrived at Mount Jerome Cemetery (the family vault) at 1 o'clock. It was headed by 500 workmen, who presented a very respectable appearance. They were arrayed in mourning and, marching in with great regularity and steadiness [*sic*], added an imposing effect to the solemn character of the cortege. The hearse and mourning coaches were followed by 239 private carriages, including those of the Lord-Lieutenant, the Mayor, Judges and representatives of the gentry, merchants and professional classes of the city. As the procession approached, the shops in the leading streets through which it passed were closed and the people, who assembled in great numbers, witnessed it with manifestation of regret.

It is not on record whether another grandson of the First Arthur, the Rev. Henry Grattan Guinness, took part in the procession through a city in which this great evangelist had for years been inveighing against, among other evils, the curse of intemperance. But it is unlikely that he would have approved of the intemperate language used against his cousin in a pamphlet promptly circulated under the title, *What it is to die a Brewer: The Burial of Sir Benjamin Lee Guinness* (the original copy of which is in the National Library, Dublin). Citing the eulogy delivered at the burial by the Bishop of Cork as an illustration 'of flattery poured forth in Dublin over the grave of Sir B. L. Guinness of double X porter notoriety' the pamphleteer, a Mr J. A. Mowatt, reminds his readers that the bishop used to be a teetotaller and 'has spoken out nobly in the cause of Temperance'. Had the bishop changed his views of intemperance and its evils 'or has the wealth of the brewery at James's Gate, Dublin, blinded his eyes?'

Clearly at odds with the bishop's remark that 'God did bless Sir Benjamin's untiring endeavours with great prosperity', Mr Mowatt castigates the brewer as 'A man who in the course of his life made more drunkards at home and abroad than, perhaps, any other in these lands; who destroyed more of the bread of men and beast; who oftener "put his bottle to his neighbour and made him drunken withal" than anyone else in these kingdoms, doubtless.' And he goes on: '...during the 70 years of Sir B. L. G.'s life, the thousands of souls which his drink hurried into an awful eternity form something fearful to contemplate. Oh, the amount of human suffering, and woe, and remorse, and sin, that Sir B. L. Guinness fostered and promoted during the 70 years of a long life as a brewer!!!'

The bishop's reference to 'that large wealth which God placed at his disposal' sends Mr Mowatt into a paroxysm of righteous polemics:

In other words, God took the poor man's wages, which ought to have gone to support his wife and family, and He placed it at Sir B. L. G.'s 'disposal' at the rate of fourpence a quart, or threepence per small bottle of double X, consumed. How fearful to contemplate this idea of the Almighty becoming Guinness's pot-boy, and disposing of his porter for him!...He built St Patrick's and gained a baronetcy by it, with all this fulsome flattery. Prior to the restoration of St Patrick's he was little known, except through his XX labels, which are the only famous literary works which he has left behind him; and they are read the world over with thick tongues, bloated countenances, bloodshot eyes and staggering gait.

Such overheated prose can hardly have impressed any but the fanatical minority already ranged alongside its author. It would certainly not have discomfited Sir Benjamin, a man of genuine evangelical piety who began and ended every day with prayers to a deity who, to his mind, was rewarding him for his honest industry and public benefactions—a God who, when it came down to it, was ritually celebrated at Mass every day by the drinking of a wine no less potent than double X Guinness. In fact, despite his wealth and the opulence of his residences, Sir Benjamin's life-style verged, as did his father's, on the austere. The glittering evenings at 80 St Stephen's Green were less a personal indulgence than a case of *noblesse oblige*.

He was the third and last of the Guinnesses to direct the brewery's affairs almost exclusively from his base in Dublin. His successors would gravitate between their Irish homes (for the Dublin 'season') and their town and country houses in England, where politics, the society of their peers and the patronage of monarchs were to occupy an ever-increasing portion of their time. With Benjamin's death a phoenix arose, fitted with wings that would carry his children and grandchildren to the dizziest peaks of the British Establishment.

4

Towards the Peak

1

If the sixth generation of 'Founder's kin' Guinnesses, maturing between World Wars I and II, is notable for its 'Guinness Girls'—the subjects of later chapters—the fourth and fifth belong to four Guinness males whose penetration of the corridors of power finds no parallel in any other British family of non-aristocratic stock. This era, encompassing the Boer War, the reigns of Edward VII and George V and premierships from Disraeli to Churchill, began with the death of Benjamin Lee, reached its peak during the lifetime of the 2nd Earl of Iveagh, and might be said to have ended with the assassination of Walter Edward Guinness in 1944.

Sir Benjamin could hardly have foreseen the lustre his grand-children would add to the family name; none of them was even born in his lifetime. But when he drew up his will it was structured so as to ensure a dynastic succession of male Guinnesses and the protection within that succession of the Guinness fortune. And since it has never been a cynicism to equate money with power in the capitalist system, it can be said, with the hindsight denied Sir Benjamin, that his will was the *sine qua non* of the glory to come. Though he had set up various family trusts before his death he was still able to leave an estate of £1,100,000 (call it, today, £26,400,000), making it the largest will ever proved in Ireland up to that date. His only daughter Anne was already married and his second son (Benjamin) Lee had taken up a career in the Royal Horse Guards. They were provided for in the will but the bulk of the estate was bequeathed in equal measure to the first son, Arthur Edward, and the third, Edward Cecil. Arthur had been sent to Eton—the first of what would be an almost unbroken line of Guinness Etonians—and he now inherited, at 27, his father's baronetcy. Edward Cecil, who had started work in the brewery at the age of 15, became a full partner in the business with his brother, though he was still six months short of his majority. This, taken together with other major bequests in the will, suggests that Sir Benjamin already had a shrewd idea as to which of the two sons was best suited to be guardian of the silver salver passed down by the First Arthur. For while he left his country estates, St Anne's and Ashford, to the new Sir Arthur, it was Edward who inherited the town mansion on St Stephen's Green—the visible expression of the brewery's civic pre-eminence.

The deed of partnership prescribed in Sir Benjamin's will stipulated that if either of his sons decided to leave the business he was obliged to turn over his half share to the other son. In compensation he would receive the sum of £30,000 plus half the value 'of the stock, good debts bills and cash on hand'.[1] The further provision, that this golden handshake should be given in eight equal instalments, without interest, would spare the remaining son any embarrassment *vis-à-vis* liquidity.

As it turned out, Sir Arthur, who married Lady Olivia White, a daughter of the 3rd Earl of Bantry, less than three years later, surrendered his partnership under far more favourable terms than this, after drawing substantial profits from the company during the years 1868–76. From the first year's profits under the partnership he took £42,000 against Edward's £2,000, but this was the year in which he agreed to enter the by-election for his father's parliamentary seat, and votes cost money. Sir Arthur's politics were staunchly Unionist at a time when the campaign for Home Rule was already attracting a nationalist element among the Protestant Establishment. Two days after the death of Sir Benjamin, *The Times* reported that 'The Liberal electors of Dublin are not disposed to accept Sir Arthur as heir and successor of the late senior member. While entertaining the highest personal respect for him on account of the name he bears, they are naturally unwilling at such a serious political crisis to entrust the representation to a young and inexperienced man whose views are likely to be antagonistic to their own.'

Despite this, he was returned unopposed and he held on to the seat in the general election later that year. Then came the bombshell. A petition accusing Sir Arthur's political agents of bribing the electorate was heard before Judge Keogh who, after examining the evidence, declared Sir Arthur's election as void. His money had been 'squandered' during the campaign and the brewers and other freemen who supported him were 'a corrupt class'. But while he was guilty of bribery through his agents, he himself, as *The Times* of 6 February 1869 reported, was not guilty of any corrupt practices.

The effect was to keep Sir Arthur out of Parliament–though not out of politics–for the next five years, when he again stood for the Dublin seat and held it from 1874 to 1880. Meanwhile, he had married into the 'quality', helped to finance the great Irish Exhibition of 1872 and poured money into converting St Anne's into an Italianate country mansion. On his 3,500-acre Ashford estate he built a massive baronial castle, had thousands of larches laid down and made it into probably the best woodcock shoot in the world, whose 'guns' included Edward VII.

His wife Olivia had never been enchanted by his connection with the brewery but Sir Arthur was unwilling to give up a partnership that yielded him a personal income of £530,000 over the eight years following his father's death–certainly not on the terms laid down in the will. His spasmodic intrusions into the affairs of the brewery were an irritant to his younger brother who in 1873 had married his cousin Adelaide Guinness, a great-granddaughter of Samuel the gold-beater, and was already concerned about the succession to his own first son, Rupert Edward, born a year later. In 1876 when the original deed of partnership came up for renewal, Edward proposed that its terms be revised to reflect the disbalance between the brothers in the management of the family business. But Guinness's trade had doubled over the past eight years and Sir Arthur was quite happy to stick with the original terms of the partnership. In the end, Olivia's hostility to Trade, in tandem with a generous financial inducement from Edward, won the day and the partnership was dissolved with a handshake for Arthur of £686,000. This, with the legacies from his father and his share of profits since 1868, left Arthur with plenty of time and wealth for the purchase of a peerage.

To this he applied himself diligently and openhandedly. He completed the reconstruction of Archbishop Marsh's library in Dublin, rebuilt the Coombe lying-in hospital and literally 'bought Killarney', saving it from speculative builders by acquiring for £60,000 the Muckross Estate, which included the shores of the famous and romantic lake. His major benefaction was in buying the 30 acres of St Stephen's Green from the householders, who had fenced it off as a private park. Arthur landscaped it with walks, flower beds and an ornamental lake and presented it to the public. For this he was rewarded in 1880 by being raised to the peerage as Lord Ardilaun[2] of Ashford and, two years later, a statue to his lordship was erected on St Stephen's Green. This was the first peerage bestowed upon the Guinness family, but unhappily the Ardilaun title ended there, for Arthur Edward died without issue in 1915. As one of Ireland's major

landlords, with estates–apart from Ashford, Muckross and Clontarf–at Ballykyn, Strandhill and Lisloughoey, his participation in
House of Lords debates was largely confined to defending Irish
landlords against the 'injustices' of the Land Act of 1896 and what he
saw as its over-generous bias towards the rent-paying peasantry.
And to ensure a platform in Dublin for his anti-Home-Rule politics
he bought the Dublin *Daily Express*, *Morning Mail*, *Evening Mail* and
Weekly Warder.

He made out his will in 1902, settling his landed estates on his only
surviving brother, Edward Cecil, 'fearing', as he put it, 'that the care
of my estates would impose too much upon my wife'. His unsettled
personal estate, valued after death duties at £495,638, went to his
wife, with his London house at 11 Carlton House Terrace, his
Dublin residence at No 42 St Stephen's Green and his St Anne's
estate at Clontarf. The London house was bought in 1916 by Benjamin Seymour Guinness of the banking branch of the family, the same
year Arthur's 66-year-old widow put up for auction the Rubens
masterpiece *The Adoration of the Magi* for which her husband had paid
1,500 guineas at the Blenheim Palace sale in 1886. It fell at 780
guineas to the highest bidder. Forty-three years later it was bought
by a wealthy British industrialist and racehorse owner, Major All-
matt, for £275,000 and donated to King's College, Cambridge. Its
cash value today is in the realm of the incalculable.

After her husband's death, Lady Ardilaun settled in Ireland,
dividing her time between Dublin, where her *salon* was popular with
the local intelligentsia, and her castle at Macroom in co. Cork, 20
miles from Bantry, the seat of her father, the 3rd Earl. At least as
intensely as her husband, Olivia Ardilaun despised the legislators at
Westminster for their concessions to the Irish nationalists and what
she saw as their timidity towards the militant republicans of the Sinn
Fein. Fire was quite literally added to her anger when her castle at
Macroom was burned by local republicans acting, as she declared
later in her will, 'on the order of an Englishman, Erskine Childers by
name'.[3] But Lady Ardilaun's opprobrium fell also, and somewhat
illogically, upon the Government's 'Black and Tans', whose occu-
pancy of the castle had provoked the republican action.

She died at her St Stephen's Green home in December 1925,
leaving an estate valued at over £900,000. Control of the rectorship
of the Protestant church of All Saints, built by her husband at
Raheny, close by his Clontarf estate, was passed to his nephew,
Benjamin John Plunket, the Bishop of Meath, with the direction that
'under no circumstances is an Englishman to be appointed as

Rector...and any such Rector must be Irish by birth and parentage'. Plunket inherited the residue of Lady Ardilaun's estate after numerous personal and charitable legacies had been taken care of. A trust of £20,000 was set up for the education of Protestant sons of the Irish gentry 'in reduced circumstances owing to loss of income from their Irish landed estates' and for assistance in the education of (Protestant) clergymen's sons. The trust would be known as the 'Lady Ardilaun Educational Endowment' and the recipients were to be called the 'Lady Ardilaun Scholars'.

Immortality was further secured with a trust fund of £500, from the income of which patients and servants at Mercer's Hospital, Dublin, were to be provided every year with a special Christmas dinner. Predictably, this was to be known as 'the Lady Ardilaun Dinner'.

The Ardilaun peerage became extinct but the baronetcy Arthur had inherited from Sir Benjamin Lee passed to his nephew Algernon Arthur Guinness, eldest son of the already-deceased (Benjamin) Lee. The strongwilled and purposive Olivia had outlived her more reserved and taciturn husband by eleven years. The consensus among the wits of her Dublin *salon* was that she had wanted to give him time to make the right connections up there.

Nubar Gulbenkian, son of the famous Calouste ('Mr 5 per cent') Gulbenkian, has written in his autobiography[4] about the enormous obstacles facing an 'outsider' aspiring to move upwards through the rigid class structure of Britain towards the end of the 19th century.

It was still held to be non-U to admit to earning one's living. Many people would have said, on hearing that my father went each day to the City: 'But fancy *having* to go to the City!' There was all the difference in the world, too, between the eldest son looking after the family 'estates' and his looking after the family 'business', no matter what the scale of it might be. Similarly, a man who had made his fortune in retail trade would meet the most formidable obstacles to acceptance by Society. First-generation wealth was disdained. Only large contributions to Party funds, the acquisition of a country 'place', a pack of foxhounds, a polo ground and, eventually, of a baronetcy, might open the door. Even then the emphasis is on the word 'might'.

Sir Arthur had played the game according to the rules by marrying an earl's daughter, getting out of 'trade' and by keeping the Conservative Party's treasurer happy. But his brother Edward Cecil held to the view that the pursuit of trade and of social distinction were in no way incompatible objectives and that the highest honours in the land were within reach so long as he matched his prosperity as a brewer with a visibly generous disbursement of his spare cash. And during the half-century left to him, from the year he became sole proprietor until his death in 1927, he proved his point to a degree unequalled by any other industrialist, before or since.

He was well equipped by temperament for the challenge. Of short and slight physique and a demeanour that would come to be described as 'scholarly' in his later years, Edward at the age of 30 was a model of the 'young man in a hurry', intolerant of fools, impatient of delay and a master of detail from the trivial to the complex. At the same time, but away from the brewery, his nature was outgoing and gregarious and he shared with his attractive cousin–wife a genuine pleasure in entertaining on the grand scale, a gift not always conspicuous in those with comparable wealth and social ambition. He was not to receive his first title, a baronetcy, until 1885 but he had set part of the scene for it ten years earlier. That was when he bought the great Victorian mansion of Farmleigh, beautifully situated on a wooded eminence overlooking the River Liffey, with a 60-acre estate stretching from Phoenix Park in Dublin to the village of Castleknock, outside the city. By rebuilding the mansion he provided an Irish seat for the earldom on which he had set his sights.

He had been drawing a huge personal income out of the family's private company. The brewery was thriving under excellent management, and high society in London was already opening its doors wide to the affluent Anglo-Irish baronet. In October 1886, the year Gladstone introduced his first Home Rule (for Ireland) Bill to the English House of Commons, the stock exchanges of London and Dublin erupted with the news that Arthur Guinness Son & Company had decided to go public.

The reaction to this bombshell differed greatly between the two capitals. No prospectuses inviting participation in the new £6,000,000 company were sent to Dublin stockbrokers nor–as *The Times* correspondent in Dublin put it on 5 October–'any measure taken to let the Irish public, who have contributed to the great success of the establishment, participate in the distribution of the shares'. The blame for this was put on the finance house, Messrs Baring & Company, in charge of the operation.

Such was the fever among investors to buy into the brewery that during one morning the applications for shares totalled £127,000,000. It had been stated in the prospectus that the chairman, Sir Edward Cecil, would keep one-third of the share capital for himself and his family and the rest would be offered for public subscription. But Baring's interpretation of these mathematics was a loose one, to put it mildly. They kept £850,000-worth for themselves, distributed another £850,000-worth among twenty of their 'near friends' and allotted £1,500,000-worth among fifty City of London stockbrokers. Hard on the outcry of disappointed would-be investors came a stern admonition from the Committee of the Stock Exchange. Messrs Baring were rapped over the knuckles for the issue of script certificates made out 'to bearer'. They were ordered to withdraw these certificates and issue new ones bearing the allottees' names. At the same time it was announced that Law Officers of the Crown and the Board of Inland Revenue would 'in future look more closely into matters connected with new issue of capital' (as reported by *The Times*, 3–17 December). But while the Irish investors had a grievance, the employees at James's Gate were given cause for celebration. To signal his retirement from sole proprietorship, Sir Edward Cecil presented each member of the brewery's commercial department with a cheque for three months' salary, and the equivalent of a month's wages went to the draymen and other manual workers, a gift that cost him around £60,000.

It was a generous gesture, and it was also a timely one. Wages and working conditions for the employees at James's Gate were better than in any comparable enterprise, other than those owned by the Quaker industrialists of 19th-century England, and it would be the company's long-term policy to maintain such a favourable wages differential. But trade unionism was on the march and Sir Edward was in no way disposed to welcome it. This he made clear four years later when the demands on his time and energies as a public benefactor obliged him to retire for several years from the chairmanship of the company. His farewell letter to the employees thanked them for their services, assured them that the traditions of the firm in its treatment of the hands would be preserved and expressed the hope, reported in *The Times* of 23 August 1890, 'that the men will not be induced by any outsiders to enter into combinations which would impair the friendly relations which have always been maintained...' These sentiments were sweetened with a parting gift of a month's pay to the clerks and a week's money to all other hands.

He was now just 43 years old and a multi-millionaire. He would stay on the board of Arthur Guinness Son & Co. until shortly before his death, guiding the affairs of the brewery as trustee for his three sons, Rupert Edward, Arthur Ernest and Walter Edward. But the fact that the eldest of them, Rupert, was then only 16 meant that the head of the Founder's kin would have to turn to another branch of the Guinness family for a replacement at the helm of the business. There were cousins galore on the clergyman side of the line from the First Arthur, through his sons William Lunell and John Grattan, but the best of them were all abroad in the world, bringing the message of the Bible to dark continents. The descendants of the First Arthur's eldest son, Hosea, had by now either emigrated to New Zealand or faded into uncommercial backgrounds in England and Ireland. So Edward turned to his wife's brother, the 48-year-old Reginald Robert Guinness, great-grandson of Samuel the goldbeater, thereby effecting, as it were, the first and only cross-fertilization between the banking and brewing lines so far as chairmanship of the latter was concerned.

Reginald presided over the board through the closing years of the 19th century and the opening years of the 20th, years that witnessed an extension of the brewery's premises, a climb in annual profits to the million-plus level and an increase in the Ordinary dividend from 14 to 22 per cent. Two years before Reginald's death in July 1909 he was knighted for his civic services to the City of Dublin, but by then there appears to have been an estrangement between him and the head of the brewery line for, as *The Times* commented on 16 August that year, there was a 'notable omission' of any reference to Sir Reginald's death in the annual report to shareholders. This had been delivered by Edward Cecil, now back in the chair—no longer as Sir Edward but as Baron Iveagh of co. Down, a United Kingdom title bestowed on him in 1891.

His elevation to the peerage had been earned by what *The Times* described on 20 November 1889 as 'the most splendid act of private munificence that had been contemplated and carried out in our time by any Englishman'. It was hardly an exaggeration. Sir Edward had placed in the hands of three worthy trustees[5] the staggering sum, in those days, of £250,000 'to be held by them in trust for the creation of dwellings for the labouring poor'. Of this sum, £200,000 would go to London and £50,000 to Dublin, and the moderate rents charged to the rehoused working-class families would be reinvested to provide further capital for an expansion of the programme. Thus was established the Guinness Trust for the Housing of the Poor, whose visible expression would take the form over the years of the 'Guinness Buildings', landmarks so familiar to the next four generations of Londoners.

An immediate and bizarre sequel to the announcement was a

'kindly' offer to the Trust, by Lord Cadogan, of an acre of land worth £40,000 situated bang in the centre of his huge Chelsea estate, one of the most lucrative privately owned residential areas of London. The land formed part of the grounds of Blacklands House, and landlord Cadogan, who was not especially noted for his charity, was not only making a gift of it but 'in order to render it immediately available' had purchased from the lessees of Blacklands House the unexpired term of their lease, which still had 14 years to run. Light was to be thrown shortly on his lordship's generosity when the lessees, Messrs Sutherland, proudly announced through *The Times* of 27 March 1890 that they would be moving their 'business', hitherto conducted at Blacklands House, and re-establishing it at Newslands House, on an isolated stretch of Tooting Common in south London.

The business in question was a lunatic asylum.

From 1890 onwards, Lord Iveagh spent more time in London than in Dublin, first in his residence at 5 Berkeley Street and later in his great Grosvenor Place mansion. This five-storey mansion in fact comprised two interconnecting houses, Nos. 4 and 5, with a total of 150 rooms and garage space for 60 motor cars.[6] It would be revealed later, in the course of the legal battle between Iveagh's executors and the Irish Revenue Commissioners, that his lordship executed a deed poll in 1920 declaring that England was his only place of residence. This was at the height of the violent civil war between the Irish republicans and the loyalist Black and Tans and, as the commissioners argued, 'Lord Iveagh must have been horrified at the condition of affairs...and being a Victorian must have thought an end had come to the social order in Ireland.' They discounted the deed poll as a lawyer's instrument rather than 'the spontaneous expression of a man's intention...in a political situation that was purely transitory'.[7]

Iveagh's social activities in England were on a level appropriate to his new status and were complemented by well-publicized benefactions of a hitherto unprecedented liberality. He joined the other trustees of his housing scheme in 1891 and by 1895 there were 5,135 people living in London's Guinness Buildings and 343 in the Dublin dwellings. These—seen later as rather bleak and austere edifices—were at the time models of working-class accommodation with community bathrooms for males and females, club rooms, laundry rooms, a shared source of boiling water for tea-making, sheds for the resident costermongers' barrows and spacious asphalted yards for the kids to play in. In the Walworth buildings

Lady Iveagh opened a nursery–'Lady Iveagh's Cradle'–where working mothers could leave their infants in the care of nurses at a cost, including food, of fourpence (or 1.66 new pence) a day. The average weekly rent of a two-to-three-room dwelling was four shillings, or 18 per cent of the tenants' average weekly earnings of nineteen shillings and fivepence. And since all rental income was invested for the Trust, its capital by 1900 stood at £307,084 in London (where 8,436 dwellers were now accommodated) and £59,882 in Dublin. Today, the Trust is known as one of England's largest housing associations and is a registered charity backed by Government loans and subsidies, with rents of the new or remodelled dwellings fixed by local rent officers.

Within three months of the outbreak of the Boer War in October 1899, a mobile hospital corps had been financed by Lord Iveagh in Dublin and put on the high seas to Cape Town. In addition to surgeons, orderlies, male nurses and dressers, the hospital was equipped with 100 beds, 30 tents, 20 wagons and 90 mules and horses. Lord Iveagh was at the Albert Docks in London to see the 80-strong contingent off to war and to hand each of them a pipe and a pound of tobacco. The corps was on active service from May to October 1900. It was the only field hospital accompanying Lord Kitchener's expedition to Prieska; later, after it had joined Lord Roberts's forces for the capture of Bloemfontein, the Commander-in-Chief mailed a soldierly tribute to Lord Iveagh: 'Very valuable addition to this Army–thoroughly satisfactory in all respects.'

Between 1902 and 1925 Iveagh made gifts totalling around £100,000 to hospitals and medical charities, including a cheque for £50,000 handed to George V in 1911 to be distributed 'at His Majesty's pleasure' among hospitals in Dublin. He also spent £140,000 on providing playing fields and a recreation centre for the poor children of that city. Other gifts ranged from sums of £1,000 to the Church Army and the Boy Scouts to £40,000 to the University of Dublin for the construction and equipment of laboratories of experimental and botanical science, for which the donor was made a Knight of the Most Illustrious Order of St Patrick. And in England he endowed with £250,000 the Lister Institute of Preventive Medicine and with Sir Ernest Cassell founded the Radium Institute, later amalgamated with the Mount Vernon Hospital.

As Iveagh's benefactions to the people of Ireland multiplied, his hostility to their struggle for political independence from England continued unabated. His position had been made clear as far back as 1870 when, at the age of 22, he had been approached by Isaac Butt,

leader of the Home Rule movement, to contest the Dublin parliamentary seat his brother Arthur had been forced to give up. At
that time the most that Butt and his supporters were asking for was a
partial repeal of the union between Britain and Ireland, a moderate
platform that was already attracting support from the nationalist
wing of the Conservative Party. Speaking for his brother in a letter to
Isaac Butt dated 25 May 1870,[8] Sir Arthur stated that '...as you
have alluded to a rumour that there was a chance of his adopting
what are commonly called Nationalist views and opinion, such was
not the case for, while none can feel more strongly a truly National
desire for the advancement of Ireland materially and intellectually,
we do not and cannot think this is to be achieved by Repeal...'

By 1912, when Edward Cecil was 65, the agitation was no longer
for partial repeal but for full Home Rule, and his lordship, now
firmly and nobly established in England, forcibly expressed his
views about that when he declared, as chairman at the annual
meeting of the Irish Unionist Alliance, 'The Alliance is now bracing
itself with confident hope to secure a final victory over the forces of
disruption.' A resolution, reported in *The Times* of 27 April, was then
passed expressing 'the Alliance's unabated hostility to Home Rule in
any shape or form and thanking the people of Ulster for their fixed
resolve to make common cause with the Unionizing of the three
southern provinces.'

Only nine months earlier, Edward Cecil had rubbed home in a
unique fashion his view that, while Guinness was undoubtedly good
for Ireland, political independence most certainly was not. On the
occasion of a visit by his friend, the recently crowned George V, to
the Dublin recreation centre referred to above, he had the Irish
children coached in the singing of 'God Save the King'. If the
performance was a little ragged there was good excuse for, as *The
Times* correspondent reported on 10 July 1911, they were singing the
British national anthem 'probably for the first time in their lives, for
till now the political trend of the Dublin populace has tabooed the
National Anthem'.

By 1918, following the landslide victory of the Sinn Fein candi-
dates in the parliamentary general election, it must have been obvious to Edward Cecil that the spectre of Home Rule—not to mention
full independence—was not so much haunting him as actually treading on the tails of his coat. It was time for the Irish Unionist Alliance
to trim its sails, just a little. Uneasiness concerning the rigidity of
the Alliance's policy had already arisen in the ranks and, in correspondence with his political colleague Lord Middleton, Edward

Cecil, while reaffirming his 'earnest hope' that the Home Rule Act would never be enforced, could foresee that the measure 'may be forced on the British Government by outside pressure'. It was not, he thought, impossible to reconcile the opposition to Home Rule 'with a prudent preparation for eventualities', and to that end he suggested that while 'presenting an unbroken front to the powers opposed to them they should neglect no means of obtaining safeguards, with such modifications of any Bill as would mitigate its worst evils'.

In the event, neither the formation of the Irish Free State in 1922 nor the birth of the Republic in 1937 had any adverse impact on the fortunes of Arthur Guinness Son & Co., and it is perhaps sad that the great-grandson of the First Arthur contributed so much to the social welfare of the Dubliners and so little to the political evolution of the Irish people.

Between 1887 and 1891, well away from the public gaze, an anonymous purchaser was active in the art world, quietly buying, through agents, every masterpiece from the famous English private collections he could lay his hands on. The American banker, Pierpont Morgan, had already started to loot these galleries for his American collection, and now it was being rumoured in art circles that a certain British industrialist had in one month purchased an array of masterpieces at a cost of £500,000. The *cognoscenti* were heard to whisper the name 'Guinness' and, in later years, with the appearance in the Winter Exhibitions at Burlington House of many great canvases lent in that name—or rather 'Iveagh', as he was to become—the rumours were confirmed.

The extent of Sir Edward Cecil's investment in paintings and drawings over a period of one month was exaggerated, but it is a fact that over the four years during which the bulk of his collection was amassed considerably more than £500,000 of his money passed through the hands of a single London firm of art dealers—Agnew's of Bond Street. The Sales Book for that period, carefully preserved by the gallery, contains four and a half pages of items bought by Iveagh, each one inscribed on one line, in minuscule handwriting. How Iveagh chose to use Agnew's, almost exclusively, in the building up of his art collection remains to this day an imperishable lesson to all would-be rivals of that great firm of art dealers.

One day he had strolled, unheralded, into another Bond Street gallery and asked to be shown some fine paintings. The partners were out at lunch and an over-cautious salesman, refusing to bring out the best of the gallery's treasures, invited the stranger to 'come back when the partners are here'. Edward Cecil left in a huff and walked on down the street to Agnew's where he repeated his request. It happened that the then partners in the gallery, the illustrious dealer William Agnew and his two sons, George and Morland, were also either at lunch or on business elsewhere. But this time, the salesman left in charge showed more discernment, producing from a back room some pictures he was not strictly allowed to show in the absence of his employers. Edward Cecil was attracted to a Boucher painting, *The Flower Gatherer*, and to Cuyp's *View on the Maas*, both of which he bought there and then for around £6,000. The date was 23 June 1887.

He returned to Agnew's nine days later and bought two Reynolds, and he was back again on 19 July to add a Romney to his incipient collection. Over the next four years he purchased, through Agnew's, over 200 paintings and drawings by masters such as the above-mentioned, plus works by Rembrandt, Gainsborough, Raeburn, Turner, Millais, Landseer, Vermeer, Watteau, Van Dyck, Guardi and Canaletto. No private collection of such dimensions was ever put together in so short a time, and his dealings with Agnew's were conducted in strict secrecy, with a code name used to conceal the identity of the purchaser. All the works went into his mansion in Grosvenor Place and they remained there until his death, on view only to his family and friends—for he was not to be tempted by offers from private collectors or from agents secretly acting on their behalf, though he could later, as noted, be prevailed upon with reluctance to lend one or two paintings to important exhibitions such as those celebrating the Rembrandt and Van Dyck tercentenaries.[9] And on occasions such as the visits by Edward VII to Edward Cecil's racing yacht *Cretonia* at Cowes it was his host's pride to have one or two full-length portraits of English beauties by Reynolds or Romney transported from Grosvenor Place and hung in the spacious dining saloon of the yacht.

Sir Geoffrey Agnew, whose great-grandfather so expertly guided the great collector, assured me that Edward Cecil bought what he liked for the pleasure his pictures gave him, and this would seem to be borne out by the fact that on one occasion he was sold a 'Romney' by a Polish countess, over a dinner table, that turned out to be by a hand other than the master's. Be this as it may, it is more than probable that he was at first spurred to visit Bond Street by the irritating fact that his friend Lord Burton, of the Bass family of brewers, was already the proud owner of a great collection of the Early British school, including the full-length Reynolds portrait of

Lady Sunderlin. Later, Lord Burton was to grumble to Agnew's that they were giving Guinness first sight of the best of the acquisitions, a fact that Sir Geoffrey confirms and which is hardly surprising, given that Edward Cecil's was the greatest single collection Agnew's has ever formed for one buyer.

Today, visitors to London can freely enjoy many of these art treasures while strolling the galleries of Ken Wood, the graceful mansion on 76 acres of Hampstead parkland that Iveagh bought in 1925 and bequeathed to the public on his death two years later. Under the terms of his will an important part of his private collection—a part valued in those days at about £300,000—was left to Ken Wood together with an endowment of £50,000 for its upkeep. Of the 63 paintings in the Ken Wood collection, 62 came from Agnew's and were originally bought by Edward Cecil at prices ranging from £3,000 to £10,000.

The Times of 1 November 1927, noting 'the priceless character of the bequest', described it as 'the most magnificent of its kind to the British nation during the present century'. It added: 'For many years Lord Iveagh has been forming his collection not only in competition with the greatest of the American millionaires but very much on the same lines—the best was always good enough for him and price was only a minor consideration.'

The rest of Iveagh's collection was left to his descendants, either directly or through the Iveagh trusts. Some of the works were subsequently sold, but two of the four magnificent Guardis he bought from Agnew's remain in the family at the time of writing and his collection of drawings by Watteau are in the proud possession of his great-grandson the present Earl of Iveagh.

If the best in art was good enough for Lord Iveagh, this was even more true of his residential life-style. Before the turn of the century he had added a sumptuous ballroom—described as the most beautiful room in Ireland—to his house at 80 St Stephen's Green, now further enlarged by the purchase and structural addition of Nos. 78 and 79. Another ballroom, featuring imported Carrara marble, was designed by the architect William Young and installed in the mansion of Farmleigh. But the greatest single *coup* affecting the Iveagh life-style was his purchase of the Elveden Estate in East Anglia from Duleep Singh, Maharaja of Lahore.

2

Duleep had been 'acknowledged' at his birth in 1838 as a son of the ageing Maharaja Runjit Singh, 'Lion of the Punjab', though it is more likely he was the offspring of Jindan Kour, the ambitious daughter of a palace doorkeeper, and a male servant with whom the decadent and partially paralysed Runjit Singh coupled her for his voyeurist entertainment.[10] At the age of six, after the death of Runjit, he was proclaimed Maharaja, with his mother acting as regent. Three years later, troops of the East India Company occupied the Punjab capital of Lahore, Jindan Kour was banished and the young Duleep taken under the 'guardianship' of the British Governor-General of India. After an uprising by the Sikhs was crushed in 1849, the independent kingdom of the Punjab was absorbed into British India and the ten-year-old Duleep forced to surrender his throne and leave the kingdom in return for a princely pension. As part of the terms of surrender, the famous Koh-i-noor diamond, the size of a pigeon egg, changed ownership from the Maharaja to Queen Victoria of England. Victoria was enchanted by the young Sikh from the day he was presented to her at Buckingham Palace, and from then on, until he turned against Britain, the queen treated him almost as an adopted son, taking a maternal interest in his education, his marriage and his general well-being in the country of his adoption.

Duleep Singh took up residence in England and lived the life of a noble gentleman, in close touch with the Court and on rented country estates where he indulged his favourite pastime of shooting game birds. He also gambled excessively, womanized, and was already in debt when he bought Elveden Hall on the borders of Suffolk and Norfolk and its 17,000 acres, mostly scrubland, with a loan from the India Office of £105,000. Here he entertained the high and mighty of the land and strove each season to achieve his ambition of slaughtering 1,000 birds, by his own gun, in one day's shooting. (The nearest he got to it was 780 partridge for a thousand cartridges.)

As his debts multiplied, he hounded the Government for an increase in his pension, using the ever-tolerant Victoria as a go-between, and finally got around to demanding the return of the Koh-i-noor, or at least its equivalent in cash. The queen's unenthusiastic response to this proposal earned her a title, from Duleep's lips, somewhat less than respectful of her status as Defender of the Faith and Empress of India. She became 'Mrs Fagin, the receiver of stolen property'. The story of Duleep Singh ends with his leaving

England, his footling attempts at stirring the Sikh nation into revolt against the British Raj, and his death in Paris at the age of 53 after an apoplectic fit.

Meanwhile the neglected Elveden estate had been slowly going to pot, its tenant farmers giving up cultivation, its mansion and other buildings in need of repair. Trustees for the India Office had taken it over and were delighted when Edward Cecil agreed to purchase the property in 1894, lock, stock and barrel, for £159,000. As George Martelli puts it in his book, *The Elveden Enterprise* (Faber & Faber, 1952), 'It was the beginning of a golden age for Elveden.'

Edward Cecil set to at once to turn the property into a country estate not only fit for a peer of the realm but magnificent enough to provide a family seat for the earldom upon which his sights were unwaveringly set. He raised the acreage from 17,000 to 23,000 by purchasing the adjoining Icklingham estate from the Gwilt family, thereby incorporating the village of that name with the villages of Elveden, Eriswell and Wangford, already part of the property.

Duleep Singh had virtually rebuilt, to his own taste, the Hall that had once been the home of the Duke of Bedford and, before him, the Earl of Albemarle. The architect, John Norton, was engaged to redesign it in the Italian Renaissance style, with a great pillared portico and the whole exterior finished in red brick with Ancaster stone dressings.

> But the interior was even more fanciful: Norton's brief was to make the main rooms reminiscent of an Indian palace, and to give him some idea of what he had in mind, the Maharaja showed him a set of watercolours brought from Lahore and photographs obtained from the India Museum. The Shish Mahal, the Glass Palace, was the inspiration for the drawing-room, with convex slivers of mercurized glass that sparkled in the light embedded in the plasterwork. The main rooms were embellished with elaborate pilasters and arches in the Mughal style; the grand marble staircase...was set with splendid cast-iron bannisters painted in sealing-wax red.[11]

Its most staggering feature, the ballroom, took 150 workmen no less than four years, from 1870, to construct. Conceived in the form of an Indian temple, its 28 white marble pillars, intricately hand-carved by imported Italian craftsmen, supported three decks of galleries dominated by a vast copper dome. With its state rooms and their richly gilded Louis XIV furniture, the individual guest suites and the solid silver fittings of the bathrooms, the whole celebrated a felicitous union—in that era of imperialist grandeur—of East and West under one palatial roof.

But if it was fit for a maharaja and his royal guests, it was a little on the cramped side for what Ernest Cecil had in mind. He overcame this problem by building a duplicate of the mansion alongside Duleep Singh's and joining the two buildings into a massive 100-room block, including a whole new servants' wing connected to the main building by passages. Nearby, in the surrounding parkland, he built a quadrangular block to house the horses and carriages and provide a game-safe for the thousands of birds he and his guest guns would blast from the skies. It is a structure not quite as large as Buckingham Palace and somewhat less classical in design. Edward Cecil also rebuilt Elveden village, which faces the main gates to the Hall, and laid six miles of roads across the estate.

There were abundant 'great shoots' in England in competition for royal patronage when Edward Cecil bought Elveden. They included Lord Leicester's superb estate, Holkham; Lord Walsingham's Merton; Lord Ashburton's great partridge manor, The Grange, in Hampshire; and the Duke of Grafton's Euston—within a partridge's flight (had it a charmed life) from Elveden. But Edward Cecil set out to develop the rabbit-infested heathland of the estate into one of the best pheasant and partridge shoots in England, rivalling even the nearby Sandringham, which his friend the Prince of Wales had acquired about the same time. The remaining tenant farmers were bought out in order to clear the land for shooting and large flocks of sheep introduced for the purpose of treading and manuring the soil.

A large acreage was always down to such crops as buckwheat and kidney vetch, which provided feed or cover for the game and had no other purpose. In 1902 some 2,000 acres were put out of regular cultivation and left to be cropped occasionally as game lands. In fact the farming—as on many other similar estates—was entirely subsidiary to the shooting and was carried on solely as a necessary accessory to it.[12]

From then until his death in 1927, eight years after being created the Earl of Iveagh, Edward Cecil's Elveden figured regularly and prominently in the sporting calendars of the Prince of Wales and the Duke of York, both before and after their ascent to the throne, as well as half the dukes and earls of the kingdom.

An inkling of what it was like to be a guest at Elveden of the 1st Earl and—until the death of George V—of his son and heir, Rupert Edward, can be gained from the recollections of one of the oldest surviving retainers, Jim Speed. Long since pensioned off and comfortably accommodated in one of the lodges on the estate, Speed served under both Iveaghs, first as oddman, then footman, finishing up as acting butler for ten years. His wife Lucy, who led her frail, almost blind husband into their little living-room to meet me, was also in service at the Hall as head housemaid. The 1st Iveagh ('about the same build as me, sir', the diminutive Speed recalls) usually invited about 30 guests–'eight guns, plus the ladies and friends'–for a typical three-day shooting party at Elveden. The permanent staff at the Hall in those days comprised a butler, underbutler, three footmen, a housekeeper, three cooks and their kitchen staff, six housemaids, a house carpenter and a nightwatchman. This staff would of course be supplemented by governesses, nursery-maids, personal valets and ladies' maids accompanying the Iveaghs and their guests on visits to Elveden. Seventy men, including game-keepers, grooms and stablemen, made up the 'outside staff', together with twenty flower- and twenty vegetable-gardeners. Guests of the 1st Earl, invariably chosen from among his social peers, would arrive by train at Thetford Station, three miles from Elveden, there to be met by his horse-drawn carriages; but when the motor-car made its first uncertain appearance, Edward VII consented to be driven by one of Iveagh's new toys as far as Thetford on his return journey, followed by an empty vehicle in case of a breakdown on the highway. Needless to say, the royal suite at Elveden, decorated in coral and green, was the last word in luxury, surpassing any comparable accommodation in the other great mansions honoured by the British monarchs.

Rupert Edward tended to favour guests from the party political world, such as Ramsay MacDonald (the 'safe' Labourite), Neville Chamberlain and Winston Churchill. But common to both regimes at Elveden was hospitality and entertainment on a regal scale, including elaborate hot meals served to the 'guns' by liveried foot-men under a great tent. Smoking inside the Hall was not tolerated by the 2nd Earl, who installed a smoking-room at the top of the lofty water tower erected by his father near to the Hall where male guests could puff their cigars around the bar or over the billiard table.

Jim Speed remembers Edward Cecil as a 'studious', scholarly man in his latter years, but still capable of the impulsive behaviour that in his younger days made his partnership with his brother Arthur Edward so prickly. On taking over Elveden from Duleep Singh he had a handsome home built on the estate for the rector of the Elveden church. But the reverend gentleman made the mistake one day of peering through one of the ground-floor bay windows of the Hall and was caught in the act as milord glanced up from his studies. Such an invasion of privacy was intolerable, and Edward

Cecil put the situation at once to rights by closing down the rectory and building a new one outside the grounds but close to the main gates, where the incumbents reside to this day. The 'Old Rectory' is now one of the homes of the widow of his grandson Lord Elveden, the former Lady Elizabeth Hare, with a permanent staff of butler, cook and housemaids in residence, while the Hall, with its memories of past grandeur, stands silent, its sumptuous furnishings draped in dust covers.

If the life-styles of the 1st and 2nd Earls of Iveagh lend a nostalgic note to the old retainer's discourse, the other reality–that of conditions in the service of Edwardian lords-of-the-manor–makes a stark contrast.

The housemaids, aroused at 4 a.m. by the nightwatchman, were required to clean, blacklead and re-lay every coal fireplace in the state rooms and private drawing-rooms of the Hall before breakfast. At 8.30 a.m., under Edward Cecil, the whole staff would assemble in the Cedar Room on the ground floor for prayers before proceeding with the interminable and backbreaking chores for which the Almighty, in his wisdom, had intended them. During the shooting season, with the Hall full of guests, these maids would often be kept ceaselessly on the go until 11 p.m., then to collapse on their beds in the servants' quarters too exhausted to get undressed. Jim Speed recalls with a chuckle that when he told the present Countess of Iveagh about the servants' working conditions in those days, 'she just couldn't believe it'. But there is no bitterness in him or his wife, only respect for the memory of the 1st Earl of Iveagh and his heir.

'Of course you never got really close to them, you know, sir. Not in those days. I mean, there was no what you might call *communication*. When they spoke to you it was simply to give you orders. Your job was to carry them out.'

Speed's present blindness is 'not too bad. I can just about make you out, sir, as a kind of shadow.' And of course these days there are audio cassettes, specially for the blind, to take the place of printed novels and so on. But hadn't he learnt to read by braille?

'It won't work for me, sir. You see, all those years of cleaning the silver–you had to use your bare hands for buffing it, you know, and there's no longer any sensitivity in my fingertips.'

Speed's predecessor as butler to Edward Cecil was an engaging character named Harris who fell in and out of favour with his employer with the regularity, almost, of a pendulum. To third parties, Edward Cecil invariably spoke of his butler as 'the scoundrel Harris' and he rarely attributed less than the basest of motives to the man's slightest initiatives. A case in point concerned The Overcoat, an old and well-worn garment, already turning green, that Edward had stubbornly clung to, year in and year out. To Harris, who rather fancied himself as a meticulous gentleman's gentleman, the overcoat was an eyesore and an affront to his own status. Since a direct complaint to his boss was out of the question, Harris decided that if the offending garment could just 'disappear' frequently enough from his employer's wardrobe its owner might finally order a new one from his tailor.

After the rediscovery for the third or fourth time of the 'lost' overcoat, Edward sent for his secretary, Mr Bliss, closed the study door behind him, and declared in a petulant hiss: 'We've got to do something, Bliss. The scoundrel Harris is trying to steal my overcoat!' Mr Bliss had many superlative qualities, but outspokenness towards his employer had never been one of them. On this occasion, however, he found the courage to suggest that perhaps the overcoat had long since seen better days and was due for retirement. He was gruffly dismissed from the room; but shortly afterwards Edward capitulated and bought himself a new coat.

The day came when 'the scoundrel Harris' so upset his employer that he was given the sack. But he found a job as butler to Lord Curzon who, on being appointed Governor-General of India, took Harris with him to the subcontinent. This was of course a splendid step-up for Harris—or would have been had he been able to keep his hands off the younger members of the female staff. To impress the prettiest of the household's chambermaids he 'borrowed' the vice-regal barge while Curzon was away and took the girl on a trip up the river where, at every station along the route, they received obsequious red-carpet hospitality. When Curzon learned of the escapade, it put an end to Harris's career in India; but it says much for the grudging affection Edward Cecil must have felt for 'the scoundrel' that he took him back as butler on his return to England.

Fourteen years were to elapse between the elevation of Edward Cecil to the peerage in 1905 and his ennoblement as the Earl of Iveagh and Viscount Elveden, of Elveden, in 1919. It was a period that encompassed World War I, the death of his cousin-wife Adelaide (1916), the entry of his sons Rupert and Walter into politics, and the development of the Dublin brewery into the largest in the world, covering an area of over 500 acres, with profits up from £1,036,305 in 1906 to £2,175,816 in 1919 (and this despite an enforced cut-back of the brewery's output during 1914–18). By then he was generally regarded as the second wealthiest man in England, surpassed only by Sir John Ellerman whose fortune derived from shipping. But any comparison between Iveagh and Ellerman began and ended with that statement of relative wealth. To the end of his days, Ellerman was a recluse. He shunned the press, made no public appearances, manipulated his vast fortune through nominees and lawyers, gave anonymously–if at all–to charity, had no reputation as a host and would have been recognized by only a handful of brokers had he appeared during business hours on the floor of the London Stock Exchange.

In contrast, Edward Cecil's personal and public lives were a game-plan (and a model one at that) of what it took in those days to be raised in one's lifetime from a plain Mister to a belted earl. With Elveden and Ashford for the shooting parties, his Grosvenor Place mansion for London's 'season', Farmleigh and 80 St Stephen's Green for the Punchestown Races and the Dublin Horse Show, and his two luxury yachts for Cowes Week, Iveagh had created for himself and his family a social status only a blue-bloodline below that of the premier dukes of England. The death of his wife and his own advanced years reduced the scale and frequency of his hospitality during the years between the end of World War I and his death, but by then his three sons, with their socially eminent wives, were more than capable of assuming the mantle and carrying on the tradition he had established for the Guinnesses as hosts to the high and mighty of Europe.

A list of the nobility that welcomed an invitation to the dinners and dances laid on at the immense town mansion created out of Nos. 4 and 5 Grosvenor Place would be tantamount to a reprint of Burke's *Peerage* and the Court Circulars of the period. A short list of the more frequent guests would include, apart from the British monarchs, the Dukes and Duchesses of Connaught, of Marlborough and of Wellington, the Earls and Countesses of Onslow, Shaftesbury and Albemarle, the Marquess and Marchioness of Hamilton, the Countesses of Arran, Buchan, Dudley, and Kilmorey, milords Churchill, Killanin, Oranmore & Browne, Desmond Fitzgerald, Cecil Manners and Hugh Cecil, Viscount Kitchener of Khartoum, and the ambassadors of Austria–Hungary and Germany. If there was little 'lionizing' of the great ones from the world of the arts, this was surely to be expected. Neither of Iveagh's friendly British monarchs (nor any British monarchs since) cared a fig about culture; and painters and writers made 'difficult' dinner companions for most dukes and earls. In any case there was always the magnificent Iveagh Collection, effectively on show throughout the mansion, to testify to the host's taste for the aesthetic.

Meanwhile, and coincidentally with his public benefactions– which included the purchase of the 500-acre Chadacre estate, near Bury St Edmunds, for the training of farm labourers' sons–Iveagh was busy setting up the network of trusts that would protect the Guinness wealth from death duties and the prodigality of any descendants, trusts that would provide incomes ranging from the handsome to the munificent for his ten grandchildren and their own descendants. Wherever investment held the promise of long-term security and appreciation, his money flowed as copiously as the flow of strong dark stout from the storage vats of the Dublin brewery. It went into land in Ireland, farms in Canada, gilt-edged stocks and real estate in Britain.

For £565,000 he secured the ground-rents income of most of the London district of Earls Court, then an unsalubrious neighbourhood but with good prospects for development. The estate was absorbed into the Iveagh Trust. In 1930, by which time its value as a residential and shopping area was on the up-and-up, it was sold to Sir John Ellerman for an undisclosed sum. But the Guinness wealth, like the rabbits on the Elveden estate, multiplied willy-nilly and on the outbreak of World War I, Iveagh, understandably concerned about its impact on the economy, had managed to expatriate funds, estimated by one of his family at around £15,000,000, from Britain to Canada where, today, they provide one of the main sources of income to his descendants.

Much of the British property and trust capital was settled on Iveagh's family between the years 1907 and 1910, well outside the five-year period within which it would have been subject to estate duty on his death. The same, unfortunately, did not hold true of his own holdings of Ordinary Stock in the brewery, increased in 1923 by a capitalization of £2,500,000 from the reserve fund, by which all Ordinary stockholders received fully paid-up new shares representing one-half of their existing holdings. For, early in the morning of 8 October 1927, the 1st Earl of Iveagh died in his Grosvenor Place mansion from a heart attack, a month short of his eightieth birthday.

His latter years had been spent living alone in London, in semi-retirement, with frequent visits by his children and grandchildren, for whom extra covers were kept laid at his dining table in case any of them arrived without prior notice. He had been ill for ten days with another of those colds that had plagued him all his life, an indisposition he had probably inherited from his mother-and-cousin,

Elizabeth. When the news of his death was broken to the Conservative Party Conference, then in session at Cardiff, the delegates stood in silent tribute to the man who had contributed so generously to the party treasury. In Dublin the flags over Trinity College and the City Hall were flown at half-mast. Five days later, while the family attended the private funeral at Elveden, memorial services were held in St Patrick's Cathedral, Dublin, and in St Margaret's, Westminster, where the King, the Queen, the Duke of Connaught and the Prime Minister were represented. And the little Roman Catholic Church of St James was filled by employees of the brewery for a votive mass in memory of the Anglo-Irish establishment's most generous patron.

In his will, Iveagh left £125,000 to the Protestant Church of Ireland, the income from which would be devoted to raising the livings of the poorer of Ireland's Protestant clergymen. The income from another £65,000 went to St Patrick's, 'during such time as the Cathedral shall be used for the purposes of the Protestant Church of Ireland'. The King Edward VII Hospital in London received £60,000, and the list of other beneficiaries, which took up three-quarters of a column in *The Times* of 7 November 1927, included every employee in his personal service, from his secretary to the tennis marker in Dublin.

Elveden, with an endowment fund of £400,000, together with the other Iveagh residences, went to his eldest son, Rupert Edward. Ashford was left to Ernest and the residue of the estate was settled on the three sons and their children, who would receive the income only for the rest of their lives. In November a provisional probate was granted for a net personalty of £11,000,000 on which £4,400,000 had been paid in death duties. With the lapse of time, while legal squabbles between the executors and the revenue authorities of the Irish Free State kept the Iveagh fortune in the news, its valuation rose to £13,500,000 or the equivalent in purchasing power today of more than £192,000,000.

The issue was settled when, after appeals and counter-appeals, it was ruled by the Irish Commissioners that Lord Iveagh had not legally relinquished his domicile of origin during the four years prior to his death, and that Ireland was therefore entitled to its whack of income tax for those years. The reluctant British taxmasters were obliged to turn over £250,000 of their own dip into the Iveagh kitty, representing the largest single payment that had ever passed into the Irish treasury from the estate of one individual.

There would be similar battles with the British authorities, well into the 1950s. In the meantime, however, the Founder's kin of the line from the First Arthur would have little need to tighten their belts. Guinness—to adapt the slogan on billboards throughout the British Isles—had been good for them. And it was going to get even better.

5

Iveagh the Innovator

1

Edward Cecil and his father Benjamin Lee had divided their time between the affairs of the great brewery and the political and social benefactions without which a British merchant family could never aspire to the social eminence bestowed by the ermine and the coronet. Much of the fruit of their industry and ambition had already been secured for Edward's son Rupert when, at the age of 30, he made his début in London municipal politics by winning the representation of Haggerston, in the working-class district of Shoreditch, giving him a seat on the London County Council. In choosing, of all places, Shoreditch as a launching pad towards Parliament, Rupert gave expression to the mix of curiosity, originality and the common touch that would characterize a lifetime wedded to the proposition that if power without responsibility is the prerogative of the harlot, then power *with* responsibility should be the province of the rich.

He had given precocious evidence of an analytical thrust in his nature when his father bought a microscope in order to make a closer study of the then relatively unknown properties of the yeast culture used in the brewing process: the seven-year-old Rupert cajoled his father into providing him with a microscope of his own which from then on, in pride of possession, out-rivalled every other diversion in the boy's playroom.

He was a slight child, not enamoured of team sports, and an early encounter with the young Winston Churchill, also born in 1874, did little to promote a taste for the rough-and-tumble of juvenile warfare. Brought face to face by their respective and fawning nannies on the occasion of a children's party, the two seven-year-olds stood staring at each other, Rupert with wariness, Winston with truculence.

The future war leader broke the silence with, 'I don't like you, Guinness!'

Rupert retorted with a heated, 'And I don't like *you*, Churchill!' Whereupon his adversary seized a silver candlestick and smote Rupert upon the head with it, necessitating six stitches to the Guinness scalp. But as Rupert grew towards manhood it became clear that, if not in height then certainly in the breadth of shoulder and the musculature of his short legs, his physical stature would outmatch that of his father. It was these same legs, described by his trainer at Eton as 'like a tree', that won him honours as an oarsman, first at Eton, as one of the eight winning the Ladies' Plate, and later at the Henley Regatta, where he won the Diamond Sculls two years in succession.

The challenge of the sea was already in the bloodstream of the male line of a family whose business fortunes and social communications before the advent of aviation were borne on the boisterous Irish Sea. The youngest of the three brothers, Walter Edward (later Lord Moyne), was probably the most responsive of all to this challenge but Rupert was never far behind. While still in his twenties, skippering his 90-foot yawl *Leander*, he outraced the Kaiser's yacht *Meteor* and the Royal Family's *Britannia* to win the King's Cup at Cowes. Earlier, when he was invited to join the crew of a German torpedo boat exercising off the west coast of Germany, his oarsmanship brought a happy ending to what might have been a tragedy when a tramp steamer rammed the German boat and cut it in half. As the *Daily Express* of 6 November 1928 reported, the crew of eight had scrambled precariously into a light Berthon dinghy—little more than a shell—but Rupert, armed with only a single scull, was able to keep it afloat and head-on to the waves until rescue arrived.

For a person who in his last years would be made a Fellow of the intellectually élitist Royal Society, Rupert had shown scant academic promise at Trinity College, Cambridge; but those who teased him for his bad spelling ('yph' for wife and, in one of his letters, the word 'horse' spelt five different ways) were probably missing the point. He was above all—as his long and varied career would confirm—an innovator and he was probably experimenting with simplified forms of English spelling years before Bernard Shaw got into the act.

Whilst still at Cambridge he had joined the London Rifle Brigade. But, being a humanitarian rather than a militarist by nature, he elected at the outbreak of the Boer War to serve with the mobile Irish Hospital his father had dispatched to South Africa for which he was mentioned in dispatches and created a CMG. He is credited as having brought into being the Royal Naval Volunteer Reserve in 1903 by proposing the need for such a body in the course of a conversation with Edward VII. 'Very well,' the monarch is said to have remarked to him, 'why don't you get on with it?' He did so, and on the outbreak of World War I, now in his 41st year, took on the job of mobilizing the London division of the RNVR as its commandant and headed a recruiting mission to Canada in 1917.

Rupert had launched himself, rather precariously, on a parliamentary career in 1908 by winning the Haggerston division of Shoreditch, a marginal seat. He lost the seat two years later when the Liberal Party received its 1910 mandate to end the blocking powers of the House of Lords, but he was back again in 1912–this time as MP for South-East Essex, a seat he retained until the end of the war. For the general election of 1918 Rupert switched constituencies again, this time to Southend-on-Sea, then one of the safest Conservative strongholds in the country, which he won comfortably. A year later, upon his father's being created an earl, he became Viscount Elveden but continued to represent Southend until Edward Cecil's death, when the Iveagh earldom passed to Rupert, obliging him to take his seat in the House of Lords. This was not, by a long chalk, the end of the Iveagh association with the East-Enders' favourite seaside resort. His wife, the witty and personable Lady Gwendolen, had politics in her bones. She had already campaigned skilfully for him in nine parliamentary elections, had for the past two years been chairman of the Women's Conservative Organization, and was an active and popular figure in her husband's constituency. She herself won the resulting Southend by-election with a handsome majority and held the seat until 1935. By then she was in her middle fifties and her eldest daughter, Lady Honor, had recently married the Anglo-American, Henry ('Chips') Channon, whose eyes were already covetously fixed on 'the best men's club in the world', the Mother of Parliaments.

Guinness–and the Guinness benefactions–had been good for Southend and there was no resistance from the Tory constituency party when Lady Gwendolen proposed her son-in-law as her successor. Channon was duly elected in her place.

The origin of the nickname 'Chips' has never been satisfactorily established, though one version has it that Channon shared rooms, after graduating from Oxford, with a gentleman called Fish. Be that as it may, the sobriquet was given further force by his fellow Members of Parliament in recognition of the seaside town's predilection for fried fish and potatoes. Channon's parliamentary career, which we shall encapsulate later, was somewhat short of brilliant but he held the seat, virtually as a Guinness 'trust', until 1958 when ill-health obliged him to stand down. Southend–home-from-home of the Cockney dynasty of 'pearly kings'–was by now so thoroughly addicted to Guinness, and the benefits thereof, that there was no hesitation in adopting Channon's 23-year-old son Paul as the new prospective Tory candidate. The following year, while still at university, he won the seat and became the youngest MP in that Parliament. He has retained it up to the time of writing and has in fact earned enough respect over the years, first as a Parliamentary Private Secretary and subsequently as a Junior Minister, to rise above the sobriquet of 'Crisp' Channon.

2

Rupert Edward had been born into great wealth, into a secured social status and with the awareness, as he grew to manhood, that an earldom was on his father's horizon and would one day be his. His father, while treating all his children with generosity, had never required them to become closely involved in his business affairs and there had in any case been no need for Rupert to contribute to a family fortune that was increasing, and would continue to increase, literally with every breath he drew. He would be on the board and a major shareholder of the brewery for as long as he pleased–but as a figurehead, a symbol of dynastic continuity, rather than a *sine qua non* of its effective operation. The titles he would inherit had been earned by his father and there was no way he could add to them even were he to marry a princess of the royal family. It was like being in a gilded and upholstered Pullman carriage, moving slowly and smoothly under its own volition over tracks leading to a preordained destination.

Politics, as a tangential route to public service, had certainly beckoned him, but he would have known that his brother Walter Edward, though six years his junior, was by nature more of a political animal than he and better equipped, intellectually, to add lustre from this arena to the Guinness name. (Walter had in fact won his first seat in Parliament ahead of Rupert and had been appointed Under-Secretary for War while his elder brother sat on a back bench in the debating chamber of the Commons.)

There were other ways Rupert could plough a furrow of his own without neglecting or compromising his inheritance and, as it turned out, the farming metaphor was appropriate. Much of his childhood had been spent on great estates, in direct contact with the earth, its produce and the men and animals that lived off it. While still in his teens he had accompanied his father to the annual hop sales at the Borough, on the east side of London Bridge, where he had watched the brewmasters judging the harvest of the Kent hopfields by scent and appearance. Scientific farming would later absorb most of his energies and innovative talents but, before that, the Guinness heir who as a boy had been so fascinated by the power of his microscope was attracted to medical science. It was he who persuaded his father to endow with £250,000 the Lister Institute for Preventive Medicine (whose constitution provides for a Guinness family representative always to serve on the governing board) and Rupert's early interest in the work of Sir Almroth Wright and Sir Alexander Fleming—the discoverer of penicillin—led to his financing the Wright–Fleming Institute of Microbiology to which he was appointed chairman in 1921.

By then, however, the pattern of his lifework as a pioneer in agricultural science had begun to take shape. Lady Gwendolen had been born on the Clandon Park estate, the family seat of the earls of Onslow, near Guildford in Surrey. In 1906, three years after marrying her, Rupert Edward bought 700 acres of the estate from his father-in-law, with a panoramic view of the Surrey downs, upon which he designed and built the beautiful country house, Pyrford Court, that would be his favourite home for the rest of his life. The site he had chosen for the house afforded his wife, from the upper floors, a view across 2,000 acres of pine trees and gorse of her own beloved family home.

During a visit to Canada in 1910 to explore on behalf of the family the possibilities for further investment in the Dominion, he was able to observe how so few of the British emigrants—particularly those of the middle and upper classes—were able to adapt successfully to the harsher conditions of working the Canadian land, and he decided then and there to do something about it. There already existed two medium-sized farms on his Pyrford estate and there was plenty of land available for the increase of their acreage. With a Canadian agricultural expert as manager, Rupert promptly established his Emigration Training Farm on the Surrey estate, where trainees from the British public schools and universities were put to a tough course under conditions as close as possible to those they would find in Canada. The scheme was an immediate success and during a visit to

Nova Scotia in 1912 to see for himself how well his former pupils were settling down, Rupert bought up a number of farms for the family's Montreal Trust to provide for a further intake of his trainees, over 150 of whom were successfully settled before the outbreak of World War I put an end to emigration. By now, to Rupert's interest in medical science was added an almost passionate involvement in the techniques and problems of farming. It was an ideal fusion of enthusiasm for someone of his inquiring and innovative nature and it was directed in the first place towards the challenge of infected milk from the dairy farms.

In those days, before the advent of TB-tested herds, the bovine tuberculosis bacilli were being transmitted to thousands of people every year and especially to children. No successful method of testing cows had yet been discovered and the conditions under which the milk was drawn, bottled and distributed were appallingly unhygienic by today's standards. Rupert had always found more time than his father had to inspect his farms and—as Jim Speed, the old retainer, put it—'to pass the time of day' with the farm hands. He had seen for himself how the dairymen, both at Elveden and Pyrford, were content with a perfunctory washing of the cows' udders before milking and he had observed the common use of unsterilized utensils in the cowsheds. The problem clearly resolved itself into finding a more reliable method for the TB-testing of herds and the education of dairy farmers and the consuming public in the virtues of sanitary production and distribution. Together with Mr William Buckley, a dairy farmer and 'clean milk' enthusiast, Rupert formed the Tuberculin Tested Milk Producers' Association in 1920, with offices at his town house in St James's Square. At the same time he put up £60,000 to help the Research Institute of Dairying—a branch of the agricultural department of University College—to acquire an experimental farm near Reading and to equip it with laboratories and up-to-date milking sheds.

The battle was a long and hard one and it was fought against the vested interests of the dairy farmers and the initial apathy of the public, but in the course of it the technique of the intradermal injection was perfected and the experimental work of the Institute, later to become the National Institute for Research Dairying, is honoured today wherever scientific dairy farming is practised. Rupert was the institute's chairman from the beginning, and the degree of Honorary Doctor of Science conferred on him in 1937 by Reading University was in recognition of his pioneering struggle to end the toll of bovine tuberculosis among Britain's children.

Since 1978, when Mr Cyril Laikin bought Pyrford Court from the family trust, the east wing has become the residence for a score of elderly gentlefolk. Ten years earlier, when the contents were auctioned off *in situ* by Christie's, the sale added around £100,000 to the family's trust funds, including the 18,000 guineas paid by Paul Getty's son, George, for a panel of Beauvais tapestry. The west wing of this lovely mansion was used in the production of the psychological thriller *The Omen* in 1975. It remains—save for the furniture and paintings—much as it was in Rupert's time, and the new owner has reserved it for his private accommodation.

It was in Rupert's kitchen-cum-workroom that he put into use another by-product of his restless curiosity—the extraction of gas from farmyard manure. Concurrently with his clean milk campaign he had put up the finance for a scientific study of the better use and storage of this substance and had invited a young chemist, Dr Hannaford Richards of the Rothamsted Institute, to make use of the dairy herd at Pyrford for this purpose. In the course of the two men's work at Pyrford it was observed that the bubbles arising from manure soaked in water were inflammable, and further exploration by Rupert established that farmyard manure, left to ferment in a container, gave off the ignitable gas known as methane. Never one to pursue a discovery that had no practical use, he constructed a plant for extracting the gas and feeding it through pipes to the kitchen underneath the bedroom, where the ovens continued to be fuelled by this source for the rest of his life. The abundance of coal gas at that time lent no incentive to farmers to profit from the discovery and a quarter of a century would elapse from Rupert's death in 1927 before a German inventor was able to announce in triumph that he had found the means to fuel tractors from the methane given off by manure...

The gas pipes and the other equipment installed in Rupert's kitchen lie there to this day, disconnected mute testaments to a private enterprise that brought him pleasure without profit. Not so, however, in the case of another discovery made by himself and Dr Richards during their experimental work at Pyrford. They found that vegetable matter such as straw could under certain conditions be converted by bacterial action into a food for plants as nourishing as the manure formed from animal droppings. Mixed with many kinds of useless garden refuse it produced the fertilizing equivalent of animal manure. Rupert saw at once that what he had here was an eminently marketable product and he formed the Agricultural Developments Company to exploit it. Today, 'Adco' is known to gardeners everywhere as the additive that converts garden refuse into soil-enriching manure, and the company set up to produce it remains a flourishing entity in the empire of Arthur Guinness Son & Co. subsidiaries.

It was the death of George V in 1936, rather than that of the 1st Earl of Iveagh nine years earlier, that freed Rupert Edward from the obligation of maintaining Elveden as a private shoot and enabled him to proceed with what was to be acclaimed as 'one of the most remarkable agricultural experiments of our times'.[1]

As custom required, he had presented himself at Buckingham Palace precisely one month after Edward Cecil's death to deliver up to the King the Insignia of the Order of St Patrick conferred upon his father. The meeting was cordial, as always, and as the new earl took his leave George V had remarked: 'I trust you are going to keep up the shooting at Elveden. I shall hope to come next year and I think the Queen would like to come too.'[2] To a loyal subject of the monarch this wish was the equivalent of a command, and it delayed for some years the implementation of a major agricultural project upon which Rupert had already set his heart. This was no less than the conversion of the barren heathland and arid, rabbit-infested soil of the greater part of the estate into arable land, supporting what was to become the largest general farm in England.

On his Pyrford estate he had already succeeded in reclaiming a large tract of unproductive heathland by planting it, initially, with potatoes. The wastelands of Elveden presented a more formidable challenge, but in Iveagh's view it was a challenge susceptible to the scientific know-how he had acquired over the years of supporting the Rothamsted Experimental Station. He had started—even before a stilled British nation was told over the radio that 'The life of the King is moving slowly towards its close'—to experiment with the sowing of lucerne (alfalfa) over a trial acreage of the inhospitable heathland. The crop took, was mown for hay and thereafter was grown in rotation with wheat and root crops. As the seasons passed and the sandy soil was gradually transformed into arable land and pastures, he extended the reclamation to more and more acreage, each tract of which, after sowing, had to be protected from the erosive East Anglian winds by a system of shelter belts and from invasion by the multitudinous rabbits by deeply buried fencework.

Meanwhile, and starting with the hundred dairy cows he had inherited with Elveden, he built up his cattle herds to 1,436 head, both beef and dairy, the latter by the importation and breeding of pedigree Guernseys which by 1950 were yielding 300,000 gallons of TT milk per year. Ten years later the once-infertile heathland had 4,000 acres down to corn, 1,000 to root crops, 4,338 to lucerne and temporary ley and with a livestock population of 2,726 cattle, 2,038 ewes and rams with a lamb crop of 2,500, and 1,886 pigs. He was now bringing under cultivation around 500 acres of wasteland per year.

6

Of Toucans – and Terrorists

If the period from the death of Sir Benjamin Lee Guinness in 1868 to the 1st Earl of Iveagh's demise in 1927 encompassed an era of the Guinness family's major investment in the trappings of social status, then the years from then on would witness a gradual unloading of the more grandiose extravagances by the down-to-earth 2nd Earl, Rupert Edward.

It started with the sale of his Grosvenor Place mansion to the Ladies' Carlton Club in 1928 and this was followed, ten years later, by the gift to the Government of Eire of the mansion on St Stephen's Green where, as already noted, it now houses Ireland's Department of Foreign Affairs. The 2nd Earl made no effort to restore the Hall at Elveden as a family residence after World War II. Farmleigh was maintained as the family's Dublin seat but in England it was Iveagh's beloved Pyrford Court and, on visits to Elveden, the comfortable and more manageable Old Rectory, from which his father had displaced the peeping vicar all those years ago. The Hall was opened up–in part, anyway–only on a few special occasions, such as the party given for the estate workers and their families to celebrate the coming-of-age of Iveagh's grandson, Lord Elveden, in 1958. To the old retainers like Jim Speed the silence that most eloquently told of Iveagh's withdrawal from the Hall was that of the numerous clocks positioned through the premises.

The 2nd Earl had always been obsessed, to the point of eccentricity, about accurate timekeeping; he himself owned no less than 18 gold watches and he insisted that all the clocks, throughout the Hall, should chime the hours at precisely the same moment. The responsibility for this lay with the house carpenter who, according to Speed, 'went almost around the bend, working to get it right' whenever the word came that his lordship was coming to Elveden.

In addition to the three watches he always carried on his person, he would also strap on a pedometer whenever he took his mandatory daily walk. The pedometer went with him even when he took his children and grandchildren cruising in the Mediterranean on one of his yachts. This was because, whatever the course being followed by his skipper, the yacht had to put into some intermediate port every single day, not for supplies but to accommodate what the family referred to as 'Grandfather's walk'.

Rupert Edward had more than justified his existence and privileged birth by his pioneering achievements in agriculture. These were recognized in 1957, when he became the first recipient of the Bledisloe gold medal of the Royal Agricultural Society, and even more prestigiously eight years later on his being made a Fellow of the Royal Society. Apart from scientific farming, the two other major claims on his time were the great brewery of which he was chairman for 35 years and the manipulation of the family fortune for the long-term benefit of his descendants.

He had taken over the chairmanship of Arthur Guinness Son & Co. at a time when sales of the stout in England were about to decline as the nation moved into the greatest slump in its history. It was therefore under his aegis that a decision was taken to embark on an advertising campaign which, as it was refined and developed over the years, achieved for its copywriters the nearest most of them were ever likely to get to immortality.

There had been virtually no Guinness advertising in the British Isles until 1928, when a limited, experimental poster campaign was tried out in Scotland. If anything, the annual expansion of its sales had presented a challenge to the brewery's productive capacity rather than the ingenuity of publicity men. But there was another reason, never publicly admitted by the family, for not engaging in the ballyhoo of sales promotion. The name Guinness, in its prime context, stood for a dark malt liquor drunk on the whole by the working class in pubs throughout the kingdom, and for the profits derived therefrom by the descendants of the First Arthur. In another context—and certainly since the baronetcy of Benjamin Lee Guinness—it stood for a family honoured by the friendship of monarchs and on its way up the social ladder from one of the lowest rungs to the top. The image of a coronet would never harmonize sweetly with that of a brewer and, while there was no disguising the connection, nor was there any anxiety—and certainly no compelling need—by Rupert's predecessors to blazon it from hoardings along the high-

ways to the race courses, the great country houses, the regattas at
Cowes and Henley.

Rupert, having inherited the Iveagh earldom, could take a less
blinkered view of all this. The coronet might sit on his brow but his
feet were firmly planted on the ground, and he raised no objection
when his fellow-directors, concerned about sales, proposed an extension, to England, of the Scottish campaign. This last had shown
promising results and it had conformed to his edict that the message
on the 16- and 48-sheet posters should be 'clean and wholesome'.
Throughout his own adult life Rupert had drunk a bottle of Guinness
every day—no other alcohol—for no other reason than his sincere
belief in its health-giving properties. He had totally approved the
final lay-out presented by the agency, S. H. Benson, though others
on the board were for rejecting it as over-simplistic. The design
featured a pint-glassful of Guinness, topped by an inch of froth,
under the slogan: 'Guinness is Good for You'. Nothing more. This
basic theme was reiterated in one form or another from hoardings
throughout the land until 1931, without any effort to add sophistica-
tion or wit. And in his 1930 report to shareholders the chairman was
able to tell them that the improvement in revenues 'coincides with
the completion of the first full year during which the company's
intensive advertising campaign was carried on'.

The 'goodness' theme would never be dropped, but from 1931
onwards it alternated with posters eyecatching in their simplicity
and gently rib-tickling as messages. Writers and artists seconded to
the campaign rose enthusiastically to the challenge of creating 'honest, wholesome and entertaining' lay-outs and included, in the early
years, the literary talents of Dorothy L. Sayers and the draughts-
manship of John Gilroy, Rex Whistler, Edward Ardizzone and
Rowland Emmett. An early play upon words—with special appeal,
no doubt, to the 2nd Earl—was the slogan, alongside a clock-face
with its hands marking the first (lunchtime) hour: 'It strikes one it's
Guinness Time'. As the thirties progressed and post-Depression
Britain got back to work, 'Guinness for Strength' and 'Have a
Guinness When You're Tired', with appropriate comic illustration,
took over. World War II imposed tight restrictions on poster-paper
supplies, so the backs of old posters were used for the exhortation of
the public to 'Keep Smiling' and for the reassurance that
'Thousands are Finding Strength in Guinness'. The fifties saw the
introduction of the famous, and precocious, Guinness animals into
the poster designs—sea-lions, crocodiles, ostriches, kangaroos and
kinkajous—all in the act of making off with their keepers' tantalizing

pint—to his anguished cry, 'My Goodness, My Guinness'; and, of course, the favourite of them all, the massively beaked Disneyesque toucan, immortalized by the accompanying verse:

> If he can say, as you can,
> Guinness is Good for You,
> How grand to be a toucan!
> Just think what toucan do.

In 1960, the brewery spent £891,000 on advertising, making Guinness the sixth largest billing—after four brands of soap powder and Stork margarine.[1]

One of John Gilroy's posters, featuring an ostrich, brought an avalanche of letters from the public, challenging the artist's logic. The great bird had apparently snatched up its keeper's glass of Guinness and swallowed it whole. There, stuck halfway down its long throat, were the bold outlines of the upright glass. *Upright?* Surely its proper position in the throat, as the ostrich raised its head, would be *upside down*! Anxious days followed, while the agency's creative people went into a huddle. Their eventual explanation of the phenomenon was grudgingly accepted by a still-sceptical public. The ostrich, it seemed, had in fact tried to imitate a sea-lion by balancing the glassful of Guinness on its beak, but its beak had opened, with the result shown in Gilroy's drawing.

By the sixties and seventies, a public conditioned to the slickness of TV commercials needed something more arresting and the Guinness posters became a little more complicated, visually. The fronts of buses proposed, 'After work—have a ƨƨϾИИIUϿ on the way back'. The simple, clean-cut drawings gave way to photographic composites, one of which interposed a glass of Guinness among cut-off bar-drinkers' hands and asked: 'Are you afraid of the dark?' Another that made a too-smart-by-half appearance in the spring of 1973 carried the wording, 'I've never tried it because I don't like it'. At the end of the seventies it was announced that the Guinness toucan was to be resurrected to star in the new million-pound campaign. Guinness's advertising was now being handled by J. Walter Thompson, who spent around £3,000 creating a radio-controlled replica of the orange-beaked bird—'Toukie'—for use before the camera. When the results turned out to be less than lifelike the agency signed up a real-life toucan on a contract providing for a fee of £75 per working day plus expenses and a chauffeur-driven limousine to and from engagements.

The affection of the British public for Guinness's distinctive brand of salesmanship humour had grown with every successive campaign and the query, 'Have you seen the new Guinness poster?' had always been good for an affirmative chuckle, whether in the public bar of the 'local' or across a candle-lit table in Mayfair. It was a concept of advertising brilliant in its undermining of sales-resistance because comfortably and unshrillingly attuned to the Englishman's presiding distrust of the hustler and the language of hyperbole.

The most persuasive and pervasive slogan of them all had of course been the magnificently restrained 'Guinness is Good for You'—as testified by a columnist in the *Observer* of 2 February 1979 on the occasion of the fiftieth anniversary of the brewery's advertising. He recalled being buttonholed by a Leftist who was outraged by an amount of money being 'wasted' on advertising in Britain. 'You take Guinness for example,' the man pontificated. 'God knows what they spend! But it has no influence on me. I drink it because it's good for me.' Similar sentiments were expressed when the brewery decided in 1951 to extend its outdoor advertising to Ireland, at a time when the average consumption of the Irishman's favourite beverage was 100 pints a year per person. The brewery's managing director, Sir Hugh Beaver, explaining that the posters on the Dublin buses were aimed at tourists rather than the natives, added: 'After all, if you went to Mecca you'd expect to see some quotations from the Koran.' But the Dubliners were puzzled by the sudden appearance of the slogan 'Guinness is Good for You'. 'Next thing,' one of them grunted, 'somebody will be telling us we should eat spuds.'[2]

During the Prohibition years in the USA the brewery had made an attempt to have its stout imported for its medicinal value, only to be rebuffed by the Treasury Department. Later, when the first small Guinness brewery opened in Long Island City, the US Treasury banned its 'goodness' slogans but passed the weaker substitute; 'A Man's Drink'. But, back in England, the famous slogan retained the nature of a simple axiom and prompted Rupert to make one of his rare interventions in a House of Lords debate. During the debate on a bill to end the proliferation of highway advertising hoardings, a fellow-peer, supporting the measure, railed; 'Everywhere I go, I am unable to see our beautiful English countryside for the billboards alleging that "Guinness is Good for You".' Rupert rose to his feet, cheeks aflame, blue eyes blazing below his white hair. 'Guinness *is* good for you!' he shouted. And with that authoritative contribution, he sat down again.

His dander was up again when a Weights and Measures inspector tried to prosecute the company on the grounds that the froth at the top of a glass of draught Guinness did not count as liquid and that the drinking public was thereby being short-changed. Guinness won the first round in the lower courts, fought an appeal brought to the High Court and were vindicated by the solemn judgement of the Lord Chief Justice, Lord Parker. The froth, m'lud ruled, was an integral part of the pint. As *The Times* of 27 June 1964 reported his ruling: 'What the customer was asking for was a pint measure of Guinness, being a composite substance, containing liquid and gas. That is exactly what he got.'

Between the management of his farms at Pyrford and Elveden, his duties as chairman of the brewery and the obligations of a pater-familias, Rupert had little time for the day-to-day business con-ducted in the House of Lords, and even less inclination. The power-shorn Upper Chamber was 'a talking shop'; beyond its precincts was where the action was, in areas of science, industry and agriculture where he could make his own decisions, unilaterally, and put them into effect through the power of his wealth and personal prestige. In the House of Lords he was merely a peer among peers, as he had learnt after taking his seat as the new Earl of Iveagh, in circum-stances that would rankle with him for a long while.

His father, before his death, had commissioned the artist Frank Brangwyn, RA, to paint a set of murals with a view to donating them to the House of Lords as part of a redecoration scheme for the Royal Gallery. The cost to Edward Cecil would be £20,000, for what the artist described as 'the most important work of my life'.

By April 1930, the Brangwyn panels, at an unfinished stage, had been seen by the Royal Fine Arts Commission and were deemed to be 'inappropriate to the surroundings'. When the matter came up for discussion in the Lords, Rupert made an emotional and moving speech appealing for a final decision to be deferred until the panels were completed and placed in position. 'I am my father's son,' he said, with a break in his voice, 'and in memory of him can I do anything else than ask you to give the fullest consideration to these pictures, whatever your final decision should be?' His plea fell on stony ears, and when he insisted on a vote, the motion to defer a decision was defeated by 55 votes to 11.

From then on—until the outbreak of World War II—Rupert was very much, as he himself sometimes put it, 'the master of my fate and the captain of my soul'. Like so many others of his class and party—with the notable exception of the 'rebel' Tory Winston Chur-chill—he refused to believe that Adolf Hitler would ever commit the ultimate folly of setting Europe on fire; he shared the view, expressed as late as January 1939 by Neville Chamberlain (and reported in *The Times* on the 3rd of that month), as he set out for a weekend at Elveden, that '1939 will be a more tranquil year than 1938'. The war submitted him and his affairs to tiresome Government restrictions, as it did everyone else, but it also triumphantly vindicated his one-man crusade to put Britain's unproductive acreage under the plough.

After the start of World War II, Elveden Hall was taken over first by the British Army and then by the American Air Force, and for the rest of the war became the headquarters of the 8th US Air Force, whose bomber airdromes were spread over East Anglia. Lakenheath, a nostalgic name today to so many thousands of former 'Super Fortress' air-crew, adjoined the Elveden estate. Meanwhile, Rupert Edward and his wife Gwendolen made their home, when at Elveden, in a five-room cottage known as the Gardener's Bothy, never again taking up residence in the great Hall.

The heaths and scrublands of the estate, as it existed in World War I, had been the site for the War Office's first experiments with tanks, and now the tanks were back again, rehearsing battle man-oeuvres over land newly ploughed up and sown to meet the embat-tled island's need of domestic food production. Rupert Edward's response to the loss, by damage, of a thousand acres of cultivated land was typical. At his own risk he set about ploughing up hundreds of acres in areas of the estate not used by the tanks, successfully applying to this poorer soil the techniques by which he had earlier reclaimed so many thousands of unproductive acreage. By the end of the war, the loss of cultivated land caused by the tanks had been made up. And from this base, over the next five years—critical to Britain's agrarian economy—the estate was created, by further reclamations, into the largest arable farm in England, with more than 8,000 acres under cultivation as a single unit.

He had done more than his bit for the war effort, but before it came to an end, and within the space of three months, two successive tragedies involving Rupert's immediate family struck the 70-year-old earl with shattering force.

The first concerned his youngest brother, Walter Edward, who had reached the age of 64 after a lifetime devoted to public service in both Houses of Parliament. Wounded in the Boer War (and men-tioned in dispatches), awarded the DSO and bar for his gallantry under fire in World War I, he had served successive Tory Govern-ments in the 1920s as Under-Secretary for War, Financial Secretary to the Treasury and Minister of Agriculture and Fisheries. He was created a baron in 1932, taking the title Lord Moyne, and although the peerage removed him from the hurly-burly of party politics in the Lower House he served with brilliance on various parliamentary committees, notably as chairman of the Royal Commission sent out to report on social and economic conditions in the West Indies. He was a moderate in politics, with an enlightened view in such areas as welfare and colonial administration, and outside politics his two abiding passions were sea-travel and the collection of exotic animals and ethnographical specimens. For cruising in European and home waters he bought the 1,447-ton steamer *Roussalka*, with a crew of 26 officers and men. When it foundered on a rock off the Galway coast in heavy fog, he and his guests escaped with their lives and he promptly bought its sister-ship, the cross-Channel steamer *Dieppe*, for conversion into a pleasure yacht. For his voyages to the Dutch East Indies, South America and Africa he used his steam yacht, renamed *Rosaura*, and enriched the London Zoo with many rare specimens, including the giant monitor lizards known as the Komodo 'dragons'.

He never remarried after the death of his wife, Lady Evelyn, in 1939, and after his close friend Winston Churchill took over the conduct of the war in 1940 Lord Moyne was appointed Secretary of State for the Colonies and Leader of the House of Lords. Six months after the Cabinet reshuffle of February 1942, Churchill sent him to Cairo as Deputy Minister of State with Cabinet rank, and in January 1944 he was appointed Minister Resident in the Middle East with political and diplomatic responsibility for a wartime territory ranging from East Persia to Western Tripoli.

After a morning's work on 6 November 1944 Lord Moyne, accompanied by his ADC and his woman secretary, was driven from his office in the British Embassy to his official residence on Gezira Island, connected to the city of Cairo by the Kasr-el-Nil Bridge across the Nile. His chauffeur, Corporal Fuller, stopped the black Humber limousine in the short driveway leading to the house and while Fuller went to open the passenger door the ADC, Captain Arthur Hughes-Onslow, strode to the front entrance of the villa. Out of the nearby shrubbery two young men emerged, revolvers in hand. The dark-haired one, Eliahu Hakim, sprang to the car and fired three shots at the white-suited Lord Moyne. One bullet entered his neck, another his stomach, and the third missed its target. In the same hideous seconds Corporal Fuller was gunned down as he leapt at the fair-haired assassin, Eliahu Ben Suri.

Before Captain Hughes-Onslow could get to them, the murderers, their bloody work done, were off across the Kasr-el-Nil Bridge on bicycles. But an Egyptian policeman, who happened to be riding by on a motor-cycle, went after them and in an exchange of fire wounded Hakim and captured both men. They turned out to be members of the Stern Gang and they would be hanged four months later after a trial and after their appeals to George VI, King Farouk, Pope Pius XII, President Roosevelt, Winston Churchill and the League of Nations had fallen on deaf ears. Lord Moyne died that night at 8.40, never having regained consciousness. He must have been aware he was high on the terrorist Stern Gang's murder list, but he had refused to be stalked by fear. Only the night before, after dining with the United States Minister, Pinckney Tuck, he had dismissed his car and walked the one and a half miles home unarmed and alone.[3]

It was not until eleven days after the news had broken in London that Winston Churchill could trust himself to address Parliament on the subject of his friend's death. To a silent and still stunned House he declared that Moyne's murder had affected 'none more sharply than those, like myself, who in the past have been consistent friends of the Jews and constant architects of their future'.[4] And in a passage that, re-read today, echoes across the intervening years with the force of a prophecy he went on: 'If our dreams of Zionism are to end in the smoke of the assassins' guns and our labours for its future to produce only a new set of gangsters worthy of Nazi Germany,' then many, like himself, would 'have to reconsider the position we have maintained so consistently and so long in the past'.

If the terrorists of the Stern Gang—then including Menachim Begin—expected congratulations from the Jews of Palestine, they were disappointed. The country's leading newspaper, *Haaretz*, spoke of the murder as the most 'grievous blow [that] has been struck at our cause' since Zionism began. Dr Chaim Weizmann, the man who was to be the founder of the State of Israel, declared in London that the shock of Lord Moyne's assassination had been 'far more severe and numbing' than the death of his own son, Michael Weizmann, in action against the Germans.

Lord Moyne's embalmed body was taken to rest in All Saints Cathedral, Cairo, before being flown to England for cremation at the Golders Green crematorium. The cortège that passed through the three main streets of Cairo on its way to the cathedral was headed by muffled drums, followed by several thousand men of all the Allied armies in the Middle East. Leading the mourners was Moyne's

39-year-old son and heir, Bryan Walter Guinness, then serving as a captain in the Royal Sussex Regiment.

Lord Moyne's estate was valued for death duties at, 'as far as can at present be ascertained', £2,000,000. Knockmaroon House and its lands, together with the Grosvenor Place mansion, went to Bryan Walter. Two-fifths of the residue of his fortune, after some minor bequests, also went to Bryan and an equal portion to his only daughter, Grania. His other son, Murtogh, who inherited the remaining one-fifth, has made no significant contribution to the Guinness saga. He lives alone, his wife having been killed in a car crash in 1976, and is much appreciated by the local 'Brits' for the parties he gives annually on his arrival at his Barbados home, Porter's Lodge.

The 'First Arthur'. Born 1725 and immortalized 224 years later by this special issue of postage stamps commemorating the bicentenary of the founding of the brewery.

Courtesy: Stanley Gibbons Ltd

Grandson of the founder and ancestor of all subsequent generations of the brewery line, Benjamin Lee Guinness was rewarded with a baronetcy for his public services, a year before his death in 1868.

Mary Evans Picture Library

Edward Cecil Guinness, host to monarchs, lord of Elveden Hall, art collector and philanthropist extraordinary. His monument is the Ken Wood museum. His most glittering bequest to the family: the hereditary earldom of Iveagh.

BBC Hulton Picture Library

Six years before the death of his cousin-wife, the 63-year-old Edward Cecil Guinness, now a peer of the United Kingdom, takes the reins at a 1910 meet of four-in-hand coaches in Hyde Park.

A widower now, and only three years short of his longed-for earldom, Edward Cecil is accompanied in the park by his daughter-in-law, Lady Evelyn, daughter of the Earl of Buchan.

© Hulton Picture Library

Before inheriting his father's earldom in 1927, Rupert Edward Guinness fought and won three Parliamentary seats including Southend-on-Sea (1918), represented to the present day by three successive 'Guinness MPs'. These pictures show him campaigning for Haggerston in 1908.

BBC Hulton Picture Library

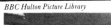

Walter Edward (right), first of the Guinnesses to hold a Cabinet post, en route from Whitehall to the House of Commons with Neville Chamberlain and Lord Birkenhead. Their sombre faces match the dark days of the 1926 General Strike.

Above left The Guinness farms in Canada, staffed by British emigrants, needed women trained in farm work. With World War I just over the horizon Rupert's wife, Lady Gwendolen, lends students a hand on the Guinness Training Farm in Surrey.

Above Lady Gwendolen, now Countess of Iveagh, stakes her claim to Southend-on-Sea in the by-election of 1927, backed by (l. to r.) her three daughters, Lady Patricia, 9, Lady Honor, 18, and Lady Brigid, 7.

Top right The bowler-hatted 2nd Earl of Iveagh beams approval as his wife charms a future constituent during the general election of 1931.

Above In 1928 Rupert Edward Guinness formally presented his father's gift of Ken Wood and its priceless art collection to the nation. His wife, Lady Gwendolen, is seated on the second chair to his right.

THE MISSIONA

Above Youngest son of the first Arthur
Guinness, Captain John Grattan Guinness
founded a line of clergymen Guinnesses,
down to the present day.

Top left Captain John's son, the charismatic
Rev. Henry Grattan Guinness, was one of
the 19th century's greatest evangelical
missionaries and preachers. Portrait by
Jean-Léon Huens.

Top right Henry Grattan's own photograph
of his second wife, Grace.

Above Henry's eldest son, Dr Harry Guinness, roused the world's conscience against slave labour in the Belgian Congo.

Left Harry's younger brother, Dr G. Whitfield Guinness, and his Swedish missionary wife, Jane af Sandeberg.

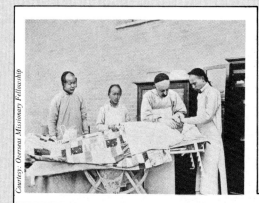

Courtesy: Overseas Missionary Fellowship

The doctor-missionary, Whitfield Guinness, operating in China at the turn of the century.

Henry Grattan's two daughters, Geraldine and Lucy, took the Bible into the darkest regions of the world.

Below Prayer meetings were held worldwide when Geraldine and her husband Howard Taylor were captured by a Chinese irregular army.

Below right Paul Grattan, the only living great-grandson of the First Arthur.

7

There's Money, in Money

1

Just as the middle name 'Lee' identifies a descendant of the Second Arthur Guinness, so 'Rundell' recurs through the line of bankers and financiers who developed an unshrill and sober empire quite separate from the brewery and with comparable success in a line of business not given (until recent years) to the pursuit of spectacular profits. The 'Rundells' have added no earls or peers to the Guinness pedigrees in Debrett's, and only two knighthoods in the five generations from their founder Richard Guinness, barrister son of Samuel the goldbeater. It is a line with no tradition of publicized benefactions and its contribution to the political ranks at Westminster has been minimal. However, while it produced only a couple of brilliant society hostesses over the years, some of its women have made their mark in the visual arts and education, and probably more signatures by the lions of literature and the stage will be found in the 'Rundell' guest books than in the brewers'.

In the blue-blood-marriage stakes the children of the banking line are not even a close second to the 'Lees'; but they make up for that in the colourfulness of many of their chosen partners. And in any case, let it not be forgotten that it was a daughter of the present James Edward Rundell Guinness, Sabrina, who came nearest of all the clan's daughters to the throne of Great Britain.

The brewery at James's Gate had already been in business for about sixty years when two of Richard's sons, Robert Rundell and his youngest brother, Richard Samuel, set up a small land agency and banking business at No. 5 Kildare Street. They were the only surviving sons of the marriage in 1783 between Richard Guinness and Mary Darley, daughter of a Dublin builder. Three intermediately born brothers died in infancy, as did one of their seven sisters. Indeed, had Samuel's son Richard not married, there would have been no line of banker Guinnesses, for his only brother and sister both died without issue. Robert Rundell and Richard Samuel were contemporaries and cousins of the affluent Sir Benjamin Lee–but there is no evidence of the brewery chief being invited to back their enterprise. The modest initial capital came from Robert, then in his thirties and, like his father and brother, a barrister; Richard Samuel gave his name to the company. Unfortunately, Richard's business acumen was no match for his brother's. He had married a daughter of Sir Charles Jenkinson, the 10th Baronet of Hawkesbury, Gloucestershire, and was already living well above his means when Robert wisely withdrew from the partnership in 1836. This first agency went bankrupt 13 years later, whereupon Richard Samuel turned his attention to politics, first as MP for Kinsale, co. Cork, then for Barnstable, Devon. He died in 1857, leaving four sons and four daughters, one of whom–Adelaide–married her cousin Edward Cecil in 1873. This alliance between Richard Samuel's line and the Iveagh succession was reinforced, as we have already seen, by the appointment of Adelaide's brother Reginald Robert to the chairmanship of the brewery.

The youngest of Adelaide's brothers, Claude Hume, was installed by Edward Cecil in Knockmaroon House, Dublin,[1] to which impressive estate he brought two successive wives before his death at the age of 43. He started his own small line of marriageable Guinness girls with one daughter, Marjorie, by his first wife, Gladys Rowley, and another, Grace Zoë, by his second wife, Zoë Nugent, daughter of the 3rd Baron Nugent. Marjorie married the Hon. Alex Villiers Russell in a union that linked this line of the Guinnesses with three impressively noble English families.[2]

Marjorie's half-sister, Grace Zoë, kept her end up by marrying Robert, the eldest son of Captain Edward Fitzroy, Speaker of the House of Commons 1928–43. Robert later inherited the Viscountcy of Daventry. Marjorie produced a son, William Rodney Villiers, but this socially promising female Guinness pedigree through Grace Zoë ended in 1966 with the marriage of her beautiful granddaughter, Belinda ('Min'), to the Mayfair gambler, John Aspinall. Their only child died in infancy and the marriage was dissolved in 1972.

While Richard Samuel turned to politics and the social game, Robert Rundell got together with an outside partner, John Ross Mahon, to form Guinness Mahon, the acorn out of which, over the next century and a half, would grow the mighty £300,000,000 oak known today worldwide as the Guinness Peat Group.

John Ross Mahon, of the landed Mahon family of Ahascragh, co.

Galway, had been serving his apprenticeship with the Richard Guinness land agency before it folded. To the new partnership he brought, with his own business acumen, the wide connections his family enjoyed with the gentry of Ireland. The capital of the company was £5,000, of which Robert contributed £3,000 and Mahon £2,000, and the profits were divided in these proportions. Between them, the partners soon developed the agency into a thriving concern and long before Robert Rundell's death in 1857 his two sons, Richard Seymour and Henry, had been taken into the business and were already beginning to build up a small banking branch of Guinness Mahon. Richard Seymour, the eldest son, had joined the firm at the age of 15, drawing a salary of £12 per annum. In 1845, when he opted for a share of the profits in lieu of a salary, he was made a partner and the profits were divided as to three-sixths to his father, two-sixths to Mahon and one-sixth to Richard. Henry became a partner in 1850, from which date the division of profits was one-third to the father, one-sixth each to Richard and Henry and one-third to Mahon.

Both sons were offsprings of Robert Rundell's first marriage to a clergyman's daughter, Mary Anne Seymour, who died when they were still children. Three years later their father married another Mary Anne, also a clergyman's daughter, who outlived him by 32 years after giving him six daughters and a son. The son, Robert, entered the church, became Vicar of Market Harborough in England and was the father of Elizabeth Maude Guinness whose career as an educationalist took her to the vice-principalship of London University's Royal Holloway College and who became vice-principal of Cheltenham Ladies' College.

John Ross Mahon lived until 1887, by which time the Dublin agency had established sub-offices in London, Strokestown, co. Roscommon, and at Ahascragh, where the Mahon family had its 'Castlegar' estate. Having no children of his own, he chose his favourite nephew, John Fitzgerald Mahon, to preserve the family connection with the agency through its Ahascragh sub-office. But this energetic and ambitious young man soon began to yawn under the soft challenge of county Galway. He took out his share of the business left to him by his uncle and went to Canada to join his brother Edward who had helped to found a small mining town in British Columbia, named 'Castlegar'.

The agency was now in the hands of Richard Seymour and his brother Henry and, as the private banking side of it developed, it had made sense for Richard to move to London while Henry attended to the land agency and the financing of corn merchants and the light railways then being laid down throughout Ireland. They kept each other informed through a daily exchange of letters but, incredibly, Richard ran his end of the business for many years without ledgers or a single clerk before opening his first (one-room) office in St Clement's Lane.[3] He had married his cousin Elizabeth Jane, child of the marriage between the Second Arthur's daughter Susanna and the Rev. John Darley, who in his turn was an offspring of the union between the Second Arthur's sister Elizabeth and Alderman Fred Darley. Thus 'three-quarters of a pint' of Guinness blood (Elizabeth Jane's) was mixed with a 'full Guinness pint' (Richard Seymour's) and possibly accounts for the fecundity of a union that produced ten children, the majority of whom outlived the biblical life-span of 'three-score-and-ten' and four of whom died as octagenarians.[4]

Henry, whose own marriage came within a year of Richard Seymour's, fathered twelve children, including seven daughters, one of whom—Lucy—married the Hungarian painter, Philip de Laszló, portraitist of two Popes, four Presidents of the United States and most of the European royalty as well as several of the Guinness ladies. Two of Henry's sons—Howard Rundell and (Richard) Noel—had joined Richard Seymour's sons as partners in Guinness Mahon during the active lifetime of both fathers. With Henry's death in 1893 and Richard's retirement on the last day of the 19th century, the land agency end of the business took second place and the private banking side began to raise its horizons, ultimately to embrace the world.

The future management of the company would flow through Henry's sons and grandsons rather than Richard Seymour's, but it was the latter's descendants who would provide the 'glamour' until then only associated with the brewery line.

The international banking activities of Guinness Mahon were put virtually on ice during World War I, and on Richard Seymour's death in 1915 three of his sons—Robert Darley,[5] Arthur Eustace and Gerald Seymour—retired from the firm. Of the three other brothers, Herbert Frederick, the youngest, had joined the Royal Navy; Richard Sidney was pursuing his own career in finance, which would take him to the chairmanship of the powerful Mercantile & General Insurance Co. and the Sterling Trust; and Benjamin Seymour was well on the road to creating the greatest international fortune of them all.

The six brothers differed sharply in character and it usually fell to the slightly built and good-humoured Arthur Eustace to play mentor and peacemaker to his brothers and their families. In sharp contrast to Arthur Eustace's urbanity was the prickly, ill-humoured nature of his elder brother Gerald Seymour, whose wife Eleanor Grace de Capell Brooke (niece of the 4th baronet of that name) died seven years ahead of him and who spent his last years in the splendid Jacobean manor, Dorton House, which he had rented at Thame.

Gerald Seymour was a snob, embittered in his later years by the failure of the Tory leadership to hand him a knighthood for his services to the party.[6] And to compound his grievances, he lost heavily in the Kreuger 'Match Crash' of 1929. Until then he had been regarded in the family as something of a financial wizard, it being largely through his foresight that Guinness Mahon moved into the rewarding area of investment banking. But he was a stern father and after his children had grown up he dominated their lives by his threats to cut them off with a penny. The eldest, Gerald Richard, married Desirée, daughter of Sir Alfred Welby, MP, in 1932. His widow, a bright and articulate old lady now living in a two-room flat at Putney Bridge, recalls the circumstances in which her father-in-law, Gerald Seymour, became the first of the Guinnesses to take his own life.

In 1933, now a widower, and suffering from nervous depression, the 71-year-old misanthropist had been persuaded by his friend and doctor to go into a nursing home. At that time Desirée and her husband were living at Dorton House and they decided to profit from the occasion by taking a trip to Scotland, the doctor having assured them that if his patient decided to return home in their absence he would move in and stay with him. As a further precaution Desirée and her husband took it upon themselves to instruct one of the manservants to take all the firearms out of the gun-room and lock them safely away, somewhere else. Returning home during their absence, and taking a look in the gun-room next to his library, Gerald Seymour demanded, 'Where are my guns?' and, on being told what had happened, ordered them put right back in their places. Within 24 hours he had shot himself.

Arthur Eustace had not been able to achieve much as a counsel to his brother Gerald, but his advice was sought about three years later when his friend Sir Arthur de Capell Brooke, a first cousin of Eleanor Grace, had to decide who should inherit his 2,500-acre Great Oakley Hall estate at Kettering, Northamptonshire. Sir Arthur had no children and his brother Edward had no interest in marrying. The closest collateral was Eleanor Grace's elder sister Catherine, who was married to Hugh Paget and already had a son, Clarence. However, and presumably on the sound principle that land plus money made music, Arthur Eustace's advice was that the estate should go to Gerald Seymour's eldest son, Gerald Richard Guinness. But there was a snag. Sir Arthur made it clear that he was perfectly agreeable to this arrangement provided Gerald Richard's children never converted from Protestantism or divorced. Whatever the legal validity of such a condition, Desirée Guinness absolutely refused to accept it. Sir Arthur then turned his attention to Gerald Richard's younger brother Anthony Wentworth, whose wife Juliette had already given him a daughter in 1930 and was about to give birth to another child which, with the luck of the Irish, would surely be a son. In the event, it turned out to be another daughter, born in April 1936 and christened Bronwyn. Sir Arthur might not have been totally discouraged by this spin of the wheel, but Anthony took it badly. He was already emotionally involved with Juliette's close friend Diana Boone, and a few days after the birth of Bronwyn he left Juliette with a regretful, 'Had it been a son, I would have stayed', married Diana immediately the divorce came through in 1938 and took off for Montreal.

This was not quite the behaviour Sir Arthur was looking for in a legatee to his estate and so, through the good offices of Arthur Eustace, he tried again with Gerald Richard and Desirée, who had given birth to a son, Hugh, in 1937. Again he sought to impose his Victorian conditions, but when Desirée again rejected them he gave in with good grace and died more or less contented in 1939, a year after his elevation to the peerage as Lord Brooke.

On Gerald Richard's death in 1975, his estate passed to Hugh, who assumed the name 'de Capell Brooke Guinness' by deed poll in 1976. Gerald's sister Hermione married John Slessor in 1923, the man who was to become one of Britain's most distinguished Royal Air Force commanders.

Whether it was the fruit of Arthur Eustace's even disposition, his happy marriage to Wilhelmine Forester, or his active life as Master of the Grafton Hunt, he outlived all his five brothers, dying in 1955 at the age of 87 and leaving a daughter but no son to perpetuate his male line. His eldest brother, Robert Darley, who had died in 1938, had left a son, Richard Smyth, whose widow Esmé is still living at the time of writing in the lovely matrimonial home at Straffan, co. Kildare, where her late husband's unique collection of model trains takes up an entire wing of the house.

Herbert Frederick, the sailor brother of Arthur Eustace, moved to England and married, but died in 1922 leaving no issue. Richard

Sidney was by now 'a big man' in the City of London and Benjamin Seymour was even bigger on Wall Street.

Richard Sidney married three times, first to Emilie Weimar, whose father was a captain in the German Imperial Guards, then Beatrice Jungman and then Ursula Blois. But it was his wife Beatrice (formerly married to the painter Nicholas Jungman) who put the banking Guinnesses on the social map of London as a hostess of eccentric flair and discrimination. At her house in Great Cumberland Place she regularly entertained and amused the brightest of young lions then on the way up in their careers, such as Noël Coward, Oliver Messel, Cecil Beaton and Evelyn Waugh, as well as the most promising young politicians of the time. Others who had already 'arrived' included Rex Whistler and Michael Arlen, favourite novelist of the Bright Young People of the late 1920s.

Loelia, Duchess of Westminster, in her autobiography *Grace and Favour*,[7] pays Beatrice the tribute of being 'the hostess who really revolutionized my young life'. 'She was heavily built with a very deep voice which was a godsend to mimics and which made her lightest utterance sound like the pronouncement of an oracle. Most of the things she chose to say were pretty devastating and she was known as "Gloomy Beatrice" from the inspired negativeness of her conversation. She countered the opening, "I've just met a friend of yours" with, "You can't have, I haven't got one."'

Breakfast dishes such as haddock and kedgeree were served at her luncheon parties, often held in a ground-floor sitting-room with the curtains drawn ('Can't face the day without breakfast'), and she was once overheard in a Mayfair milliner's telling the assistant, 'I want a hat for an ugly middle-aged woman whose husband hates her.'

The two spirited daughters by her first marriage, Zita and Teresa ('Baby') Jungman, would cringe whenever their mother, a merciless tease, loudly and publicly demanded of her daughters' escorts to state their intentions, and the Duchess of Westminster remembers seeing her 'force the unfortunate Teresa to get up and do a solo Charleston for the benefit of a young man before whom she particularly did *not* want to make a fool of herself'.

Teresa, herself, was no slouch when it came to legpulling and outrageous behaviour. An early success was her posture, at the age of 15, as 'Madame Anna Vorolsky', an aristocratic refugee from the Red Terror. Suitably costumed and made-up, she was able to bring tears to the eyes of more than one London sophisticate with her tale of how she had sold her jewels in order to educate her 'poor little boy'. Later, in the early 1930s, the great Evelyn Waugh himself came under Teresa's spell and might have married her had he not converted to Catholicism after his first marriage, thereby—as he viewed it at the time—debarring himself from remarriage.

Between the world wars, Richard Sidney added to his chairmanship of the Mercantile and General Insurance Co. the chairs of the Anglo-American Debenture Corporation, the Railway Debenture & General Trust Co., the Railway Share Trust Agency Co., the London & Scottish Assurance Association, the Debenture & Capital Investment Trust, the Share & General Investment Trust and the Sterling Trust, formerly the Alabama, New Orleans, Texas and Pacific Junction Railways Co., Ltd.

Beatrice died shortly after the end of World War II, during the course of which, on being dug out of the bomb debris after her London home had been hit by the Luftwaffe, she is reputed to have risen above her characteristic glumness by declaring, 'I knew I should be wonderful, and I was.' Another story has it that on being rescued, unscratched, she answered the question, 'Why didn't you get yourself out?' with, 'I wanted to see if Dick would mind.'

2

Benjamin Seymour Guinness, the fourth son of Richard Seymour, was undoubtedly the most outstanding individual capitalist of the entire Guinness clan. He was the first of them to sniff, in the 1890s, the prospects for lucrative manipulation of Wall Street where the early training in his father's London office, with its international ramifications, together with his own restless mental energy, had built him a formidable empire of corporation directorships years before his father's death in 1915. They included the New York Trust Co., Lackawanna Steel Co., Kansas City Southern Railway, Sea Board Airlands, Duquesne Light Co., Pittsburg, and United Railways of San Francisco. He had joined the Royal Navy as a student–cadet at the age of 14, retiring at 23 with the rank of lieutenant, and after marrying a daughter of Sir Richard Williams-Bulkeley in 1902 he set up a home on Long Island where he fathered one son, Thomas Loel ('Loel' from here on), and two daughters, Meraud and Tanis. Benjamin, when he was not making money, liked to tinker with motor-cars, and he brought Loel up to share his hobby, teaching him at the age of ten to drive a yellow racing Stutz acquired by Benjamin after it had broken the world's speed record at Sheepshead Bay.[8]

He commuted–if a suite in the *Berengaria* comes within the term–between his English and American homes, and during the 1920s Mrs Benjamin Guinness outshone her sister-in-law Beatrice in the stylishness, if not the drollness, of her entertainment as a hostess. British and European royalty came to the fêtes at her country house, Sunnyhill Park, Ascot, and to the dances she gave in the ballroom at 11 and 12 Carlton House Terrace, the town mansion overlooking St James's Park. Here her grown-up children and those of Benjamin's American associates rubbed shoulders with royal princes and dukes, the cream of Debrett's and most of the foreign diplomatic corps.

In 1929, sensing the first tremors of the Wall Street earthquake, Benjamin–in his sixties and a multi-millionaire–began to shed his American interests. At the same time he took steps to ensure that his fortune would never be decimated by British death duties. He gave up British residence by making over the mansion in Carlton House Terrace to Loel, stayed at the Ritz during his brief visits to London, but spent most of his time in Paris or at his house in Mougins, in the hills above Cannes, described by guests (and reported by the *Daily Telegraph* of 6 January 1931) as 'one of the most delightful villas on the Riviera'. Here, on 5 January 1931, his wife Bridget died. The only Guinnesses at her funeral in Cannes were Benjamin and his children, but the family turned out in force for a memorial service in London, where Princess Helena Victoria and Princess Marie-Louise headed the mourners.

Three years earlier, after training at Sandhurst for a short commission in the Irish Guards, the 20-year-old Loel had started on his turbulent matrimonial career by marrying Lord Churston's daughter, the 19-year-old Hon. Joan Yarde-Buller. It had been no big secret that Churston and Benjamin had set their hearts, years earlier, on a union between these offspring and were conspiring to that end. In the event the couple fell genuinely in love without prompting. The wedding took place at St Margaret's, Westminster, of course, and was one of the social events of the year with hundreds of invited guests, including Mrs Patrick Campbell, running the admiring gauntlet of a rubber-necking London throng. By now, Loel was piloting his own plane, for which a landing strip had been laid down in his parents' Mougins villa, where he flew with his bride for the honeymoon.

His father's delight at the marriage of his only son was somewhat marred at the time by a legal dispute that, in its own way, throws a certain light on the character of the great financier.

A professional tennis coach named Hubert Courtenay Evans was taking him to court, claiming breach of an agreement under which he was to have accompanied Benjamin to Cannes in the winter of 1925 and coach him at tennis for two hours every weekday for a fee of 12*s* 6*d* an hour, plus travelling expenses and accommodation. The action was heard in the High Court of Justice, London, where Benjamin denied ever having engaged the coach to go to Cannes with him. He had merely expressed his opinion that he might be able to find a job for him there. Mr Justice Roche accepted the coach's version of the affair. As reported in *The Times* of 26 and 27 April 1928, on giving judgement for £153 17*s* 6*d* he said that, having seen both parties, 'the recollection of the plaintiff commended itself to me'.

As a small child in New York, Loel had been asked by one of his father's friends, the Tammany politician, Bourke Cochran, what he was going to do when he grew up and had stoutly replied, 'Help dadda in business.' There is no evidence of his having been a pillar of strength to the paternal empire before 1929 when, with his 23rd birthday coming up and his vast inheritance already secure, it was the siren call of politics rather than high finance that sounded the more sweetly in his ear.

Britain's first ever Labour Government had fallen to the Tories in 1924 and when the General Strike of 1926 paralysed the country, Loel and his undergraduate friends rallied to the support of Prime Minister Stanley Baldwin and his Home Secretary, Winston Churchill, by taking over, unpaid, some of the striking workers' jobs. The strike was broken but, as unemployment mounted and another general election (1929) approached, the challenge of Westminster became irresistible and Loel put himself forward as Tory candidate for Whitechapel. It was a brave choice of constituency—a working-class Labour stronghold where the sitting Member was president of the massive Transport and General Workers' Union.

Loel did his best to woo the cloth-capped electorate of Whitechapel, even declaring (as *The Times* of 22 May 1929 reported) to his underwhelmed audiences that he himself had once undergone the rigours of honest labour, as a meter inspector and a train driver. How he had found the time for this during his brief adulthood was not disclosed, but the sceptics who suspected he was referring to his activities—three years earlier—during the General Strike had the satisfaction when the votes were counted of seeing the Tory candidate at the bottom of the poll with 3,478 votes.

But he had fought the good fight and two years later, when internal dissension in the Labour Government forced Prime Minister Ramsay MacDonald into another general election, Loel returned to the hustings, this time as candidate for the safe Tory seat of Bath. Here on 27 October 1931, he romped home with a majority of 16,455 votes.

Conventionally, the long road to 10 Downing Street—secret Mecca of every new young backbencher—starts with a good maiden speech and subsequent appointment as unpaid Private Parliamentary Secretary to a Government minister. In Loel's case the appointment came first. The Under-Secretary for Air, Sir Philip Sassoon, was a good friend of his and the godfather of his son Patrick, born three months before Loel's adoption by Bath. Loel was also a pilot in Sir Philip's Auxiliary Royal Air Force Squadron, 601. It did not therefore stun the House when Sir Philip named Loel as his PPS. As the subject of his maiden speech, seven months later, he chose the complex problems of Britain's foreign exchange position and was loudly applauded when he sat down, not least by that wizard of parliamentary oratory, Lloyd George. A lobby correspondent for the *Daily Telegraph* declared on 11 June 1932 that it was 'one of the best maiden speeches heard in this Parliament' and added: 'He has a confident and easy manner and his first essay in the House led members to predict that he will go a long way.'

Loel was to remain PPS to Sir Philip throughout the four-year term of that Parliament, travelling widely on his minister's behalf to explain Britain's airmail policy to the various countries served by the national airline. And it was during one of these trips—to Australia—that his marriage to Joan went down in flames. His own version of the story, given in testimony at the divorce hearings in November 1935, was that he had arranged for his wife to spend a holiday in Switzerland while he was away, but on his return he learned that she had gone to South America. Later she told him she had 'formed an attachment' for Prince Aly Khan, son and heir of the Aga Khan. The attachment was in fact a mad infatuation, propelling Joan from the arms of her very English husband into those of the amorous and dashing prince. Evidence was produced showing they had occupied a suite together at a Paris hotel. The action was undefended and Loel won costs and the custody of his son. There were compensations for both parties, for Loel was returned to Parliament less than two weeks later in a landslide general election victory for the Tories, and Joan went on to become the Princess Aly Khan, until she was obliged to share the title with the Aly Khan's next wife, the Hollywood 'sex goddess', Rita Hayworth.

A year after the divorce Loel took as his second wife Lady Isabel, the 19-year-old daughter of the Duke of Rutland and a niece of Loel's friend, Lady Diana Cooper. The difficulty—a real one in those days—of a divorced person's being given a church wedding was solved through the good offices of the divorce-law reformist Dr Geikie-Cobb, rector of the tiny City of London parish of St Ethelburga's. There being no hotels in the parish where bridegrooms or brides could check in for the legal 'residential' term of seven nights, the good rector had provided three spartan bedrooms in a dwelling house behind his church for the use of such persons. The house was in a back alleyway bearing the challenging name of Wrestler's Court and was unapproachable by car. For seven nights, therefore, the reddish-haired, slightly balding Loel was driven by his chauffeur from his home in Belgravia to a dark archway in Camomile St, thence to proceed on foot to Wrestler's Court and the narrow bedroom with its one small window overlooking a dairy shop. The sacrifice was rewarded with a marriage that lasted 15 years, and was blessed with a son and a daughter. The guest list for the reception at Benjamin Guinness's mansion in Carlton House Terrace filled a column of *The Times* and was headed by the Duke and Duchess of Gloucester, the Duke of Kent and Prince Arthur of Connaught.

To his skills as a racing motorist and aeroplane pilot Loel had by now added a master seaman's certificate, and he skippered his first yacht, the 216-ton *Atlantis*, across the Atlantic and back for his honeymoon with Isabel, making this one of the few yachts of its size to do the double crossing in winter.

Shortly after the outbreak of World War II, Loel—still MP for Bath—was promoted from an RAF flight-lieutenant to squadron leader, then to group captain in command of the famous wing of the Tactical Air Force formerly commanded by 'Sailor' Malan, Britain's highest scoring fighter pilot.

Benjamin Seymour had survived to enjoy his gallant son's brilliant wartime career and on Benjamin's death in 1947 Loel would automatically have become one of the wealthiest men in Britain but for two tiresome snags. One was the apparent absence of a will;[9] the other the survival of Benjamin's second wife, the Italian princess Maria Nunziante (the daughter of the Duke of Mignano), whom Benjamin had wed in 1936, thus becoming, in line with Italian aristocratic custom, the only member of the Guinness family entitled to call himself 'prince'. There had been no children of the marriage and while Loel was searching for the will at his father's homes in New York, Berne, Paris, Normandy and the South of France, battle lines were drawn up between himself and his stepmother for a legal conflict that would persist over the next four years, revolving around a dispute as to whether Benjamin's domicile had been in Switzerland or in France.

Shortly before his death, he had consolidated the greater part of his worldwide fortune into a trust company under the name Ebit SA. The trust was for the benefit of his children and was administered after his death by his sagacious Swiss secretary, Mr K. Haller. For Loel and Haller it was argued that Benjamin's domicile had been in Switzerland, and that his will—since discovered—had been drawn up in that country and death duties paid there, and that his widow (who had not been provided for in the will) was therefore not entitled to a maintenance allowance as prescribed by French law. His stepmother argued back that her husband had deliberately avoided becoming a Swiss resident for tax reasons, and that his Swiss homes were never in his name but were usually rented by his secretary, Mr Haller. She asked for a £9,000 annuity from the trust.

Loel not only resisted this claim but demanded that his stepmother hand over to him certain items of property ranging from paintings and jewellery to a wooden pepper mill—items the *principessa* claimed were presents from Benjamin. Further, he insisted that since the Guinness villa at Cassino, Italy, had belonged to his father, the compensation payable for war damage should go to him rather than to his father's widow. This attitude—surprising, perhaps, in one already so well endowed with worldly goods—did not necessarily reflect a longstanding personal animosity between Loel and his Italian stepmother. It was in line with his father's and his own rooted concern never to dissipate on 'outsiders' the family wealth built up so diligently over the years. (A droll example of this occurred on an occasion when Benjamin, having broken a motor-car journey in France to eat at a restaurant, was presented with a bill for 300 francs. On his protesting at the amount, the waiter went into an exhaustive account of the high cost of food at the time, ending with the exaggerated claim that 'a kilo of butter, alone, costs us a hundred francs'. Benjamin's answer was to send Loel along the street to buy three kilos of butter, which he handed to the dumbstruck waiter in full settlement.

The battle over the will was fought through courts in Paris and Berne and the mounting legal costs forced the *principessa* to sell much of her personal jewellery. Thereafter, there was no further reportage of the case in the press, from which it may be assumed that an out-of-court arrangement was reached.

In the meantime Loel's marriage to Lady Isabel had ended, with a scenario straight out of a Judith Krantz-style novel.

Gloria Rubio was born in Mexico in 1913, the daughter of a writer, José Rafael Rubio, who—according to her version in *Time* magazine of 26 January 1962—had taken her to New York 'after he had crossed ideologies with Dictator Porfirio Diaz'. Since Diaz had already been overthrown and obliged to exile himself from Mexico in 1911, it would seem that Gloria was either over-romanticizing her background or confused about her own birthdate. What is not in dispute is that she arrived in Europe in 1933 and, with her gleaming black hair, long-necked Nefertiti profile and svelte figure, was soon in demand as a Paris fashion model. Here, in 1935, she met and married Count Franz von Fürstenberg, one of Hitler's aristocratic fans, and they settled in Berlin where Gloria gave birth to two children, Franz and Dolores.

According to the *Time* version, 'when Hitler came to power, Gloria and her two children . . . fled to Madrid while her husband stayed on in Germany'. This account delays Hitler's historic access to power by at least two years; but exquisite creatures like Gloria should be granted the prerogative of muddling their dates. It is, of course, a fact that Franz von Fürstenberg became ADC in Paris to the infamous Otto Abetz, Nazi boss of Occupied France during World War II. And it is probably true that during that time Gloria 'fled to Madrid' and obtained a 'friendly divorce'.[10] After the Liberation she returned to Paris, where she resumed her career as a fashion model and was a frequent guest at the British Embassy on the Faubourg St Honoré, then presided over by Duff Cooper and his wife Lady Diana. (The Coopers and the banking Guinnesses were old friends and one of Benjamin Seymour's last acts of generosity was to make a present for life of one of his flats on the Rue de Lille to the Coopers upon Duff's retirement from the ambassadorship, two years after Labour's landslide election victory in 1945.)[11] By then Gloria had married Ahmed Fakry whose father, Fakry Pasha, Egyptian Ambassador to France, was related to the Egyptian royal family. The union was opposed by Ahmed's family and not recognized in Egypt, but it was arranged by proxy in Mexico and it ended in divorce in 1949.

In that same year 'Princess Gloria Fakry', as she was now known in Paris, met Loel on a Mediterranean yachting trip. Love blossomed between the 42-year-old Loel and the elegant 36-year-old Mexican and was consummated, according to Lady Isabel's affidavit in the undefended divorce action, at the Trianon Palace Hotel in Versailles.

They were married by the Mayor of Antibes, off one of Loel's two yachts, the *Sea Huntress*, in circumstances of such secrecy that the regulation banns were not published and the witnesses were two directors of the local shipbuilding yards. Loel handed the cooperative mayor a cheque for £100 to be distributed among the poor of Antibes. Lady Isabel had agreed to give him a divorce only on the condition that he buy her whatever house she most fancied. In the event she chose their friend Captain 'Bobby' Cunningham-Read's house, 'Westmeads', in Warwickshire, and Loel bought the place for around £35,000.

It was reported (in the *Evening Standard* of 9 June 1962) that Benjamin Seymour, in his will, advised Loel to 'safeguard your freedom of movement at all times', a policy to which the old man had long been faithful and which his son certainly had the means, in abundance, to pursue. He now owned houses in London and Paris, Arthingworth Manor at Market Harborough, Leicestershire, and a stud farm and castle in Normandy. To these he would add a house in Lausanne (with a bowling alley in the basement), a mansion (with nine bathrooms) at Manalapan, Florida, which he later sold to the du Ponts, a palatial villa on his own private hillside at Acapulco, an apartment in the Waldorf Towers, Manhattan, and in his later years the magnificent property 'Piencourt' near Deauville. And for ease and convenience of transport he bought a private Viking plane equipped with luxury bedrooms, a bathroom and a bar, and later added an Avro Commander for short hauls around Europe, a £250,000 twin-jet Lear and a helicopter. A third yacht, the 330-ton *Calypso*, would help take care of the more leisurely voyages from place to place.

His marriage to Gloria was happy and amusing, and over the next 14 years all seemed to be for the best in the best of all possible worlds. His elder sister, Meraud, had married the Chilean artist, Alvaro Guevara, in 1929 and had settled with him in the South of France. Two years later his younger sister, Tanis Eva, married one of Loel's fellow-pilots in the 601 Auxiliary Squadron, the Hon. Drogo Montagu, youngest son of the Earl of Sandwich. (This first marriage was a failure and ended in divorce after three years.[12] Subsequently Tanis married, in succession, Howard Dietz, the head of publicity for Metro-Goldwyn-Mayer, and Lieut.-Commander Ed Phillips. And between her first two marriages she caused a sensation on both sides of the Atlantic by breaking off her engagement to the Earl of Carnarvon on the eve of their planned wedding in New York. Carnarvon later married the Viennese-born dancer, Tilly Losch.)

Patrick Benjamin, Loel's only child by his first wife, Joan, had grown into a dashing heir to the family fortune and was already flexing his vocational muscles with a finance company in New York when he delighted his father by falling in love with his own step-sister, the 19-year-old green-eyed daughter of Gloria's first marriage—the Countess Dolores von Fürstenberg. They were married in New York in 1955 and produced three grandchildren for Loel over the next five years.

There could hardly have been a cloud on Loel's gold-plated horizon in October 1965. His wife had been nominated by the New York Couture Group's experts as the second best-dressed woman in the world, after Jacqueline Kennedy. They drifted at their own pace and peerless style from one luxurious residence to another, accompanied always by a 'skeleton' staff made up of two chefs and a kitchen maid, Gloria's personal maid and Loel's valet, plus three chambermaids. In Lausanne they entertained such friends as Truman Capote, Noël Coward, David Niven and Yul Brynner; in Paris, the Duke and Duchess of Windsor; at Lake Worth, Florida, the Kennedys. The devoted Gloria divided her time between playing hostess and writing fashion articles for *Harper's Bazaar* and she resisted the temptation to take on any loftier literary challenges that might put a strain on the marriage. (A play she had written in 1962 was accepted by a London producer but she pulled out when she realized it would mean leaving Loel alone for the weeks of the pre-London tour, saying, as she told the *Evening Standard* on 2 November 1967, 'I would rather have the husband than the play.')

Such an idyllic life almost invited the intervention of the jealous gods and the tragedy, when it struck, was spiked with a special poignancy for Loel. Patrick Benjamin, who shared his father's pleasure in driving fast motor-cars at the kind of speeds they were designed for, had recently escaped unscathed from a near-fatal collision on the Swiss highways. The police had suspended his driving licence but it was restored to him through Loel's good offices. A few days later, on 5 October 1965, he crashed his Italian sports car on one of the roads near Lausanne and was killed.

It was the first of a series of car crashes that would claim the lives of Guinness heirs over the next ten years, and it was a tragedy from which Loel would never fully recover. He was left with his two children by Lady Isabel: the 26-year-old William Loel and the 24-year-old Serena Belinda ('Lindy' to the family). William would perpetuate the male line from Benjamin Seymour with two sons, born 1972 and 1973. Lindy had married her cousin 'Sheridan', the

5th Marquess of Dufferin and Ava, a year earlier at Westminster Abbey, with Princess Margaret, the Earl of Snowdon and Princess Alexandra among the guests.

At the memorial service for Patrick, held in the Guards Chapel of Wellington Barracks a month after his death, one friend of Loel's, noting the grief already etched into the 60-year-old's features, saw it as marking the end of what until then had seemed 'a perpetual quest for amusement'. This was perhaps an unduly pessimistic judgement, but if there was anything left of the quest it surely ended on November 1980 with Gloria's death from a heart attack at her home in Lausanne.

8

Samuel, and the Great Anglo-Texan Hoax

1

As already noted, the progress of Guinness Mahon & Co. in London was virtually halted by the outbreak of World War I and the retirement of Richard Seymour's sons from the family business. But Richard's brother, Henry, had left five sons, two of whom—Howard Rundell and (Richard) Noel—formed a new partnership in 1916 to take over such of the London business as could be handled from Dublin, and the future of Guinness Mahon & Co., merchant and investment bankers, would lie in their hands and those of their sons.

In the Appendix we briefly sketch the career of Howard Rundell's eldest brother, Henry Seymour, who so diligently and objectively researched the origins of the Guinness family. It remains to add that he outlived all his brothers, dying in 1945 at the age of 86 and leaving four daughters by his only wife, Mary.

In 1923, with the world of finance returning to normal, the 60-year-old Howard Rundell moved to London and set up business at 20 Bishopsgate, leaving Noel in charge of the predominantly land agency work of the Dublin office. With Howard went his three sons (Henry) Samuel, Edward Douglas and Arthur Rundell, all now active partners in the firm.

Neither of his youngest sons, Frederick Roberts and Brian Cecil, took up permanent careers with Guinness Mahon. Frederick Roberts ('Bobs' to the family) was summoned in the City of London for allegedly applying to his own use a cheque for £450 given to him by a Mr W. C. Powers for the purchase of a motor car. The prosecutor charged that the cheque had been cashed but the complainant had received neither the vehicle nor the return of his money. The hearing was adjourned for a fortnight while the papers went to the Director of Public Prosecutions and there was a happy ending a fortnight later, when it was announced that the DPP did not propose to prosecute, leaving the magistrate to conclude that the defendant was innocent of any fraud in the matter.[1]

In the official Guinness pedigree, 'Bobs' is listed as having only two children, both boys, by his marriage in 1925 to Nora Shelton. In fact there was a daughter, Patricia, born out of wedlock and much to the embarrassment of the grandparents, Howard Rundell and his wife May. A family conference was held and the situation resolved, with results more appropriate to a Mills & Boon novelette than to real life.

The grandparents' home was Elm House, in West Clandon. Here, their children had been in the care of a nanny, Mrs Scarborough, whose husband Dick was employed as a porter at the Guinness Mahon offices in London. The Scarboroughs still lived in the village and they agreed to take the infant Patricia and to bring her up as their own daughter. The truth of her real parentage was kept from the girl and from the two legitimate sons of 'Bobs' and Nora until, to the dismay of all concerned, the eldest son, Howard Michael Guinness, and Patricia Scarborough—now in their teens—fell in love with each other. Their romance dissolved promptly and poignantly in the harsh light of revealed truth. 'Bobs' took his family to South Africa where he became first a director and then chairman of Dreyfus & Co., an export–import firm, and where he died in 1979, with his eldest son safely married to a Cape Town girl and Patricia living in Canada.

Both as a banker and human being—so often seen as mutually exclusive terms—Samuel was the most impressive of the three banking brothers. He lived into his 86th year, by which time (1975) the Guinness family, while still controlling the largest block of shares in the financial empire started by his great-grandfather, had only three of Robert Rundell's descendants on the 16-strong board of directors of the parent company.

Samuel himself was deprived of a male heir by a tragedy, the circumstances of which remain to this day a mystery to his descendants. In 1931, Samuel's only son, George Francis, aged 15, killed himself with a gun in an outhouse of his father's London home at Cheyne Walk, Chelsea. The coroner's verdict was 'misadventure': the boy had died while cleaning the weapon. Samuel's wife Alfhild will not talk about the tragedy, even to her grandson James Greene, whose mother, Helga, was away from home at the time of the tragedy and, according to James, knows as little as he does about the circumstances leading up to it.

Samuel had met Alfhild Holter, a 17-year-old Norwegian girl, during his freshman year at Balliol College, Oxford. They were married in 1913, and his love affair with Alfhild and her country continued to his death.[2] (Alfhild is still alive at the time of writing—a frail but spirited old lady, still living in the Cheyne Walk home, attended by a devoted nurse and a housekeeper.)

Shortest in stature of all his brothers, Samuel had a heart that more than compensated for his lack of inches and possessed an excellent head for finance. He was also the most robust of the brothers, both as an oarsman at Winchester and Balliol and, later in life, as a tireless hill walker in his beloved Norway, often accompanied by his close friend, King Haakon VII. He was elected to the board of the Provincial Bank of Ireland and, five years later, when his father reopened the London office of Guinness Mahon, he became a partner. He joined the board of the National Discount Co. at 38 and pioneered British investment in European electric power companies as a director of Electro Trust Ltd. And he added these duties to his tireless travel, worldwide, building the Guinness Mahon empire up to his retirement in 1968. In 1953 he joined the board of an investment and shipping finance company, Viking Tanker, that had had a close banking relationship with Guinness Mahon since 1936. Ten years later it was announced that Guinness Mahon and Viking were to merge under the name of Guinness Mahon Holdings.

Outside banking and shipping, his scholarship was limited, and his first son-in-law, Sir Hugh Carleton Greene, a former governor of the BBC, recalls with amusement how, during a visit to Berlin, Samuel bought up half a shopful of bound volumes, 'quite literally by the yard', without even checking their contents. With all his earthiness and his shrewdness in finance there was an endearingly naïve side to his personality. Hugh Greene had met Samuel's eldest daughter Helga in Munich, where he was working as a foreign correspondent and she was being 'finished'. They married in 1934 and as a wedding gift Samuel presented the young and unpretentious couple with a limousine *and* flesh-and-blood chauffeur. The chauffeur, needless to say, was released by his embarrassed employers as soon as Samuel's back was turned.

For his wartime service to Norway, Samuel was decorated in 1947, simultaneously with his wife, with the Chevalier Order of St Olaf. Next to his ties with that nation came his affection for the people and institutions of the United States, and it was this that led him unwittingly into the role of 'straight man' in a hoax perpetrated in 1953 by Hugh Greene's brother, the eminent novelist Graham Greene, in collusion with his film producer friend, John Sutro.

The story of this hoax has, until now, been kept under wraps by its perpetrators out of a commendable concern for those in high places—including a past editor of *The Times*—upon whose august faces dollops of shattered egg must seriously detract from the respect due to the institutions they represent. In fact, there came a point in this wickedly conceived prank when Graham Greene was tempted to cry 'Enough!' and confess all, but by then, as his co-conspirator might have observed, 'this thing is now bigger than both of us'. And as Greene himself concedes, 'I have learned that nothing can be more difficult to stop than a practical joke which succeeds too well.'

Greene's antipathy towards certain aspects of North American culture is well known to his friends, as is his opinion that these aspects find especially unappealing expression in the make-up of the typical Texan. From this it follows, with all the logic proper to mischievous intent, that he should be inspired by a liberal—and, as it turned out, singularly appropriate—intake of 'Black Velvet' (a mixture of champagne and Guinness) on the Edinburgh-to-London express to propose to his companion, John Sutro, the foundation of an Anglo-Texan Society, dedicated to the advancement of amity between the ten-gallon sombrero and the bowler hat. There and then, Sutro pledged his support and on 22 August 1953 the following letter appeared in the columns of *The Times*:

Sir,

May we beg the courtesy of your columns to announce the formation of the Anglo-Texan Society? The society has the general object of establishing cultural and social links between this country and the State of Texas which occupies a special historical position not only in relation to the United States but also in relation to Great Britain. It is hoped, when funds permit, to establish special premises in London for welcoming visitors from Texas and—if our ambitions are realized—of providing them with a hospitality equal to that which Texas has traditionally given to English visitors. Those interested are asked to communicate with the undersigned at 1 Montague Square, London W1.

We are, Sir, yours, etc.

GRAHAM GREENE, President
JOHN SUTRO, Vice-President

The noble letter, duly copied in the newspapers of Dallas, Houston and Fort Worth, triggered an immediate and enthusiastic response. And, on the bowler-hatted side of the Atlantic, influential allies in the cause of Anglo-Texan solidarity pressed forward. They included the well-known banker, Samuel Guinness, and his friend Sir Alfred Bossom, MP.

Graham Greene was by now already on his way to report the Mau Mau rising in Kenya for a Sunday paper and, if his co-founder, Sutro, had braced himself for a confession of perfidy during his first meeting with the banker, he was promptly unbraced by the genuine warmth of Samuel's tribute to the Greene–Sutro initiative and his eagerness to get in on the act. He accepted with grace his nomination as Vice-President of the Society.

Upon Greene's return a second letter appeared in *The Times*:

Sir,

You were kind enough to print a letter in which the formation of the Anglo-Texan Society was mentioned. We had a strong response to this letter and the Anglo-Texan Society has now been inaugurated. The officers include Mr Samuel Guinness and Sir Alfred Bossom, MP. Those who are desirous of joining and have not already written to the honorary secretary at 1 Montague Square, W1 should do so now.

Yours faithfully,

GRAHAM GREENE, President
JOHN SUTRO, Chairman
Anglo-Texan Society
1, Montague Square

Meanwhile a churlish note of suspicion had been struck by one newspaper, the *New York Times*.

We could not believe our eyes. We remembered only too vividly Mr Greene's controlled but consuming anger towards us because of what he considered was a reactionary reign of terror over here...We can feel scepticism, like a calcium deposit, residing right in our bones. Mr Greene may be on the side of God, but he has created some fascinating diabolisms and plenty of hells in his time, and we wonder whether Mr Greene doesn't have some insidious plot underfoot. Maybe like getting Texas, our richest, vastest, proudest state to secede from the Union.

Such cynicism was treated by the Society with the contempt it merited. The seeds of Anglo-Texan comity, sown by Greene and Sutro, had sprouted into a flourishing plant, and over the next ten years the Society's admirable activities would be regularly reported in *The Times*, in the column devoted to 'Social News'. Graham Greene's frequent journeys abroad allowed him to duck such early delights as the lecture (with film) by a lady member on her recent visit to Texas and the dinner at the Traveller's Club to celebrate Texas Independence Day, with Dr Myron Koenig, Cultural Attaché of the US Embassy, as one of the speakers. And John Sutro held the fort for him as when fifteen hundred men from the American Air Force, with their civilian fellow-Texans in Britain, joined members of the Society and their guests in a giant barbecue at Denham Film Studios. Hillbilly bands played 'Beautiful Texas' and 'San Antonio Rose' while the celebrants tucked into 2,500 pounds of prime beef donated by the Houston Fat Stock Show. The United States Ambassador, Mr Winthrop Aldrich, appointed Texan Ambassador for the day by the Governor of that State, delivered the flag of Texas to an unblushing Sutro.

Subsequently, at an Anglo-Texan dinner given by Samuel Guinness at his Chelsea home in honour of Mr Nieman Marcus, the Dallas store-owner, Graham Greene suffered something of a crisis of conscience. Mr Marcus had seemed somewhat ill-at-ease with his 'honorary' Texan dinner companions and, after taking a turn with him in the garden, Greene unburdened his guilt, after swearing Mr Marcus to secrecy. 'At that moment,' says Greene, 'I think he began to enjoy his evening.'

On 1 April 1955 the novelist submitted his resignation as president to Samuel Guinness on the ground of his too-frequent absences abroad and he received in reply a letter couched in suitably valedictory terms:

Mr Guinness read your letter of resignation as president at the last meeting of the Council on 4th April. It was very regretfully received by us all as it arrived at the same time as Mr Sutro's resignation as Chairman. You and he were the Founders of the Society and did so much at its inception to get people together and to get things going. I am sure that I express the feelings not only of the Council but also of the members of the Society when I say how grateful we shall always be to the two of you for what you did.

Graham Greene was formally replaced as president by Sir Alfred Bossom and from then on, until 1959, an annual dinner was thrown by the Society in the House of Commons. The venue was changed to the House of Lords upon Sir Alfred's elevation to the British peerage in a year that also saw his appointment as an admiral of the Texas Navy, with a formal presentation of credentials by the Governor of Texas's representative, Dr Norris, specially dispatched from the Lone Star State for the purpose.

An apogee in the Society's affairs was reached in February 1962 when, at the annual general meeting, Lord Bossom was able to announce with pride the appointment, as honorary vice-presidents, of the Governor of Texas, Mr Price Daniel, and the Vice-President of the United States of America, Lyndon B. Johnson.

The doings of the Anglo-Texan Society were religiously reported in *The Times* until the death in 1965 of its president, Lord Bossom.[3] By then, Samuel Guinness was in his 77th year and perhaps not up to any more social jollities with back-slapping cattle ranchers and oil men. But the Society was still listed in the London telephone directory until 1979 against the address of 5 Manor Close, Warlingham, Surrey. When, that same year, the present writer called to inquire about membership, I was told by its secretary, Captain W. R. Mitchell, that the Society had just folded. He agreed that this was a great pity but, 'Well, all good things come to an end, sooner or later.'

If this exposure, 27 years after the event, raises the spectre of a 'Graham Greene Society', founded by vengeful Texans, one can be sure the celebrated man of letters will accept his dues with fortitude.

2

The untimely death of their son George Francis left Samuel and Alfhild with three daughters, two of whom—Helga and Marit—have brought literary and artistic accomplishment to a line of Guinnesses otherwise almost totally wedded to finance. Samuel and Alfhild—a superb amateur soprano, welcomed in all the Guinness homes for both her talent and her charm—seem to have taken pains to encourage their daughters to 'do their own thing'. At the age of 15, Marit was sent to study painting in Munich, Florence and Paris, completing her training in London where she met and married Carl Aschan, the only son of a Swedish judge and a baroness mother.

The couple were set up by Samuel with a house in Chelsea Park Gardens, and a nearby studio where Marit began to develop her special and pioneering technique as an enamellist working with materials—often including gold—fired at temperatures up to 1,000 degrees Centigrade to produce plaques of extraordinary translucence and beauty. With 25 individual exhibitions, worldwide, already behind her and her enamels on show at the Victoria & Albert Museum and in ten public collections throughout the United States, she more than merits the tribute paid her by the leading art magazine *Apollo* in January 1974: 'Her position as the leading contemporary enamellist has been recognized for some time....She has revitalized the age-old technique of enamelling to produce highly original work which is entirely contemporary in spirit.'

Today, at 62, her hair still an unfaded 'Guinness red', Marit works daily in the same Chelsea studio, taking as long as three months on one work and developing 'new and exacting techniques... with qualities of voluptuous appeal seldom found in contemporary art'.[4] She remembers her father Samuel as 'a man of vision, who believed in people'. And she speaks of his many and unpublicized benefactions which included paying for the further education at Balliol College of several promising but financially unendowed students, in memory of his son's death.

Marit's daughter Juliet Marit married a gentleman farmer in 1980 and is the managing director of Grand Tours, a highly successful operation offering guided tours of the British cultural inheritance. Juliet, too, had wanted to be a painter at the age of 16, but by then her grandmother Alfhild was beginning to take up the brushes and her father took the view that the family's quota of artists had already been reached. So Juliet went to work as a picture restorer under the tuition of the National Gallery's Helmut Ruhemann and by the age of 21 was expert enough to be included in the team Ruhemann took with him to work on the damaged art treasures of Florence. In her spare time she developed her natural talent as a painter, and in 1972 Alfhild, Marit and Juliet pulled off a remarkable 'treble' by having a total of nine of their paintings, all landscapes, accepted for the annual exhibition at the Paris Salon, the equivalent of London's Royal Academy.

Helga's motivation towards a career in the arts was probably a need to escape the traditional role of a Guinness heiress and what Hugh Carleton Greene recalls as the 'rather stifling appurtenances of wealth' in her parents' big Edwardian house on the Earl of Onslow's estate. Divorced from Hugh in 1948, she soon afterwards set herself up as a literary agent in London, and in 1955 she met a 66-year-old American writer with whose last few years of life she would become both emotionally and professionally embroiled. They were introduced by Jessica Tyndale, the American representative of Guinness Mahon, who had shared a table with the famous Raymond Chandler[5] during a *Mauretania* crossing from New York to Southampton.

Chandler was still mourning the death, after 20 years of marriage, of his wife Cissy whom he had married when he was 36 and she 53. Helga helped to find him a rented flat at 116 Eaton Square, just around the corner from her own London home, and was delighted to take him on as a client. For tax reasons he was obliged to return to his home in La Jolla, Southern California, later that year, but he corresponded regularly with Helga and began the up-and-down courtship that would continue to his death.[6]

He was now embarked on his last Philip Marlowe novel, *Playback*, but his heavy drinking took him intermittently into nursing homes and it is doubtful that he would have finished the book had Helga not flown out to help him in November 1957, though she herself was ill at the time. 'Her arrival,' Chandler's biographer Frank MacShane records, 'worked like a tonic,'[7] and the book that had been promised the publishers by 1 April 1958 was delivered three months ahead of schedule. As Chandler himself put it: 'With Helga around I feel as though I could write anything—sonnets, love poems, idiocies, plays, novels, even cookbooks. [They in fact planned to collaborate in writing a 'Cook Book for Idiots'.] What on earth happened between this rather cool, aloof woman and me?'

Frank MacShane essays an answer:

Chandler evidently wanted to place Helga Greene on a pedestal. He pictured her as a badly hurt and lonely woman who was too shy to speak of the sufferings that afflicted her after her divorce from Hugh Greene. But the image wouldn't stick...She was a very energetic and efficient literary agent, the mother of two sons whose upbringing engrossed her and, as the daughter of a rich banker, hardly in need of financial support...Her great value to Chandler was that she was far more honest and considerate than a number of women he became involved with.[8]

One of these women was an Australian divorcée with two young children whom Chandler had taken on as a secretary, more out of his Galahad instincts than for her professional efficiency. Later, after she had returned to Australia, from where she importuned him for money, he made her a present of the English rights to *Playback*, which Helga bought back from her for £2,000 so that she could have the cash, since Chandler had given her 'practically all the loose money he had'.[9]

By the time he returned to London in February 1958 he was drinking a bottle of whisky a day. There were a few final revisions Helga thought he should make to *Playback* and she kept him going by making him eat regularly and, whenever possible, surreptitiously watering his drinks. They took a trip together to Capri, stopping at Naples, where the famous American crime writer had set up an interview with America's famous crook, 'Lucky' Luciano. But Helga continued to refuse his offers of marriage, right up to February 1959 when she flew to La Jolla to put the now hopelessly alcoholic writer into hospital. Here, she finally agreed to marry him, when they returned to England, hoping it might add years to his life if she could look after him in that more tranquil atmosphere.

They stopped *en route* in New York where Samuel Guinness happened to be on business and to whom Chandler wanted to make a formal request for his daughter's hand. This bizarre first meeting between the suitor and the father–both in their 71st year–failed to win Samuel's approval of the marriage.

Although this in no way weakened Helga's commitment, Chandler's feelings were hurt. On top of this, the frail author had caught a cold in wintry New York and he decided to put off London in favour of Californian warmth. Back in La Jolla he wrote, somewhat naïvely, to Helga: 'It seems very strange to me that your father should have turned so completely against me, when you said I behaved beautifully the night he had us to dinner. I know he thought I was a bit old–but he is a bit old himself. Someone must have told him things to my discredit...'

Out of Helga's care, he went back to hard drinking, fell ill with pneumonia and died in hospital on 26 March 1959. Upon Helga's agreement to marry him he had changed his will, making her the beneficiary, in place of the Australian divorcée, as well as his literary executrix. The Australian went to court, charging Helga with exerting undue influence, but the judge rejected her case 'with prejudice', thus ruling out any further actions in the future.

Helga still controls the Chandler copyrights, together with the affairs of a few of her favourite clients, though she is now semi-retired in Grosseto, Italy, with her second husband, Stuart Connolly, a former tea planter and later an executive with the P & O shipping line. The two sons of her marriage to Hugh exemplify their literary inheritance. Graham Carleton Greene is vice-chairman of the prestigious Jonathan Cape publishing company as well as being on the board of the Guinness Peat Group, with a block of shares inherited from his grandfather, Samuel. James Greene is himself a poet[10] and the translator of the Russian poets Osip Mandelstam and Afanasy Fet, and his poetic works and psychoanalytic writings are regularly featured in a wide range of British periodicals. Helga's youngest sister, Ingrid Louise, married an accountant, Winston Williams, who committed suicide in 1971, leaving a daughter and a son.

The death of Samuel's only son meant that the next generation of banking Guinnesses would be the sons of Samuel's two brothers

Edward Douglas and Arthur Rundell and those of his first cousin, Henry Eustace, the only son of Noel Guinness.

Noel had stayed on in charge of the Dublin end of Guinness Mahon & Co. after 1923. He had earlier kept up the family tradition of combining banking with the law by becoming a solicitor on graduation from Oxford at the age of 22. Two years later he married Mary Stokes, an active women's emancipationist in Irish politics, and set up home on the Hill of Howth, with its magnificent view of Dublin Bay. His first love was sailing, a pastime he shared somewhat reluctantly with his overseeing of the Dublin office, but he served Guinness Mahon as faithfully as he courted the breezes of Dublin Bay.

In 1942, in the middle of World War II, Guinness Mahon & Co. announced the formation of a separate legal entity, Guinness & Mahon, to carry on the firm's banking business in Ireland, with an authorized capital of £1,000,000, all of which would be held by Guinness Mahon. On 7 February 1942 the writer of City Notes for *The Times* explained that 'As this country is a belligerent and Ireland is a neutral, it may well be that the partners have found the respective rules and regulations corresponding to this difference of status a fruitful breeding ground of all sorts of complications.' At the age of 72, Noel became the first chairman of the new private company and his 45-year-old son, Henry Eustace, became managing director. He would take over the chairmanship on his father's retirement but although he is described by one of the bank's historians as a 'born banker',[11] this is not precisely how his family remembers him and it seems he, like his father, served the bank as much out of family loyalty as from a personal dedication to the business. His chief interest was in alpine plants and rock gardens, in which field he became a recognized expert. According to his daughter-in-law, Mary, it was the opinion of Henry Eustace's sister Margaret—two years his senior and 'a very strong character'—that she would have made a better banker than Henry. He had been somewhat dominated from childhood by Margaret, and his resultant and chronic shyness had earned him the family nickname of 'Henry the Hare'. This, at least, is one commonly held explanation of the sobriquet. His widow Beatrice, a tall, strong-boned woman, still very much alive at the time of writing and living with her small staff in the house built by Noel on the Howth peninsula, has another explanation. She says the nickname arose from Henry's requests as a child to have the same children's story, featuring a hare, read to him, over and over again.

Between 1942 and 1973 the Guinness banking empire evolved through a complicated series of conversions, mergers and takeovers into the present structure whereby a holding company, the Guinness Peat Group, controls all the group's activities through its subsidiaries, Guinness Mahon Holdings Ltd, Guinness Mahon & Co. Ltd and Guinness & Mahon Ltd. When 'Henry the Hare' died in 1972 he left two sons, (Anthony) Peter and John Henry, on the boards of the Guinness Mahon companies.

Peter inherited his grandfather Noel's love of the sea and at the age of 35, with his second wife, Susan, and two friends, he sailed the 12-ton *Rob Roy MacGregor* from Falmouth to Vigo and back, a distance of 1,232 miles, in 28½ days, for 18 hours of which they were hove-to in a force 9 gale. For this feat he was awarded the Royal Cruising Club Founder's Cup. And four years later he made another name for himself by becoming the only Guinness to straddle the lines of the banking and brewing empires when he joined the board of Arthur Guinness Son & Co. as financial director.

9

The Banker's Girls

John Henry succeeded his father as chairman of Guinness & Mahon and a director of Guinness Mahon Holdings, both of which posts he holds today.

In the event, only one of Samuel's brothers–Arthur Rundell–provided a son and heir to carry on the banking line into the seventh generation from Richard of Celbridge. This was James Edward Rundell Guinness, about whom more anon. The second eldest brother and partner, Edward Douglas ('Ned' to the family), made no outstanding impression on the world of merchant banking but made a fortune for himself by buying up every bicycle repair shop he could lay his hands on in the British West Indies.

One of his sons, John Ralph, joined the Foreign Office after graduating from Trinity Hall, Cambridge. At the Foreign Office, he soon gained a reputation as one of its most talented functionaries. He was also, alas, destined to father another Guinness boy whose life would be taken in a road accident.

His two sons, Peter and Rupert, were respectively 4 and 7 years old when John drove them back to his farm in Norfolk after picking up their nanny at King's Lynn Station for the start of a summer holiday in 1978. His wife Valerie and their daughter were waiting for them at the farm when John's car had a head-on collision with another one being driven on the wrong side of the road by a local septuagenarian married couple. The couple were killed in the crash and little Peter, rushed with his brother to the intensive care unit at King's Lynn Hospital, died later of multiple injuries. It was one of four tragedies to strike the Guinnesses in as many months that year and the London newspapers splashed the news under their boldest headlines.

Arthur Rundell, the third of Howard Rundell's sons, married his wife Patience when he was 28, on becoming a partner in Guinness Mahon. As the family bank developed its overseas connections, Arthur travelled widely from capital to capital, building up contacts and alliances with a network of foreign concerns. In common with most of his fellow-bankers of the West, Arthur Rundell was impressed by the 'stability' and discipline created by Adolf Hitler during the pre-war years of the Nazi regime, and in 1937 he attended a congress of the International Chamber of Commerce in Berlin, as a member of the British team. Here he declared, in a speech to the plenary session, reported in *The Times* of 2 July, that 'subject to a far-reaching scheme for European political conciliation, a large gold credit or loan at a reasonable rate of interest should be granted by the United States and Great Britain to Germany to allow her to get rid of exchange control, get back to freedom of currency and abolish the restrictions which hindered German foreign trade'.

'Political conciliation' was, of course, far from the mind of the author of *Mein Kampf*, but the good will of European capitalism was at the time most important to his long-term plans, as Dr Goebbels no doubt stressed when he and his wife entertained the British delegates during the congress. The Führer could not get along for this occasion but he sent presents to Arthur Rundell and his colleagues as a mark of his appreciation.

From 1943, Arthur Rundell was one of the pillars of the International Chamber of Commerce, serving the British National Committee of the ICC as Chairman, Vice-President and President until his death in Bombay in 1951, aged 55. By then he had become the first—and to date the only—Guinness of the banking line to win a knighthood, being dubbed 'Sir Arthur' in 1949 for his services to overseas trade.

Patience had given him two sons. The younger, Ivan Douglas, showed no propensity for finance, married an Irish girl, Mairead FitzGerald, at the age of 25 and bought a small market garden near Yeovil, Somerset, together with a bungalow in which he lived. It was here, on the evening of 14 August 1956 that Ivan Douglas collapsed and died while having a tooth extracted under an anaesthetic. A verdict of misadventure was recorded at the inquest, and a doctor gave evidence that the 29-year-old Ivan was a chronic alcoholic. The county pathologist found signs of acute heart failure and a liver that was 'almost destroyed'. The expectation of life, in his opinion, was 'not more than about three months', and the inhalation of an anaesthetic to one in Ivan's condition 'was bound to have been fatal'.[1]

The elder of Sir Arthur's sons, James Edward Alexander Rundell, was born in 1924 and educated at Eton and Oxford. He is only the second of all the Guinnesses to have been given the name James. His father, Sir Arthur, wishing to break away from the confusing recurrence of Christian names throughout the Guinness pedigree, had intended to give all three of his children (including his daughter Pamela) names that had not hitherto been used by the clan. Presumably he decided that the James born in 1803 to the Second Arthur's brother Edward did not count, since that James had died unmarried at 22. In turn, James Edward and his wife Pauline baptized their own five children with exotic Guinness 'firsts'. Their first set of twins were named Sabrina and Miranda, the second set Hugo and Julia, and the daughter in between, Anita. All four girls were born between 1955 and 1959 and between them they have done for the banking line of Guinnesses what the celebrated 'Guinness Girls' did for the brewery line in the 1920s and 1930s. But with a difference. The Guinness girls of two generations back, as we shall see in a later chapter, flowered in a pre-war society in which débutantes were presented at Court instead of curtseying to a cake in a Mayfair ballroom, a society that regarded engagement to the son of a duke as the indisputable proof of a girl's successful London 'season'. The war and the subsequent downgrading of the 'old school tie' as a necessary passport to social acceptability put an end to all that. The new idols were pop singers, writers and actors of proletarian stock and TV 'celebrities', rather than the blue-blooded scions of the aristocracy. There were, of course, pockets of parental resistance to this heresy, mostly by the war-rich and the *parvenus* of the middle class; who were now 'coughing up' for finishing schools and daydreaming of a title in the family. But the daughters of James Edward were never obliged to keep a copy of Burke's Peerage at their bedsides, or even to 'do' the London seasons, when more exciting or worthwhile challenges beckoned to them.

On the face of it, James has conformed closely enough to the prototypic English gentleman of means. His hobbies are listed in *Who's Who* as 'hunting, fishing and shooting'. He hunts in Hampshire and his comfortable estate at Mattingley, near Hockfield, has a trout stream running through the grounds. With friends, he also owns a nearby shoot of about 2,000 acres. His town house in Phillimore Gardens, Kensington (currently valued at over £500,000), is equipped with a swimming pool and a tennis court, in what must be one of London's largest private gardens. But the family's holiday residence is not at Gstaad or in Sardinia but in the little village of

Gassin, a few miles from St Tropez, and the big villa is alive during the summer with his daughters' current idols, few of whom could sit a hunter unpreccariously or play a salmon. Undoubtedly, most of the credit for this informal and classless ambience must go to James's effervescent wife, Pauline. Formerly one of the most beautiful of London's high-fashion models, her adventurous nature had led her, while still single, to hitch-hike 19,500 miles from South Africa to Egypt, a feat beside which even her daughters' spirited romps flicker palely. And she has always preferred, as they do, the company of movie stars and jet-set singers to that of her husband's city colleagues and their public-schooled offspring.

James Edward, for his part, has never discouraged his children from going out into the world and doing their independent 'thing'. And this has had to include paying their own way, with no access before marriage to the great family fortune he holds in trust for them.

The first of the girls to untie this purse string was Julia, the blondest and youngest of them who, in March 1980, at the age of 20, was married to 27-year-old Michael Samuel. It was a union that will bring a rare infusion of Jewish blood into the family by linking the banking Guinnesses with the great merchant bank of Hill Samuel, whose deputy chairman is Michael's father, Peter Samuel, an old friend of James Edward's. And perhaps it illustrates the wisdom of James's 'long leash' policy with his unmarried children, for although Julia is probably the most conventional of the sisters, she shared their interest in media-created 'celebrities', took a job as secretary in a London publishing house, but ended up marrying an Old Etonian whose uncle, Viscount Bearsted, is one of Britain's richest men.

Her twin brother Hugo shows little sign, so far, of carrying on the banking tradition of the 'Rundell' Guinnesses. His father had hoped that, after Eton, Hugo would train as an accountant, but instead he took a job with an advertising agency and is today one of the youngest copywriters in the business.

Miranda, like her twin sister Sabrina, took an early training in the Montessori system of teaching and at 19 worked in the Gorbals slum of Glasgow for a child rehabilitation scheme. In her early twenties she shared for a while in Sabrina's overseas adventures before settling down in London as an editorial assistant on the fashion magazine, *Harper's and Queen*.

Described by friends of the family as 'potentially the brightest' of the four pretty sisters, Anita, the only non-twin, is another example of the 'long leash' paying off. At 18 she accompanied an aspiring pop singer, Anthony Russell,[2] to New York, in pursuit of fame. And with all the bravado of youth they declared their intention, should fame elude them, of forming a cook–butler team in the service of wealthy Americans. In the event, and despite the 23-year-old Russell's aristocratic credentials, the team made no hit in either sphere and shortly afterwards Anita transferred her affections to (and later married) Amschel Rothschild, the amateur racing driver son of Lord Rothschild and brother of Jacob, the international banker.

With Sabrina, the 'long leash' policy would appear to have come unstuck, though only in the unique circumstance of events that would build to the proportions of a national guessing-game. It started in the summer of 1974 when the lissom, honey-blonde Sabrina, with the blue 'bedroom' eyes, came into contact with the nine-year-old Tatum O'Neal at the London nursery school where the child star of *Paper Moon* was a pupil and Sabrina a student-teacher. The rapport between the vivacious 19-year-old Guinness girl and the precocious American nymphet was immediate; and, to the delight of both, Sabrina was invited by the divorced father to spend the rest of the summer in his Californian home as companion to his child, on completion of his movie.

It was as exotic an interlude as any young European lady could wish for, with a continuous flow of Hollywood personalities through the O'Neal beach house at Malibu and occasional evenings out at a film première or a star-studded 'A' list party. So much so that when the holidays were over and Tatum had to go back to school, Sabrina stayed on through the spring of 1975. There was never any question of a romantic liaison between Sabrina and the 34-year-old Ryan O'Neal. A genuine affection had developed between the two girls and, as Sabrina observed, they still had each other's company every weekend and, as the *Daily Mail* of 20 November 1974 reported, 'There is plenty to do while she is away, keeping the house together.' A first-class air passage was provided by O'Neal for Sabrina to spend Christmas 1974 with her family, and on her return to Malibu her little super-star friend made her a present of an £8,000 Porsche. But life with Tatum must have had its trying moments, and when British Lion offered Sabrina a job as production assistant in their Hollywood office, she accepted it. The film company was then preparing to make *The Man Who Fell to Earth*, starring David Bowie, with whom Sabrina had already made friends and whose wish to have her as his 'girl Friday' during the production had been as good as a nod to the British Lion front office.

Again, there was no evidence of an emotional involvement between the Guinness girl and the married–and confessed bisexual–'superstar' Bowie, and this is confirmed by someone who had every opportunity to share her confidences at the time. Ian La Frenais, the pocket-size 'Geordie' and co-creator with Dick Clement of the highly successful TV series 'Porridge' and 'The Likely Lads', had come to work in Hollywood where he now operates a production company, Witzend, from an eye-trapping blue-and-white house on Highland Avenue, between Sunset and Hollywood Boulevards. He had been a welcome guest at the Guinnesses' house in Phillimore Gardens, Kensington, and when Sabrina found herself homeless he leased her a room in the house he had first taken, hanging over a jungly avenue off Benedict Canyon.

'Sabrina always paid her share of the rent,' says La Frenais, 'and was an ideal person to share with. She stayed clear of the Hollywood scalp-hunters but was really enthusiastic about the film business, even to the extent of applying for membership of the Screen Actors' Guild. But like her sisters Miranda and Julia, who also came over looking for work at the time, she ran into the usual permit problems.'

With the Bowie movie finished and nothing particularly exciting on the horizon. Sabrina returned to her parents' home in England. She was with them in November 1978 when her mother nearly died. The daughters had gathered at Mattingley to celebrate their parents' silver wedding; later that night Pauline took some sleeping tablets, collapsed, and was rushed to an intensive care unit of Basingstoke Hospital, four miles away. The cause of her collapse was withheld from inquiring reporters; all they were told by the hospital secretary, Nigel Walsh, was, 'She is very critically ill. It would not be right for me to say what the cause is.' Asked if she was suffering from an overdose of drugs, he replied: 'We must say nothing.'[3]

In Britain, Sabrina provided gossip-columnists with nothing more noteworthy than her appearances in public with celebrities such as Mick Jagger, Jack Nicholson, Robert Powell and Rod Stewart. Whether or not there was substance to reports of a romance with the handsome young Tory MP, Jonathan Aitken, their friendship survived his engagement in 1979 to the Swiss beauty, Lilitza A. Zucki, and by then the *gamine*, soft-lipped features of Sabrina Guinness were decorating the pages of a thousand newspapers and magazines throughout the world.

The daughters of James Edward were no strangers to the Princes Charles and Andrew. They had many friends in common and had mingled with the royal princes at dozens of the social gatherings to which the popular press has no entrée. Only on the rarest of occasions were their names ever linked publicly with the princes—as in

1978 when it came out that the 17-year-old Andrew, escorting Julia, was refused admission at Annabel's nightclub until he put on a tie. But Sabrina had missed two London 'seasons' while she was in California and had grown, by the summer of 1979, from a star-struck teenager into a desirable and relatively sophisticated young woman. Certainly her conversation and sense of humour would have made a refreshing change from the simpering inanities of most of the 'eligible' young females in the princes' little black books.

The first hint at potential headline material came at the end of June 1979 when Charles and Sabrina were spotted together at a performance of the Fats Waller musical *Ain't Misbehavin'*. Less than a month later, after a weekend's polo at Cowdray Park, Sussex, the heir to the British throne was *paparazzi*-ed sneaking off in his Aston Martin with Sabrina seated beside him—and the balloon went up.

There could be little doubt, during the rest of that year, that the friendship between the young people had grown into a romance. There were discreet weekends together in country houses of friends, and in September Sabrina was invited to meet the Queen at Balmoral Castle—checking in for the flight to Scotland as 'Miss Mander' (her mother's maiden name) and returning to Heathrow with the Duke of Edinburgh in an Andover of the Queen's Flight. By October the headlines of the tabloid press had changed from the cautious *My Goodness, Sabrina!* and *Life's More Fun with a Guinness!*—to IS SABRINA THE NEXT QUEEN OF ENGLAND?

A marriage between the ravishing Sabrina and the future King of England—unthinkable a generation back in view of the young woman's showbiz background—would probably have won the hearts of a British public reared in the present climate of an unstuffy monarchy 'humanized' by Charles's father, Prince Philip, and his aunt, Princess Margaret. There would have been resistance, even so, from the Establishment, spearheaded by the Archbishop of Canterbury and very possibly by the Queen herself. But if Charles had been ready to declare his love, after unofficially canvassing the good-will of the Press barons, the ordinary people of Britain would have rejoiced.

He must have been aware of this, and he was also aware of the growing constitutional urgency to lead a future queen and mother down the aisle. It follows from this either that he was not in love, but simply infatuated by the physical allure and bright companionship of the Guinness girl, or else, though being in love, the royal prince, superbly trained as he is for his future role, had made the regretful decision that Sabrina was not of the calibre of a Lady Diana Spencer, in short, not of the stuff it takes to make a future queen of England. Meanwhile, and until Sabrina's novelty began to wane, he could indulge the affair in the absolute assurance that their intimacies would never be made public.

This was not just a matter of Sabrina's natural good taste and invulnerability to chequebook journalism. There is perhaps no family in the land more defensive of its privacy than the Guinnesses or more united in all its branches when that privacy is threatened. There would be no recurrence of the indiscreet interview given to the press in July 1979 by Sabrina's predecessor in the prince's affections, the blonde and curvesome divorcée Jane Ward. It can be taken as written that, so far as Charles's skills or deficiencies as a lover are concerned, the dewy lips of Sabrina Guinness are forever sealed.

Guinness Peat was the result of a merger between Guinness Mahon Holdings Ltd. and the old-established merchandising and commodity trading company, Lewis & Peat Ltd. The effect of this was to coordinate under one great international umbrella the activities of both companies which, in the case of Guinness Mahon, were primarily in the field of merchant banking, with commodity trading a secondary interest—roles which were reversed in the case of Lewis & Peat. A full list of the subsidiary trading and banking companies now wholly controlled by the group would take up several pages of this book. Other than those incorporated in Great Britain, they embrace scores of subsidiaries in Europe, the United States, Canada and the Third World and encompass activities ranging from insurance and commodity brokering to pharmaceuticals and aviation.

James Edward Rundell Guinness became deputy chairman of the group, with Lord Kissin as executive chairman, and in 1979 held 870,516 of the total of 2,772,546 ordinary shares held by the other directors and their families. With a nominal value of 25p each and a market value at the time of writing of around 115p, his holding is worth over a million pounds. He and his cousin Helga's son, Graham Carleton Greene, are the only two of the family now on the heavyweight board of the group, the chairmanship of which was relinquished by the 66-year-old Kissin in 1979 to make way for the former cabinet minister and Secretary of State for Trade, Mr Edmund Dell. But James Edward remains chairman of Guinness Mahon Holdings and a director, with his cousin John Henry, of Guinness Mahon & Co., while John heads the board of the Irish subsidiary, Guinness & Mahon, of which his brother Peter and James Edward are directors.

With a turnover for 1980 of £686,000,000 and trading profits of £23,000,000, the Guinness Peat Group has carried the banking Guinnesses a long way indeed from the modest land agency set up in Dublin in the early 1800s by their ancestors Robert Rundell and Richard Samuel.

10

Guinnesses for God

T he Rev. Paul Grattan Guinness is the historian of the remarkable line of Guinnesses who descended from the First Arthur's youngest son, John Grattan. Born in 1908 to a 73-year-old father and a 31-year-old mother, Paul is the only great-grandson of Arthur alive today and has settled with his Canadian wife Jean on the Balearic island of Ibiza where he recently completed a history of the renaissance of Israel, entitled *Hear O Israel*.

He has been to some pains in his correspondence with the present writer to propose a connection between the evangelical work for which his line of Guinnesses is famous and the devoutly Christian atmosphere in which the First Arthur reared his large family. A connection could, of course, be argued, but at the best it was a tenuous one. Lynch and Vaisey have written[1] that 'the family were...evangelical in their persuasion and their second birth in Christ was to them an event of unique importance, by the side of which nothing else could be said to matter'. Yet the First Arthur was probably no more pious in his religious faith than the majority of Anglo-Irish Protestants of his generation and class, none of whom founded a line of 'born again' missionaries comparable with that of the 'Grattan' Guinnesses.

The Second Arthur was indeed a deeply religious man, notably in his later years, but despite his interest in the evangelical preachings of John Wesley and the Calvinist George Whitefield, he remained a pillar of the established Church of Ireland until his death. Nor is there any reason to doubt that the First Arthur would have been happy if all the sons had made their careers in the family business. The pride he undoubtedly enjoyed from his first son Hosea's rectorship of a famous Dublin church would certainly have been matched by a relief that three of his sons, Arthur, Benjamin and William, had not followed Hosea's vocation. The fact that they were already active partners in the brewery when the youngest son was still in his teens would have taken the sting out of John's decision at the age of 15 to choose the Army as a career. John fought as an infantryman in the East India Company's armed forces at a time when those forces were engaged in the bloody Mahratta campaign against the princely rulers of India. As an infantry captain he led the Company's mercenary Indian troops into battle for twenty years before his retirement in 1824 after the conquest of Lower Burma, a country of ominous import to the Guinness family, as we shall see later in this history.

A more persuasive clue to the evangelical motivation of this line of Guinnesses is in the fact that Captain John Grattan had been 'born again' during his service in India, and, on his settlement in Cheltenham ('God's ante-room' for retired Indian Army officers), chose a Congregational church for his religious devotions. The handsomest of all of the First Arthur's sons, he had married Susanna Hutton, daughter of a Dublin alderman, while on home leave in 1810, and she gave him two sons, John Grattan junior and Arthur Grattan, before her death in 1826, shortly after the end of her husband's brief partnership with the brewery's Liverpool agency (see above, p. 16).

Three years later, at the age of 47, he married the widowed Jane Lucretia d'Esterre.

The name d'Esterre had already provided a colourful footnote to the history of Ireland's struggle for emancipation. Early in 1815 Daniel O'Connell, the Liberator, had made an attack upon the Corporation of Dublin, employing a term which one of the Protestant aldermen, a pork-butcher named John d'Esterre, took as a personal slight. O'Connell had merely described the Corporation as 'beggarly', a mild enough adjective in the repertoire of a master of invective. But it was common knowledge that d'Esterre was in financial difficulties and, with or without justification, he decided that O'Connell's allusion was as much, at least, to himself as to the Corporation. And he had another, and more practical reason for calling the Liberator out. A few years earlier he had actually opposed an anti-Catholic resolution by the Dublin Corporation. Now he was intending to stand for election as one of the city's Sheriffs, a post that would help in the retrieving of his fortune, and it was important he should be able to convince the Protestant political machine he was no longer 'soft' on the Catholic issue and its leading protagonist, O'Connell.

D'Esterre sat down and wrote a truculent letter to the Liberator, protesting at his language and demanding 'your reply in the course of the evening'. O'Connell's reply, next day, was unconciliatory. A second and even more abusive letter from the alderman reached O'Connell and was returned unopened. D'Esterre then put the word around Dublin that he was going to horsewhip the Liberator, that day at the Four Courts, where O'Connell practised as a lawyer–a threat that vastly tickled the fancy of the Dublin citizenry, given the fact that O'Connell, in physical terms, was the equivalent of about two d'Esterres. However, the horsewhipping would clearly be only the prelude to a duel with pistols, and here the advantage would probably be with d'Esterre who, apart from presenting a smaller target, had been an infantry captain in the Indian Army and earlier, as a young naval lieutenant, had shown his mettle when mutineers threatened to hang him from the yardarm of his ship. None of this discouraged O'Connell from stepping out of the courts to meet his challenger, but d'Esterre, brandishing his whip, had moved off along the Quay to take up his post in front of Brian Diebson's drapery shop in College Green, an establishment O'Connell would have to pass on his way home. But the teeming throng of excited Dubliners aborted a confrontation that day.

Next morning Sir Edward Stanley, a friend of d'Esterre's, called on the Liberator's second, Major MacNamara, requesting an apology from O'Connell. He was turned away and the duel was arranged to take place at a rendezvous in Kildare, just across the borders of County Dublin, at 3 p.m. that day.

Stanley tried hard to obtain a postponement, but MacNamara would not yield. For his part he suggested only that, as the principals had no private quarrel, honour should be satisfied by the exchange of a single shot. But Stanley's temper was now roused. 'No, Sir!' he answered. 'If they fire twenty shots each, Mr D'Esterre will never leave the ground until Mr O'Connell makes an apology.' To which MacNamara replied heatedly: 'Well then, if blood be your object, blood you shall have, by God!'[2]

Snow had fallen on the sloping field where the duel was to take place, and by the time d'Esterre arrived, an hour behind his opponent and accompanied by practically the entire Dublin Corporation, the news had not only brought a great crowd of peasants to the scene, but rumours had reached a jubilant Dublin Castle to the effect that O'Connell had been shot and killed.

The seconds took over. D'Esterre won the toss for position and the two men advanced to the prescribed ten paces of each other. As the handkerchief fell, d'Esterre stepped quickly to one side and fired. His shot missed, but O'Connell's, fired simultaneously, found a home in d'Esterre's stomach. He died of the wound two days later, leaving an 18-year-old widow and two small children. O'Connell immediately offered to share his considerable income with the widow, but all she would accept was an annuity for her daughter, which the Liberator paid until his death thirty years later.

John Grattan Guinness took Jane Lucretia d'Esterre as his second wife fourteen years later. Described by her son, Henry Grattan, as 'a woman of deep Christian convictions, an authoress, poet and musician', she bore three sons over the next ten years, all of whom were ordained in the Established Church and the eldest of whom, Henry Grattan, would bring to the name of Guinness a lustre totally unconnected with beer or banking.

Neither of the sons by John Grattan's first wife Susanna 'took the cloth'; and the eldest of them, John, strained the Christian forbearance of his parents—and especially that of his uncle, the Second Arthur, and his cousin Benjamin Lee—to the limits. He was the one who was sacked in 1838 for 'mixing with degraded society', and twenty years later tried to relieve his abject poverty by suing Benjamin Lee for wrongful dismissal, a suit that was promptly dismissed on his cousin's evidence. Meanwhile he married the daughter of a Dublin alderman who gave him two sons. The official Guinness pedigree offers no data beyond their birth dates but Brian Guinness confirms that one of them—Arthur Lee Albert Grattan—was the great-grandfather of the logician and mathematician Ivor Owen Grattan-Guinness whose works include *The Development of the Foundation of Mathematical Analysis* (Cambridge MIT Press, 1970).

When we turn to the careers of Henry Grattan and his descendants we are into a Guinness story so romantic and wide-ranging as to make those of the 'Lee' and 'Rundell' lines seem almost pedestrian.

Only 14 when his father died in 1850, and with no interest in joining the family brewery, Henry Grattan went to sea three years later as a midshipman where he 'fell into evil company and evil ways'.[3] According to his son Paul Grattan, he decided upon his lifetime vocation in his twentieth year when, 'recuperating from an illness on a farm in Ireland, leaping a ditch with gun in hand, he sprained his ankle and the days of enforced inactivity gave him time to think'. Reading the Bible with new understanding, the vision of Christ crucified, risen, glorified, so captured his imagination...he began immediately to share his discovery with others and to resolve to devote his life to missionary work.

Returning to his widowed mother's home in Cheltenham, he threw himself into local evangelical work while awaiting admission to New College, London. He was admitted in 1856 but started his studies with some misgivings. He had already observed what he considered to be the 'dampening effect' of academic learning on evangelical zeal and he recalled later how 'with many tears I besought God on the night of my admission, walking the streets of the great city, to keep me from backsliding and growing cold about Divine things'.[4] It was hardly the most positive approach to academia. Nor were his studies advanced from then on by his compulsive sorties onto the streets, where he would spend long evenings handing out tracts or preaching to street corner audiences. He left the college without completing his second year and for the next five years lived the life of an itinerant evangelist, tramping from one meeting to another, mostly on foot, the horse-buses not having yet made their appearance.

While still at college he had been invited, on the strength of his sermons from the pulpit of the Whitefield Tabernacle in London, to become its pastor but he chose instead to be ordained as an inter-denominational evangelist and it was as such that the handsome young preacher with the golden voice began to draw crowds in their thousands to meetings throughout the British Isles.

There had been intermittent revivalist movements in the United States and Britain over the past 60 years and both nations were soon to experience a major upsurge of religious fervour. Henry Grattan Guinness, who in his own words 'only longed to be a burning and shining light for God among men', took his Bible and his riveting oratory to the great cities of England and Wales where his growing reputation as an evangelist had already preceded him. Unlike the commercialized and affluent 'hot gospellers' packing today's audiences into the stadia of America and Britain, Henry Grattan lived from hand to mouth during this time, never quite sure where he would find his next meal or lodgings. He had his mother's constant moral support but she was living on an Army widow's pension and when Henry was informed that his uncle, the Second Arthur, had willed him the sum of £400 he had it remitted to his mother, at a time when his personal monetary assets were in the region of half-a-crown.

Earlier hostility by the Anglican Church towards the evangelism of Wesley and Whitefield, with its emphasis upon inner religion, had by now virtually disappeared, and when Henry Grattan was invited in 1858 to preach in Dublin's York Street chapel, the cream of the

Protestant Establishment turned out to hear the message of this fiery maverick from the great trading family of Guinnesses. As the Dublin *Daily Express* reported:

Few preachers have addressed congregations more influential...The wealth, the respectability, the cultivated intellect as well as the evangelical piety of the city, have been represented in a measure unprecedented, we believe, on such an occasion in this country. The Lord Lieutenant, the Lord Chancellor, the Lord Justice of Appeal, judges, Members of Parliament, distinguished orators, Fellows of Colleges, the lights of the various professions and, to a considerable extent, the rank and fashion of this gay metropolis, have been drawn to a dissenting chapel, which was thronged by more than sixteen hundred even on weekdays, by this new attraction.

Outside Dublin, in the stronghold cities of Roman Catholicism, it went without saying that the Rev. Henry ran into a certain degree of sectarian hostility, expressed in the characteristic Irish mode of the times. When he attempted to preach the love of Jesus to an open-air meeting in Limerick, he was, as *The Times* of 6 May 1864 described, 'pelted, hooted and knocked down [and] was saved from the vengeance of the populace by Captain Jones of the depot battalion'.

Meanwhile he accepted an invitation to preach in the United States, then being swept up in the great religious revival of 1858–61, and he stayed for seven months, including ten weeks in Philadelphia and seven in New York, and made evangelical missions to a number of other cities in the USA and Canada. During this time he had been preaching up to nine sermons a week and when his tour was finished he spent the summer holiday at Ilfracombe in Devonshire. And it was here, at the age of 25, that he met the woman who would share the next 38 years of his life's mission.

Fanny was the eldest child of the ill-fated Edward Marlborough Fitzgerald, related to the great Anglo-Irish family of that name. His first marriage, to a Roman Catholic girl of the lower middle classes, had estranged him from his parents and when the marriage itself broke up he went into the Army, rose to the rank of major, and at the end of his service entered upon a successful career in British journalism. His second marriage, to the young daughter of Admiral Stopford, was an exceptionally happy one and produced five children. It ended eleven years later in double tragedy with the death of his wife and only son, Gerald. Edward Fitzgerald booked passage, alone, on a channel steamer to France, sat down in the saloon to write a farewell letter, then sought out an isolated section of the deck and plunged into the sea.

In a London office, Arthur West, an actuary and member of the Society of Friends, was reading a newspaper account of Fitzgerald's death when his partner handed him a letter. Written on the channel steamer's notepaper and signed 'Edward Fitzgerald', it expressed concern for the future of his four little girls for whose needs he would 'soon be unable to provide'. And it ended: 'Before this reaches you, I shall be out of reach of any answer.'

Fitzgerald's despairing appeal had been addressed to the right person. Arthur West talked it over with his childless wife that evening and they decided to adopt the eight-year-old Fanny and find homes for the other three girls among members of the Tottenham Friends Meeting House. Fanny remained with the Wests for nearly twenty years until–her plans for a visit to Paris having fallen through–she settled for a holiday in Ilfracombe. She was introduced to Henry Grattan after hearing him preach to a local congregation. They were married three months later.

A turning-point in Henry Grattan's career was reached in 1886 as he was on his way to a preaching appointment in the north of England. His daughter Lucy pinpoints the moment in her book *For Such a Time As*:

Walking along the dreary street of a Yorkshire town, he paused to read a notice newly posted on the wall of a house. With his hands clasped behind his back, his high-crowned hat pushed to the back of his head, he read the poster with mounting indignation. It announced a series of lectures to be held in the neighbourhood when a famous infidel would attack the character of Christ and the authority of the Bible.

The 'infidel' was Charles Darwin, whose book *On the Origin of Species by Means of Natural Selection* had only recently been published. Darwin's theory of evolution was, of course, in direct conflict with the prevailing interpretation of the Scriptures, but it was a work that had not yet reached the mass of the people, 50 per cent of whom were in any case illiterate. Now they were going to hear about it from the lips of the anti-God himself!

Overwhelmed by the thought of the damage Darwin and his adherents could do to the very foundations of Christian belief, and at the same time only too aware of his own deficiencies as a scholar, Henry Grattan cut short his itinerant evangelism, sought out all the books he could find touching on this new apostasy and studied them closely with a view to finding answers and refutations from the Christian evidences. When he felt better prepared for the arming of his fellow-Christians against the heresies of the evolutionists he and

Fanny rented a large Georgian home in Baggot Street, Dublin, with the intention, initially, of inviting young men to meet him there for the study of Christian evidences and theology. It would also be his and Fanny's first settled home and a place where she could bring up their family, consisting then of a five-year-old boy and a baby girl.

But, fervent evangelist and born missionary that he was, his classes in Dublin were not long confined to finding answers to the agnostics. Out of them grew two missionary training colleges, from which 1,500 students went out in the world to serve under societies of a wide variety of denominations. (One of their students, pursuing his training in a London hospital, was so appalled by the number of homeless boys wandering the streets of the city that he decided to stay there and dedicate his life to their care and rehabilitation. By the time of his death in 1905 he had founded 136 institutions for this purpose and his name–Dr Barnardo–had become a household word.)

It was in 1873 that Henry Grattan and his wife founded the East London Institute for Home and Foreign Missions, otherwise known as Harley House ('under a pressing sense', as the evangelical litera- ture put it, 'of the claims of the eight hundred millions of heathen who are in this 19th century still utterly unevangelized'). They also established Cliff College in Derbyshire, the Livingstone Inland Mis- sion in Africa and others in South America and India, later banded together under the title 'The Regions Beyond Missionary Union'.

Fanny Guinness, who came to be known as the 'Mother of Harley House', was a practical, down-to-earth woman who, apart from her domestic duties, attended to most of the financial problems of Harley House as well as relieving her husband from classroom duties during his tours to recruit new students. Many years later, one of the first twelve Harley men, Joseph Adams, was asked on the eve of his return to China to give students something that would benefit their missionary career. With a smile he said he could do no better than begin with Mrs Guinness's final words to him when he first left for China. 'Feeling the solemnity of the occasion,' he said, 'I sharpened a pencil and took a notebook to record her farewell advice. Presently she said: "I have one piece of advice to give you which I earnestly hope you will remember all your life." I felt for the pencil; it was all ready. I listened eagerly. "Whatever part of the Mission field you may be in," she said, "always be sure to keep your hair tidy."'

Fanny Guinness's book, *The First Christian Mission on the Congo*,[5] had paid tribute to the work of the missionary-explorer David Livingstone and the journalist-explorer Henry Stanley, whose

eight-month search through east-central Africa for the lost Livingstone had ended on the shores of Lake Tanganyika with the immor-
tal greeting, 'Dr Livingstone, I presume?' At first separately and
then together, until Livingstone's death in a native village, these two
men, by mapping the River Congo, showed the way for the missionary societies to the interior of the dark continent where, as Fanny
Guinness described it, 'A new and populous world of vast extent is
laid bare to our view; its millions buried in the darkness of ignorance,
error and sin, hateful in their ways and hating one another, sunk in
cannibalism and crime, degraded by domestic and foreign slavery,
trembling in superstitious bondage through fear of death, and having no glimpse of another and better life.'

In 1892 Fanny suffered a stroke that left her a semi-cripple until her
death in 1898. Henry Grattan was then 62, a tall fine-looking man
with commanding blue eyes set in a strong and handsome face
wreathed by a shock of white hair. Five years later he took for his
second wife the 26-year-old Grace Hurditch, youngest daughter of a
lifelong friend, Charles Russell Hurditch, who was the founder and
director of the Evangelical Mission. Three of his children by Fanny
had died in infancy–two on the same day in 1878, of diphtheria–and
the remaining four, Harry, Geraldine, Lucy and Whitfield, were
now respectively 42, 40, 38 and 34, already married and deeply
committed to the missionary field.

Immediately following his second marriage in 1903 Henry Grattan began a five-year journey around the world speaking in
churches, conferences and universities and renewing contact with
students previously trained at Harley and Cliff Colleges. He took
with him a letter which had been addressed to him, just before he left
England, by Balfour in which the Prime Minister told him of his
interest in Henry's books, which he had 'studied closely'.

In Philadelphia he preached in the Memorial Church built on the
site of the one in which he had preached 75 times during the revival
in 1859. In Shanghai he spoke twenty times in eight days to large
audiences in the Free United Church, and was invited to address the
Shanghai Zionist Association in the Royal Asiatic Hall. For over an
hour he held the attention of the audience with an eloquent address
on 'Zionism from a Christian Standpoint', a full report of which
appeared in the local Jewish paper.

Henry and Grace's first son, John Christopher, was born in
Australia in 1906 and their second, Paul Grattan, on their return to
England in 1908. John would become a pioneer in progressive

education, and Paul would develop his father's researches into biblical prophecy and broaden the vision of reconciliation between Jews and Christians.

Incredibly, over the years 1870 to 1908, Henry Grattan found time to write more than twenty books, the first of which, *The Approaching End of the Age in the Light of History, Prophecy and Science*, went into 14 editions and gained the author the award of Doctor of Divinity; and the last, *Creation Centred in Christ*[6]–with its 600-page Astronomical Appendix–led to his election as a Fellow of the Royal Astronomical Society.

He had read and been deeply impressed by the findings[7] of the Swiss astronomer, Jean Philippe Loys de Cheseaux, to the effect that the prophetic periods of Daniel and the Apocalypse, *interpreted on the year-day scale*, are astronomical cycles of extraordinary accuracy.

He therefore began a 40-year-long study, relating cryptic prophecies of the Book of Daniel–together with known dates of world history–to precise astronomical data, which enabled him to compile a chronology of history and even to anticipate future fulfilment of prophecy. He finally reached the conclusion that:

The cycles of astronomy hold the key unlocking the mysteries of prophecy which measure the Ages of Redemption history.

This was the basis of his Judaeo-Christian synthesis and of his understanding of the time of Israel's renaissance, which–in prophecy–is related to the eventual coming of the Messiah and of the Messianic Age.

His findings were incorporated, with supporting astronomical tables, in such works as *The Approaching End of the Age* (1878), *Light for the Last Days* (1886), *The Divine Programme of the World's History* (1888), and *Creation Centred in Christ* (1896).[8] They express his understanding of the duration of the Jewish Diaspora–the twenty-five centuries of Jewish dispersion which began with the Babylonian Captivity in 604, 598, 587 BC etc., and which culminated in Jewish restoration to Palestine between 1917 and 1948.

He pinpointed 604 BC as a principal starting point of 'The Times of the Gentiles'. Measuring from that date, and from the starting point of the Mohammedan Calendar in AD 622, he calculated that 'the year 1917 is consequently doubly indicated as a final crisis date...clearly most critical in connection with Israel.' It was, of course, in this year, in November and December 1917, 31 years after the publication of Henry Grattan's book, that the British Government issued the Balfour Declaration (pledging British support for a Jewish National Home in Palestine), and that General Allenby liberated Jerusalem after centuries of Ottoman and Muslim domination.

In June of that year, General Sir Beauvoir de Lisle called on Allenby at the Grosvenor Hotel in London to congratulate him on his appointment as Commander-in-Chief, Middle East. In the course of their conversation de Lisle said: 'Nothing can prevent you being in Jerusalem by 31st December.' When Allenby asked, 'How do you make that out?', de Lisle told him of Dr Grattan Guinness's book, *Light for the Last Days*.

Henry Grattan's last two years of retirement were spent in Bath where he continued to write in his study, furnished with three thousand volumes. When news of his death reached the 1910 Edinburgh Missionary Conference, under the chairmanship of Dr John R. Mott, the twelve hundred delegates rose spontaneously and sang the hymn: 'For all the saints, who from their labours rest . . .'

Henry Grattan was without a doubt the most charismatic of all the Guinnesses. He left an estate valued at £4,600 net.

Fanny's son, Harry, had been born in Canada in 1861 during one of Henry Grattan's tours. He had inherited his father's good looks and histrionic gifts and, after graduating as a doctor of medicine from the London Hospital, he sailed for Australia.

Harry was an evangelist with a genial, extroverted personality that appealed at once to the down-to-earth colonials of the Antipodes. On the strength of his first few sermons to Tasmanian congregations, he was kept in Australia for the next two years, preaching to overflowing halls throughout the continent. For one of his lectures to a male audience in Melbourne, 15,000 applications for seats were received. When he preached in Brisbane, the Primate of Australia and Tasmania took the chair.

The earliest of Harry's conquests in Tasmania was the heart of Annie Reed. They were married in London in 1887 and became joint honorary secretaries of the missionary-training institute founded by Henry Grattan and Fanny. By the time Dr Harry paid his first visits to the missionary stations of the Upper Congo, King Leopold had settled the squabbles with Portugal and France by taking over, under his personal sovereignty, the newly formed Congo 'Free State', opening it up to the trade of all nations and allowing them to line their pockets from the sweat of the populations bordering the great river.

Appalled by the working conditions he witnessed at first hand during these visits, Harry made spirited appeals in three hard-hitting audiences with King Leopold. When they fell on the deaf ears of the monarch—himself the greatest profiteer among all the Congo traders—Harry took his case first to the British Foreign Secretary, Lord Lansdowne, and then to President Theodore Roosevelt at a meeting in Washington in 1907. No doubt he followed, on this occasion, the great president's advice to 'speak softly...' though he carried no big stick to a statesman dedicated to foreign expansionism. This was finally provided by a wave of international protest over the treatment of the Congolese people, leading to the appointment of a Belgian commission of inquiry which in due course confirmed that the 'Free State' was founded on slave-labour. As a result the Belgian Parliament stepped in over the head of Leopold and converted the traders' paradise into the colony known until 1960 as the Belgian Congo and now—following the murder of its first premier, Patrice Lumumba, on the instigation of the CIA—as the Republic of Zaire.

The moderate measures of reform instituted in the Congo by King Albert after the death of his father Leopold in 1910 freed Harry from his commitment to the cause and turned his attention to the work of his missions in India until his death in 1915, having outlived his father by only five years.

As the 19th century drew to a close, the disparate branches of the Guinness family—brewers, bankers and missionaries—were vigorously pursuing their varied interests in virtually every corner of the globe. A triple-stout Guinness beer, 'West Indies Porter', had long since been lightening the white man's burden in the Caribbean and in a dozen other colonies of the farflung British Empire. Banker Richard Seymour and his son Benjamin were in correspondence or personal contact with a network of overseas financial institutions, wherever an honest buck was to be made. But neither of these branches could match, in adventurousness and energy, the deeds of the 'Grattan' Guinnesses, spurred as they were not by materialistic ambition but by a deeply felt, inherited faith in what they believed to be the civilizing power of the Bible.

Harry's sister, Lucy Evangeline, had studied in Paris. Later, she accompanied her father on his journey throughout India and again, after the death of Fanny, travelled with him through Egypt and Palestine, where he addressed delegates to the Zionist Congress in Jerusalem. During a second visit to Egypt she met the German missionary–explorer, Dr Karl Kumm, who was about to undertake an extensive journey through the Sudan. At the end of the tour in 1900 they were married in Cairo.

In many respects the brightest of Henry Grattan's children and the most gifted as a writer, Lucy had already published several books, evangelical in theme, including *The Neglected Continent* (South America) and *Across India at the Dawn of the Twentieth Century*. She had only five more years to live from the date of her marriage and in that time she worked with her husband in setting up the Sudan Mission and helped him to compile his informative study, *The Sudan*,[9] for which she wrote the introduction shortly before her death. Dr Kumm dedicated his book, 'To the memory of my fellow worker, my teacher in many things, my helpmate, my wife', and his preface begins, 'This book was conceived in tears...'

Her father, Henry Grattan, was in Australia when the news of Lucy's death, after an operation for cancer, reached him. Her half-brother, Paul Grattan, then unborn, was later told by his mother, Grace, that the 71-year-old Henry Grattan left Sydney and sought out the solitude of a quiet bay on the coast of New South Wales where he sat for a long while with bowed head, oblivious to the crash of the sea. A hand came to rest on his shoulder and in the accented voice of an Aborigine came the New Testament line, 'Let not your heart be troubled, ye believe in God, believe also in me.' He turned and looked up into the wrinkled face of an old black woman.

He went back to Sydney and wrote his lines on *The Transfiguration of Sorrow*:

> Sorrow! to pluck it up the world hath sought,
> To cast it out, to bring it to an end,
> By any means, nor cared has man for aught
> If from its ills he might himself defend.
>
> But Jesus of another mind possessed,
> From scenes all sorrowless in love come down,
> Transfigured sorrow, clasped it to His breast,
> And wore it on His forehead as a crown.

Lucy left two sons by Karl Kumm, Henry and Karl. The elder became a Rockefeller Foundation research doctor, working on the problem of Yaws Disease, and later served as President of the Polio Foundation of America. The younger was ordained in the American Episcopal Church, became a chaplain with the US armed forces in

North Africa and Europe and subsequently vicar of an Episcopal church in the USA.

Even to an agnostic–perhaps especially to the unbeliever–there is something daunting about the spirit in which the foreign missionaries in the 19th and early 20th centuries made their way across the great oceans and the land masses of the heathen world, embracing with steady fortitude the perils and physical hardships of their vocation. The common cause that inspired them in many cases to lay down their lives strikes an anachronistic note to today's world, in which the cold-blooded torture and butchery of young militants, intellectuals, and socially conscious clergymen has become a rule of conduct to 'Christian' dictatorships in the 'neglected continent' of South America and elsewhere. But ideals and idealism, as the mainspring of sacrifice, transcend both time and purpose, and the guts of the urban guerrilla battling in the darkness of a police state is of the same brave stuff that the missionaries took with them on the crusades into their own 'dark regions'. Whitfield and Geraldine Guinness were two such 'guerrillas for Christ'. And their battleground was China.

The China Inland Mission had been founded by the Englishman, Dr Hudson Taylor, in an era when China was being ravaged by domestic rebellions and carved up, economically, by the Western powers, led by Britain and France. Geraldine Guinness joined the mission in 1888 and by the time her younger brother Whitfield followed suit in 1894 she was already married to Hudson Taylor's son, Howard. The young Emperor Kuang Hsü, influenced by an enlightened faction of reformers, was in the process of breaking the power of the Manchu officials and regional warlords and transforming China into a modern constitutional monarchy when he was put under house arrest by the reactionaries under the sway of the Dowager Empress, Tzu Hsi, sparking the campaign of terror known as the Boxer Rebellion. The objective of the uprising was the expulsion of all foreigners from China, and the first of its victims were the Christian Chinese and the foreign missionaries isolated in the north-eastern provinces.[10] When the slaughter spread to the capital, Peking, the surviving missionaries took refuge in the foreign legations quarter until Peking was relieved and occupied by the troops of Britain, France, America, Germany, Japan and Russia.

Geraldine and her husband had been spared the horrors of the Boxer Rebellion while on a speaking tour of Australia, New Zealand and America on behalf of the China Inland Mission. They had come to love China and its people despite an earlier experience when on a working visit to the mission station at Taikang, in Honan province, they came close to losing their lives in a riot instigated by a local Buddhist nun resentful of the mission's presence in the city. The province was in the middle of a severe drought which had brought destitution to thousands, and when the nun circulated a report that the foreigners would be handing out cash, on a certain day, to any Chinese who presented themselves at the mission, the stream of eager callers turned into a riotous mob. Useless for Howard and his male colleagues to explain that they had no money to give away. The mob stormed past them into the house where the two unmarried missionary ladies and Geraldine had taken refuge, smashing and pillaging as they went. One of the two ladies managed to escape to a friendly neighbour's house, the other was physically assaulted and stripped. When Geraldine went to her aid she not only received the same treatment but her head was cut open by a woman wielding a hoe. As she stood there, the blood streaming to her shoulders, she was saved from a worse fate by the arrival of a friendly Chinese named Wang who managed to restrain the mob until a young mandarin and his escort of soldiers reached the scene, just in time to save Howard from being stoned to death in the front courtyard.

Later, Dr Whitfield Guinness, who had come out to China as a medical missionary on the eve of the Boxer Rebellion, also escaped with his life when his mission was attacked and destroyed and he and two colleagues had to be hidden in a loft by Chinese converts. The nearby river, the only safe escape route to their base in Shanghai, was almost dry at this time. But after thirty days in the loft, unexpected rains raised the level of the stream and they were able to make their escape by boat.

Over the next three years, Whitfield was the only qualified medical missionary working in Honan province. He nearly died of diphtheria in 1904 and on recovery took his furlough in England, returning to China in 1905 where, in the course of a journey with Hudson Taylor, he met Jane af Sandeberg for the first time. There is no record of the impression then made on Whitfield by this young niece of Prince Bernadotte of Sweden, but he was shortly to receive a letter from his father, Henry Grattan, asking if he or his sister Geraldine knew the young lady, who had recently joined the China Inland Mission. (Henry had been staying as a guest of Bernadotte's in Sweden where he had seen and been greatly impressed by a portrait of Jane.) Trusting his father's judgement in all things, Whitfield sought Jane out again and they were married in Shanghai that same year. After honeymooning in Japan they returned to Honan province, to the newly constructed mission hospital at Kai-Feng, the only one in a region as large as England and Wales. Here, Whitfield worked as a doctor-missionary until his death. His story is told in the biography, *Guinness of Honan*,[11] written by Geraldine.

When Sun Yat-sen's Kuomintang party was taken over in 1925 by General Chiang Kai-shek and the purge of its Communist members began, China was again set ablaze with inter-factional warfare. The fighting in the east of Honan province was already filling Whitfield's hospital with wounded soldiers and civilians when he wrote to his son, Henry:

We may have to evacuate. If the southerners reach Honan, they will make it hot for Britishers and for the Chinese Church. Missionaries in the centre and west of the province are leaving for the east and Shanghai is crowded. Borodin is a trained agitator of ability, striving to raise the Communist revolution in different parts of the world. At Canton he has been successful, and now in Hankow and Wu-chang. The northerners are trying to prevent their coming to Honan...

When one of the wounded soldiers brought to the hospital was found to have typhus, Whitfield agreed to having him admitted to an isolation hut where he himself would attend to the patient. A week later, as Kai-feng was about to fall to the southern force, all missionaries were ordered to evacuate to the northern capital of Peking. By then, although he did not know it, Whitfield had contracted typhus. A retreating northern general had offered him a box-car on a military train and during the journey of two days and two nights the dreaded rash appeared...

He was buried in the British Embassy cemetery, a few miles from Peking.

When Whitfield died at the age of 58, his sister Geraldine was already 64. She had spent almost half of her life in China and was fluent in the language, but had long since been taken off routine missionary work to concentrate on publicizing the China Inland Mission through her writings and her lecture tours, with her husband Dr Howard Taylor, throughout Australia, New Zealand, the United States of America and Canada, as well as in the United Kingdom. Her major two-volume biography, *The Life of Hudson Taylor*,[12] had been published and there would be twenty missionary biographies from her pen before her death in 1949, two years after that of her husband. But China kept calling her back. She had returned there, after six years' absence, with her husband and father-in-law in 1905 and was at Hudson Taylor's bedside in the mission house at Changsha when he died. She was there again for the three years 1919–22, writing her book *The Call of the Great North-West*, and was one of the survivors, in Lanchow, when the great earthquake of 1919 struck, killing 200,000 people.

In February 1922, as she and Howard were in the course of a field tour of the western provinces and about to enter Yunnan, they were captured by the irregular troops of 'General' P'u Kiang-kuin, then being hunted as outlaws by the army of the provincial government. Her journal, written during her captivity, records the experience.

We are passing field after field of opium. On both sides of the road it seems to be all opium, and this when large portions of Kweichow are in a state of semi-famine. The people are forced to grow it in many cases by rapacious officials...

It is not an hour since we fell into these brigands' hands. They rushed out upon us from behind some brush-wood, firing their guns, and one of the leaders drawing his knife with shouts of excitement and a face horrible in its fury...My chair was in front, and I got out at once and met them...I turned to see if Howard was coming, and found that they were carrying him the other way. I understood in a moment: a hostage!...I managed to hold my ground and explained that Dr Taylor was deaf, and I would not leave him. So we have the comfort of being together, thank the Lord.[13]

When they were brought before 'General' P'u in an outlying village he politely explained that they would be killed if the Government troops attacked his own army of 4,000 men. Their release depended on the response he received to a letter calling for certain terms, a letter that would be taken to the provincial headquarters in Yünnanfu by the Chinese evangelist, Mr Li, who had been captured as he came out to meet Geraldine and Howard. Later, P'u changed his mind and ordered Geraldine to take the letter herself while her husband remained as hostage. She at first demurred, but 'Howard urged it, speaking of our chair-bearers, seven men for whom we are responsible [and who] would all be allowed to go with me'.

For the next five weeks, while the world's press carried the story and prayer meetings were held throughout America and Britain, Geraldine went from one official of the Government to another, pleading in vain for action to secure Howard's release. The drama ended with a change of heart–or perhaps tactics–by P'u, and the release of Howard Taylor.

They resumed their world travel on behalf of the China Inland

Mission until, in 1944, Geraldine suffered a stroke that left her partly paralysed for the remaining five years of her life. In 1947, her husband and senior by only one month died in their Tunbridge Wells home after a protracted illness.

There had been no offspring to follow in the evangelical footsteps of Geraldine and Howard but the barrenness of this one limb of the 'Grattan' tree was more than compensated by the fruitfulness of the others.

Harry's Tasmanian wife, Annie Reed, had presented him with seven sons and two daughters (a third daughter, Margaret, died in infancy), all born during the first 18 years of their marriage. Four of these sons went into the Church. John Frith Grattan, whose descendants made their homes in Rhodesia and Australia, became rector of various parishes in Norfolk. Gordon was a Proctor in Convocation and Canon of Winchester before his death in 1980. Howard Wyndham served as an RAF chaplain in World War II before becoming Rector of St Barnabas's, Sydney. From there he took over the rectorship of St Michael's at Vaucluse in New South Wales, retiring at 68 to Wentworth Falls, where he died eight years later.

His younger brother, Desmond, spent six years with the China Inland Mission until the Japanese invasion in 1938, and 25 years as vicar of Laleham, Middlesex, until his recent retirement. Of the three non-clerical sons, Henry went to Australia in his teens, won an MC in World War I and subsequently went into the film industry as a producer of newsreels; Alexander, a surgeon, married the daughter of the French Consul in Calcutta, and set up practice in South Africa; and Victor joined his sister Geraldine ('Geen') as manager of the private school she founded in Sussex.

There was only one son, Henry, by Whitfield's marriage to Jane af Sandeberg. Brought up in China, he joined the Inland Mission in 1931 and married Dr Mary Taylor (not related to the founder, Hudson Taylor). He and his wife, the last Europeans in Nanking when the Chinese Communists took over the city, were kept under house arrest for a year until the Red Army was dislodged by Chiang's forces. They continued their work in the mission's hospital at Kai-Feng until World War II, when the advance of the Japanese started them on a long, perilous march towards India. During this 1,000-mile trek through flood, famine and plague they lost two of their infant sons before being air-lifted by the RAF to Calcutta. After the war, and until their retirement in the 1960s, they continued their missionary work in the Far East. The surviving son is Os (Ian

Oswald) Guinness. His two works to date—*Dust of Death: A Critique of the Establishment and the Counter-Culture and the Proposal for a Third Way* and *In Two Minds (The Dilemma of Doubt and how to Resolve it)*—embody a more contemporary view of religion than that found in the works of his great-aunt Geraldine, but in a recent letter to his great-uncle and fellow-author, Paul Grattan, he wrote that 'The vision and example of previous generations of Guinnesses is never far away from my awareness of what [my wife] and I are about.'

The literary talent that flows so strongly through the female line from Henry Grattan and his first wife Fanny found its most precocious expression in a child biography written by the younger of Whitfield and Jane's daughters, Mary Geraldine, using her family name of Pearl. Written before her death at the age of nine, *Pearl's Secret* ran into many thousands of copies at the end of World War I. Thirty years later her elder sister Joy Guinness (baptized Isabel Gordon) published her major work, the biography of her Aunt Geraldine referred to earlier in this chapter.

Today, the only surviving son of Henry Grattan is the Rev. Paul Grattan Guinness. Educated in Europe, New Zealand and America, Paul married his wife, Jean, in 1935 after they graduated together from Northwestern University, Chicago. He served as an army chaplain in World War II, spent 12 years in Geneva directing the YMCA's world publication programme and another 12 years furthering his father's vision of a Judaeo-Christian messianic partnership born of Hitler's holocaust and the creation of the State of Israel. One of his sons, the recently ordained Peter Grattan, personified his parents' dream by marrying a Jewish girl, Michele Gilbert. The other, John Elliot, married a German girl, Christiane, and is now vice-president of the American space technology giant TRW, with headquarters in Cleveland, Ohio.

Intermarriage between Guinness children—a feature of the brewery line and, to a lesser extent, the bankers'—played almost no part in the genealogy of the 'Grattans'. The one exception concerns Paul Grattan's elder brother, John Christopher, who in 1935 married his great-niece Karis, daughter of 'Geen' Guinness's marriage to Ian Mackenzie. (That Karis happened to be only five years younger than John is explained by the fact that John was born in his father's 71st year.)

John Christopher Guinness, who died of cancer at Virginia Beach in 1979, earned a unique place for himself as a progressive educationalist during his 15 years as headmaster of Long Dene

School, in Kent. In his youth he had joined the Liverpool Repertory Company as an actor, sharing roles with contemporaries such as John Gielgud and Robert Donat. This early training served him well as headmaster of a school which, under his direction, laid special emphasis on the arts and was noted for the professionalism of its theatrical productions. Ex-pupils such as Humphrey Burton, the author–illustrator Angela Ogden and actor Nick Simons retain vivid memories of sitting spellbound in the darkened hall of Long Dene while the headmaster, with the beautiful voice inherited from his father Henry Grattan, stood at a lectern, reading from the classics to the entire school. There was no 'fagging' imposed on juniors in this co-educational private boarding school. Pupils grew and ate their own natural food, untouched by chemicals, and were encouraged to develop freely their own potentialities. There was no religious indoctrination–a radical break from the Grattan tradition of evangelism. (John Christopher's own leanings were in fact towards Buddhism, with an 'ecumenical' leavening of Christian tenets.)

In partnership with his wife he had opened Long Dene in 1939, four years after their marriage, and their children–Lindis, Chloe and Anthea–became pupils. The painful decision to close down the school in 1954 was forced upon the Guinnesses by a national slackening at that time in the flow of fee-paying entrants to, independent boarding schools and by lack of support from the local educational authority.

His eldest daughter, Lindis, had trained as a dancer in Britain, but her height (both her parents were over six feet tall) was against her. She had great beauty, however, and a superb figure, and her thoughts turned towards an acting career in Hollywood. The going was rough. With no track record as an actress, in a city where beautiful young girls were literally queuing for movie work and where the name Guinness had no magic, Lindis, in her own words, 'sat starving in a Beverly Hills room waiting for the telephone to ring'.

To pay the rent she posed for the well-known photographer of nudes, Mario Casilli, and recalls with a chuckle a letter she received from her mother some months later. Her parents had been scanning a book-stall while waiting for their train at Victoria Station when her father's eye fell upon the cover of a girlie magazine called *Midnight*. 'My God,' her father spluttered, 'it's Lindis!'

She would not be the only Guinness girl to pose topless for a photographer (see below, p. 202), but she was certainly the first.

Meanwhile, nothing was happening for her on the movie front and at 21, when she was offered work as a bare-breasted showgirl in Las Vegas, she took the job, changed her name to Fiona, and paraded her spectacular charms for two years, first at The Mint Hotel in downtown Las Vegas, then in a classier show at The Stardust, under the banner 'Artists and Models'. She returned to Los Angeles when her parents and their two other daughters moved over from England, and she began to get small parts—'usually as a secretary or a whore'—in TV and feature films, together with one or two lead roles in local theatrical productions. She appeared in such cinematic gems as *Grave of the Vampire*, *The Hippy Murders*, *Black Stockings* and *Love, Boccaccio Style* before her first good break came around in 1975 with a featured role in the three-part TV mini-series entitled *The Law*.

Meanwhile, her father had started giving private music classes, using a special version of the recorder adapted for easy tuition to children, while his wife taught piano and violin. 'He even,' says Fiona, 'started up a small workshop to manufacture and market the pipes, but the poor dear wasn't much of a businessman and it never really got off the ground.'

Both her sisters had been drawn to Oriental philosophy, Chloe to the more practical benefits of yoga and polarity therapy, while Anthea was drawn to the spiritual aspects. When Chloe moved to Virginia her parents joined her and bought a little house on Virginia Beach, where Karis still lives at the time of writing. Chloe is now married to a professor of English, Will Wadsworth, and living in Washington, DC. Anthea, the brainiest of the three, left for India in 1975, took her PhD in Relative Religions in 1980 and is now a respected, Urdu-speaking adherent of the Punjab ashram, 'The Dera'.

There was never any social contact between the family of John Christopher and their wealthy relatives of the brewing and banking lines. Whenever the young girls raised this question with their father his invariable response was, 'We couldn't afford to live up with them.' But it is something of an irony that today, when Arthur Guinness Son & Co. is investing millions in film production through its Hollywood subsidiary, the Film Finance Group, a great-great-great-granddaughter of the Second Arthur is living in a two-room apartment on Lexington Avenue, West Hollywood, working as secretary for an insurance agency while awaiting another small part in movies.

11

The 'Gentlemen' Line

While the generations of 'Lee' Guinnesses brewed their beer, while the 'Rundells' gave service to Mammon and the 'Grattans' to God, two further lines from the First Arthur procreated progeny down to the present generation, for the most part unnoticed by the chroniclers of Society, the Stock Exchange and the evangelical church. These were the lines from the Rev. Hosea Guinness, founder of the family's senior branch and from the second youngest of the First Arthur's sons, William Lunell.

Hosea married Jane Hart, the seventeen-year-old daughter of an Anglo-Irish colonel, who presented him over the next quarter of a century with six sons and seven daughters. One of the daughters died in infancy and this was probably also true of another two daughters and a son. Only two of the surviving five sons—Arthur and Francis Hart—were left to perpetuate the senior line from Hosea.

Hosea's eldest son, Arthur, became curate of Loughall in co. Armagh, and left two sons to carry on his line. The first-born, Arthur Hart, moved to England and his descendants add little interest or lustre to the Guinness story. The poorest of the 'poor Guinnesses', they became a genealogical tributary totally remote from the mainstreams of Guinness wealth and glamour, and the continuity of this branch rests today with the recently married, 31-year-old Kevin John Guinness, a clerk in the Department of Health and Social Security in London.

The younger of Hosea's two grandsons, Thomas Hosea, remained in Ireland and sired seven children, only one of whom is listed in the official family pedigree as having married. This was Charles Davis, who partly compensated for his siblings' inertia by marrying the Hon. Lucy, daughter of the 6th Baron Massy, and siring two sons, one of whom—the bachelor Hugh Spencer—became a Customs officer in Peking and died at sea in 1922. His brother, Owen Charles, rose to the rank of major in the Worcestershire Regiment and his branch of the senior line of Guinnesses is secured today by a son, Paul Dennis, and grandchildren.

The most distinguished of Thomas Hosea's children was undoubtedly Miss May Guinness, his eldest daughter and a painter of solid repute. Awarded the Croix de Guerre in World War I for her bravery as a nurse with the British army in France, she outlived all the family, dying in 1955 at the age of 91.

For the finest fruition of Hosea's tree we must turn to the offspring of his youngest son, Francis Hart, the only Guinness to become a policeman. After 15 years in Calcutta Francis sailed in 1852 for New Zealand with his wife Catherine and their children aboard the immigrant ship, *The Tory*, and served as Sub-Inspector of Police in Canterbury from 1858 to 1862. During the last 20 years of his life he was the resident magistrate, first at Ahaura and then at Ashburton.

Four of Francis Hart's sons, Arthur Robert, Edwin Rowland, John Clephane and Frank Hart, had all been born in India but brought up in New Zealand. The eldest, Arthur Robert, was the third member of the entire Guinness clan to win a knighthood[1] and the first and only one to earn it by his labours in the cause of social justice. Articled as a lawyer and admitted to the bar of the crown colony's Supreme Court in 1867, he quickly won the respect of the more humanitarian of the colonists by his brilliant and persistent advocacy on behalf of the 'Fenian' prisoners, seven Republican Irishmen charged with sedition for setting up a cross in the Hotikita cemetery 'in loving memory' of two fellow-countrymen executed for the shooting of a police sergeant. Later, both as a lawyer and an elected member, first of local councils then of Parliament, he played a prominent part in the political struggle against the large land-owners, to win the land reforms and to pioneer the social legislation for which New Zealand became the world's pace-setter. Before the Conservatives, campaigning as the 'Reform Party', regained power in 1912, Arthur Robert saw one of his causes, the provision of old-age pensions, reach the statute book, and another, the granting of votes to women, set a precedent for the rest of the world.

He served as Speaker of the New Zealand Parliament from 1903 until his death in 1913, two years after receiving his knighthood. He had married a colonist's daughter, Elizabeth Westbrook, in 1878 but there were no children.

New Zealand paid a heavy price for its defence of the Empire during World War I, with 56,000 men killed or wounded out of the

100,444 sent to Europe. Two of Arthur Robert's nephews died in action–Arthur Grattan at Passchendaele and Francis Benjamin at Gallipoli–and a third Guinness nephew of the same generation, Cecil George, died on the Somme.

John Clephane, the most prolific of the first generation of New Zealand Guinnesses, had no less than six sons by his two marriages, all of whom married and produced sons and grandsons to perpetuate the senior line.

Only one of Cecil George's three elder brothers–Sidney Oswald–sired male children and the eldest of them, Cecil Warren, was killed in Italy during World War II. But the other two sons, Guyon William and Griffen Sidney, added eight children to the seventh and present generation of New Zealand Guinnesses.

William Lunell, like his brothers, the Second Arthur and Benjamin, began as an apprentice in the brewery at the age of 15. After the death of Benjamin, he shared with the Second Arthur and John Purser in the management of James's Gate, retiring in 1839, by which time his brother's two sons, Arthur Lee and Benjamin Lee, had taken over effective control of the business. His only son, William Newton, was born about three years later than his cousins Arthur Lee and Benjamin, but the call of the brewery was less peremptory to him than the clarion of religion. He took holy orders, was married three times and served as rector of the affluent Protestant Church at South Yarra, Melbourne, where a stained-glass window perpetuates his memory today, 87 years after his death at the age of 83.

There would be no other clergymen in the male line of descent from William Lunell, but with his son's first and second wives, daughters of a rear-admiral and a colonel, already inscribed in this branch-pedigree of what, until then, was a family of traders, the line of 'Gentlemen Guinnesses'–as its living descendants now half-jokingly dub themselves–came into being. Gentlemen of leisure they certainly were not. William Lunell had inherited £1,500 on his father's death in 1803 and he lived very comfortably on his income as one of the brewery's management, but his clergyman son and heir, the Rev. William Newton, left no fortune and two of his own sons ended up with salaried jobs in the Empire–(Robert) Cecil with the Hong Kong and Shanghai Bank and Edward in Australia, where he became Crown Solicitor of Victoria and the founder, down to the present, of four generations of Australian Guinnesses. Of the remaining four sons, two died unmarried, a third rose to the rank of brigadier-general with the Royal Irish Fusiliers and a fourth became a doctor of medicine. One of William Newton's daughters, Mary Alice ('May' to the family), warrants a place in this history by virtue of becoming the wife of her banker-cousin Howard Rundell Guinness.

A further instance of intermarriage, this time *within* the 'gentlemen' line of Guinnesses, occurred in the next generation when the brigadier-general's son, Alan Henry—who had followed his father into the army, fought in both world wars and was taken prisoner by the Japanese after the fall of Hong Kong—took his uncle Cecil's widowed daughter, Barbara, as his wife. There were no children of the marriage and it ended in divorce ten years later—the only case of divorce in any of the Guinness intermarriages.

Alan's younger brother, Patrick, died at 19 of Bright's Disease. The third and youngest of the brothers, Maurice West, became an executive with Shell International and spent his first ten years with the company in Puerto Rico where he met and married Gloria Ashford, daughter of the distinguished Dr Bailey K. Ashford.

Maurice himself, now 83 and living in London, combined his lifetime profession as an oil company executive with a passion for the best of detective fiction, in particular the works of Raymond Chandler. The two men became correspondents and met frequently in London, especially during the writer's last stay in the capital, in 1958, when he was pressuring Maurice's cousin, Helga Greene, to marry him. Frank MacShane, in his biography of Chandler, describes how Maurice, on his way home from work, would occasionally stop in to see Chandler at the flat Helga had taken for him in Chelsea, at 8 Swan Walk.

> Chandler was always what he called a 'horizontal man' who preferred lying down to sitting up...When Guinness paid his visits, Chandler would mix them drinks, and the two men would lie down on the bed, side by side and converse. Then Guinness would go home.[2]

It was probably during one of these horizontal sessions that Maurice talked his friend into the idea of at last marrying off his famous fictional character, Philip Marlowe, to his girl friend Linda Loring. The author did in fact write the first few chapters of a novel incorporating this marriage but he never finished the book. Before his death the following year he had second thoughts about marrying Marlowe off, and he chided his friend with an inscription written on the flyleaf of the copy he gave him of his last Marlowe novel, *Playback*: 'For Maurice—the man who ruined my career.'

Maurice and Gloria Guinness have just one son, Gerald Newton, born in Puerto Rico in 1931 and now Associate Professor of English literature at the University of Puerto Rico. Exceptionally handsome and youthful-looking with, as his mother puts it, 'girl friends all over the place', Gerald chose for his PhD thesis the subject of erotic poetry of the 17th and 18th centuries. He seems to be under no compulsion to end his bachelorhood and is probably the last of the 'Newton' line through his brigadier-general grandfather.

Any contact in the past between this line and the brewers and bankers has been purely accidental. Indeed, Maurice—with only the suspicion of a twinkle in his eye—stoutly refuses to acknowledge more than a 'remote' relationship with the 'other Guinnesses', though he shares a direct blood-line with them from the First Arthur. He recalls meeting Loel Guinness whilst Loel was honeymooning in Jamaica with his second wife Lady Isabel. He found his cousin 'amusing but rather superficial, mainly interested in having his fun'.

The gentlemanly line of Guinness military officers was carried on by all three of Maurice's first cousins. Eric Cecil, only son of (Robert) Cecil, was a captain in the Royal Irish Regiment. His son Patrick Robert opted for the Royal Navy, married a naval commander's daughter in 1940 and was killed on active service four months later. Both of Ernest Whitmore's sons were commissioned officers, Eustace John as a captain in the Royal Navy and Dennys Robert as a colonel in the Royal Engineers. In 1946 Eustace married Angela Frisby, the widow of a war hero and daughter of Lady Gwendolen Hoare of the well-known banking family. Their son Timothy Whitmore, now 34, chose banking as a career, and became the only one of the William Lunell line to go into the firm of Guinness Mahon & Co.

Dennys Robert, by his Philadelphia-born wife Elizabeth, had one son, born 1933, whose death by suicide gave the British press yet another opportunity to juxtapose the words 'Guinness' and 'Tragedy' in a headline. Major Dennys Key Guinness had married a naval commander's daughter, Veronica Terry, in the 1950s, but by 1978 they had separated and early in July of that year came the news that Veronica was seeking a divorce and the custody of their four children. The major, who was jobless, had gone to live with his elderly parents in Hampshire and on the night of 4 July, at the Lamb Hotel in Hartley Wintney, he flourished a revolver and informed the locals drinking with him at the bar that he was going to use it first on his wife and then on himself. The police were notified and the major arrested, charged with illegal possession of a firearm and released on

Rupert, the 2nd Earl of Iveagh (third from right, front row) with one of his shooting parties at Elveden. Queen Mary sits in the centre, with the reigning King George V behind her, and Lady Iveagh on her left. Also in the group are Bryan Moyne standing at the extreme left, Ernest Guinness standing fifth from left with the Duke of Abercorn on his right and the Marquess of Hartington on his left. Three of the 'Golden Guinness Girls' are seated on the extreme left, Oonagh and Maureen on the ground, Aileen between them on a chair.

The south front of Elveden.

BBC Hulton Picture Library

Above Maureen was 26, and married to a cousin – the ill-fated Marquess of Dufferin and Ava – as she arrives for a Buckingham Palace garden party with her father, Ernest Guinness, and her mother, Cloe.

Right Maureen Guinness with Britain's man of destiny, Winston Churchill.

Courtesy: Maureen, Lady Dufferin and Ava

Left Oonagh, third and youngest of Ernest's daughters, with her first husband, the Hon. Philip Kindersley, in 1933. Three years later they were divorced.

Below Dufferin and Ava *(left)* flexes a rod during a Yorkshire houseparty.

Keystone

Above Aileen and the Hon. Brinsley Plunket at the christening of their baby, Marcia, in 1933, but, sadly, she died three years later. The marriage between these cousins ended in divorce. Their first-born, Neelia, completes the picture.

Above middle The American 'Chips' Channon has 'arrived' – leading his bride, Lady Honor Guinness, from their wedding-of-the-year at St Margaret's in July 1933.

Above He was born to succeed to his father's earldom but died in action at 32. Arthur Onslow Guinness with his bride Lady Elizabeth Hare, daughter of the Earl of Listowel.

Left The assassinated Lord Moyne's funeral cortège passes through the streets of wartime Cairo. His son and heir, Captain Bryan Walter Guinness, led the mourners. (Radio photograph from the back page of *The Times*, 10 November 1944.)

Central Press Photos

The 1929 marriage of Bryan Walter
Guinness (now the 2nd Lord
Moyne) to his first wife, the
18-year-old Diana Mitford,
loveliest of Lord Redesdale's
celebrated daughters.

Topham

Bryan Walter with his second wife, Elisabeth.

Lady Brigid and her husband, Prince Friedrich Georg Wilhelm Christoph of Prussia, alias George Mansfield.

Topham

Prince Friedrich of
Prussia focuses on
his third child by
Lady Brigid, the
newly-christened
Victoria, proudly
cradled by her
grandfather, the 2nd
Earl of Iveagh. Her
paternal
grandmother,
Princess Cecile of
Prussia, is on
Iveagh's right.
Victoria's brothers
Andrew and
Nicholas are in front.

Maureen's daughter,
Lady Caroline
Blackwood, with her
first husband, the
painter Lucien
Freud.

Keystone

bail. The next night he was found dead in his bed, an empty bottle of barbiturates by his side.

Confirmation of the total estrangement between this line and the brewery Guinnesses came the next day, when the Hon. Jonathan Guinness, a director of Arthur Guinness Son & Co., was told of his kinsman's death. As the *Belfast Telegraph* of 6 July 1978 reported: 'I did not know him,' he said, 'or what relation he was to me. I think he was *some* relation.'

12

Titles Galore

1

We left the saga of the brewery Guinnesses with the assassination in Cairo of Lord Moyne. His brother, Rupert Edward, the 2nd Earl of Iveagh, was then 70 and the succession to his earldom rested with his son, Arthur Onslow Edward.

Arthur Onslow had succeeded to the courtesy title of Viscount Elveden as a 15-year-old boy at Eton and, at 21, had come into the inheritance from his grandfather's trusts. He was Lord Moyne's only nephew (his uncle Ernest had no sons) and he idolized the explorer-politician whom he accompanied on the 1935–6 expedition to the East Indies. His intention was eventually to follow his uncle's example by standing for Parliament. But first he would get married, which he did in 1936 to the younger daughter of the 4th Earl of Listowel, Lady Elizabeth Hare. Again following the example of his uncle, the young viscount served his apprenticeship in local politics, as a member of the West Suffolk County Council; but by the time he felt ready to launch himself into national politics the Munich crisis had stirred Britain into belated preparation for war and Arthur had himself transferred from the Territorial Army to the Anti-tank Regiment of the Suffolk and Norfolk Yeomanry.

On 14 February 1945, just 13 weeks after the assassination of Lord Moyne, it was announced that the Earl of Iveagh's son and heir, Major Viscount Elveden, RA, had been killed in action.

Although Arthur Guinness Son & Co. had been a public company since 1886, it had been the board's concern—no less than that of the earls of Iveagh—that it should always be a direct male descendant of the 'Lee' line who would give the chairman's report to the annual general meetings of the company in London. Arthur Onslow's death levelled a grievous threat at this tradition. The 2nd Earl of Iveagh was now almost 72. His surviving brother, Ernest, was vice-chairman of the brewery but of late had taken little part in its administration, was living most of the time on his Glenmaroon estate and was in less robust health than his elder brother.

There had been only three other male Guinnesses of the 'Lee' line in the 2nd Iveagh's generation: Sir Algernon Arthur, Kenelm Edward Lee and Nigel Digby Lee, all of them the sons of the 1st Iveagh's soldier brother, Captain (Benjamin) Lee. None of them was actively involved in the brewery, and Edward Cecil's doubts as to Algernon's business perspicacity had long since been justified. Algernon had known that on coming of age, he would inherit a life interest in Irish properties willed by his father, yielding an income of £3,700 a year, the rough equivalent in spending power today of £80,000. But he could not wait to get his hands on it and he went to moneylenders, borrowing on the strength of his forthcoming legacy. In part, this was to finance his passion for motor racing.[1] In other part, it was to live the good life, at a rate of expenditure greatly in excess of the income that would shortly come his way. At the age of 27 his personal extravagance, compounded by extraordinary naïvety in business affairs, landed him in the bankruptcy court, with, as *The Times* of 30 June 1911 reported, gross liabilities of £185,462 against assets of £28,565.

The public examinations by the Official Receiver bracketed a period during which Algernon's cousin, Rupert Edward, was awarded a CB in George V's Coronation Honours List. It must have been intensely embarrassing to him to have the rather seedy details of his nephew's financial affairs prominently reported in the press at this time but he obviously felt under no compulsion to bail Algernon out, though he could have done so with a few strokes of his pen before the Official Receiver was ever brought in.

It came out that Algernon had mortgaged his Irish properties for £44,000 but was still in need of £65,000 when he met a certain Captain de Courcy Bower who put up a 'scheme' for borrowing £150,000 from an insurance company. In the event the scheme collapsed, after Algernon had paid out commissions of £16,000 by going again to the moneylenders. At the public examination on 29 June 1911, the Official Receiver put it to him: 'Your difficulties were caused by extravagance and you tried to get money in any way you could, eventually in a very foolish way.' 'As it turned out,' Algernon wryly acknowledged.

Later, the Receiver proposed another, and presumably more soberly conceived, scheme for calming the creditors. It included the sale of Algernon's estates, but the full details were not disclosed in *The*

Times report of 25 June 1912. At the age of 45, Sir Algernon married
Winifred Mounteney. He served with the RAFVR in World War II
and died in 1954, leaving a daughter.

Algernon's youngest brother, Nigel, made little impact in any
direction and produced no male heir, but Kenelm, like his brother
Algernon, was one of the pioneers of motor-car racing. Together,
they had helped in the construction of the first great racing track at
Brooklands, and by 1924 Kenelm, too, had set up a world record for
land speed. His other claim to fame was as the inventor of an
improved sparking plug which he named after his own ini-
tials—KLG—and which his own company manufactured on a large
scale until 1927 when he sold out his interest to Smiths Accessories.
By then he had retired from racing, following a crash during the San
Sebastian Grand Prix in which his mechanic was killed and he
himself suffered head injuries that left him in a coma for several days.
He married a daughter of Sir Thomas Strangman in 1928 and over
the next few years seemed to be in full possession of his mental
faculties. Indeed, it was during this time that he invented the first
hydro-pulsator for the treatment of gums by water-jet massage. But
in later testimony, reported in *The Times* of 12 April 1937, his doctor
described how his patient had begun to suffer delusions of persecution, including the conviction that he was being hunted by gangs of
American blackmailers. His marriage was dissolved in 1936, with
custody of his two young children to his wife, and fifteen months later
Kenelm Lee gassed himself in the bedroom of his Kingston Hill
home. The coroner's verdict was 'suicide while of unsound mind'.

His son Kenelm Ernest Lee—'Kim' to his friends—inherited his
uncle Algernon's baronetcy. His daughter Geraldine ('Deena') married the Armenian Mikael Essayan, child of the marriage between
Calouste Gulbenkian's confidential secretary, Kvork Essayan, and
Calouste's only daughter, Rita.

At 81 Rupert Edward could look back on a lifetime of signal accomplishment, the highest reward for which had been bestowed upon
him, seven years earlier, when it was announced that Her Majesty
Queen Elizabeth II had invested him with the insignia of a Knight
Companion of the Most Noble Order of the Garter. He would be the
916th recipient of this honour—the oldest and most prestigious order
of knighthood in Great Britain—since its inception by Edward II in
1346, and it meant he could put up his shield in St George's Hall,
Windsor Castle, together with those of his fellow-recipients, the then
Prime Minister Sir Anthony Eden and the former Labour Premier,

Earl Attlee. At the installation ceremony in the Chapel of St George, he sat next to Sir Winston Churchill, his childhood protagonist, who had been the last knight installed in the order, two years previously. On this occasion there was no candlestick within reach and no provocation to resort to one; the two men were now bound in friendship.

Rupert's wife Gwendolen, the 75-year-old Countess of Iveagh, witnessed the solemn and colourful ceremony from her seat beside Princess Alexandra. She had been an active and supportive partner in her husband's campaigns for clean milk and scientific farming and was about to hand over to the National Trust the Onslow family seat of Clandon Park, together with a substantial endowment for its upkeep. She was the well-loved matriarch, by now, of three daughters and thirteen grandchildren and would live to celebrate her diamond wedding anniversary, three years before her death in 1966. Rupert died the following year at Pyrford Court.

He had so arranged his affairs that the bulk of his wealth was transferred to family trusts for the benefit of his successors well before 1962, after which date the whole of his personal estate would have been liable to death duties. The Canadian assets incorporated in the Montreal Trust remained intact. The property on Fifth Avenue, New York, had been sold, back in 1956, for a reputed figure of $17,000,000 and the proceeds re-invested by the American trust. To avoid the break-up of Elveden, Rupert had long since sold his life interest in the estate to the family trustees and had become a plain tenant farmer on the property. Similarly, the Burhill Estate in Surrey and the 15,000 acres of property in Bedfordshire, Hampshire, Suffolk and Hertfordshire had been incorporated in two estate companies, the shares in which were transferred to his children more than five years before Iveagh's death. Family trusts set up by Iveagh's father and grandfather already controlled the greater part of the family's holding in the brewery and its empire of subsidiaries and his personal holding was transferred to his grandson and to his daughters before it could be trapped for estate duty.

All that was left for the taxmasters were his Pyrford estate and investments in Ireland with a value of around £295,000. In total, these amounted to £543,880 from which Britain and Ireland shared death duties of £178,113. During his lifetime the 2nd Earl of Iveagh had been unstinting of his wealth so far as the financing of agricultural research was concerned, but he had been under no compulsion—as his father had been—to donate vast sums to public benefactions. There were no charitable bequests in his will. The balance of his personal estate, after taxation, went–apart from a few small legacies–to his three daughters.

With his death and that of his brother, Lord Moyne, an era in which descendants of the First Arthur embellished the name of Guinness through public service, as distinct from spectacular hand-outs, came to an end.

2

Between the years 1904 and 1920, seven daughters were born of the marriages of the 1st Earl of Iveagh's three sons. All seven would inherit great wealth. Between them, they would marry into five different titled families, produce nineteen children and make a corporate impact on the social scene in many ways more charismatic than that of their contemporaries 'the Mitford girls', the six daughters of Lord Redesdale.

As if from an aversion to one-upmanship, the wives of Rupert and Ernest had presented their husbands with an equal number of daughters–three each. The seventh Guinness girl was the only daughter of Walter Edward, the 1st Lord Moyne. In terms of inheritable wealth there was little to choose between the Rupert threesome and Ernest's, since the bulk of Iveagh's fortune (far greater than his brother's) had been entrusted, according to family traditions, to the male line via his son and grandson. But in other respects the two sets of siblings were made of differing stuff. All three of Rupert's daughters–Honor, Patricia, and Brigid–became entitled to the prefix 'Lady' from 1927 when their father inherited the Iveagh earldom. Honor was then eighteen years old, Patricia nine and Brigid seven. They had been born in England, brought up on their father's English estates and regarded Ireland as their second home. By contrast, Aileen, Maureen and Oonagh, the three daughters of Ernest, most 'Irish' of the three brothers, spent the greater part of their childhood on his Irish estate, Glenmaroon, until the end of the 1914–18 war when their father took up residence at No. 17 Grosvenor Place, and on his Surrey country estate, Holmbury House.[2]

There were other factors making for a distinction in temperament between the two sets of Guinness daughters. Physically, Ernest's were a good deal prettier than their more stockily built cousins, and in their early years they must certainly have got more fun out of life. Their father had been trained in every department of the brewery and would remain its vice-chairman until his death, but he did not have the heavy responsibilities devolving upon his brother, the 2nd Earl, as head of the family, nor did he share his younger brother Walter's involvement in matters of state. The air, the sea, and everything to do with the carriage of people across those two elements were a lifelong passion and he brought to this pastime a professionalism and inventive flair at least comparable to his elder brother's work in the field of agriculture.

A first-class yachtsman and member of the Royal Yacht Squadron, Cowes, he bought *Fantom II* from the Duke of Westminster after World War I and made her one of the most famous of private ocean-going vessels. Formerly a French trading ship, the 600-ton four-masted schooner was fitted with twin-screw motors, each of 320 bhp giving a speed of around ten knots. And in 1923, when his three daughters were still in their teens, he set sail with them for a 40,000-mile cruise around the world that would take them across the Atlantic and thence through the Panama Canal, to Fiji, the Far East and back through the Suez Canal—a journey of eleven months.

In his fifties he became one of the oldest aviators of his time to qualify for a pilot's licence and he bought a three-engined biplane flying boat for ferrying his family and friends between Southampton and Ashford Castle, co. Galway, and for cruises over the great Irish lakes. Not content with that, he supervised in 1930 the design and construction, at the Supermarine Works of Vickers, of a three-engined duralumin-hulled monoplane with a wing span of 92 feet and a top speed of 120 mph. The seaplane had open cockpits aloft and accommodation below for six passengers, comprising a luxuriously furnished saloon, several cabins and an electric lighting and ventilation system that earned it, in those days, the description of 'an air yacht'.

He was the most romantic and imaginative of the three brothers and his taste for drama had somewhat embarrassing consequences on one occasion, when he was serving as an infantry officer in France during the 1914–18 war. He had spotted a young man, heavily-bemedalled, in the uniform of a British officer, riding on a bicycle through the lines. Reasoning, with logic, that no young officer could possibly have acquired so many decorations, Ernest came to the conclusion that the cyclist was a German spy, and he promptly triggered an alarm. The 'spy' turned out to be the young Prince of Wales (later the Duke of Windsor), who from then on had to do without his bicycle.

All the Guinness girls, as they grew to womanhood, were endowed with the charm compacted of expensive schooling and their Irish blood; in Rupert's girls the quality might be described as 'gracious'; in Ernest's a more apt adjective would be 'elfin'. Be that as it may, by the early thirties they had all been launched into London society with a series of 'coming-out' balls to which every eligible bachelor in town sought an invitation. Especially in those days, it would never have occurred to daughters of the landed gentry to seek training in a profession. 'Coming out' had as its prime object the introduction of the girls to a leisured society that would sooner or later provide them with 'suitable' husbands. Meanwhile they were encouraged to take up some form of part-time charitable work, and Maureen, especially, threw herself into this with energy and enthusiasm. The pattern for her work, later in life, on behalf of the sick and needy was set in the late twenties when the petite, flaxen-haired Guinness girl, accompanied by her best friend 'Baby' Jungman, the daughter of 'Gloomy' Beatrice, ferried hot meals three times a week from the soup kitchens of London to bedridden invalids in the slums of Paddington.

Her eldest sister, Aileen, was the first of the daughters of Ernest and Rupert to go to the altar. Following the example of so many earlier Guinnesses she married her cousin, the Hon. Brinsley Sheridan Plunket. The barony had passed to Brinsley's eldest brother, Terence. With the title had gone the Plunket estate, Bray, in co. Wicklow, so Ernest bought the young couple an estate and castle of their own. He chose Luttrellstown, a magnificent Gothic castle adjoining the Iveagh family seat of Farmleigh, surmounted by battlements and turrets and featuring on its parkland an ornamental lake from the centre of which rises a gleaming Doric temple. Aileen divorced Brinsley Plunket in 1940 and he was killed a year later in combat as a flight-lieutenant in the RAF.

Maureen likewise chose a husband from the ranks of the Anglo-Irish aristocracy. This was the handsome, 21-year-old (Basil) Sheridan Hamilton-Temple-Blackwood, who had already won distinction as a history and languages scholar at Eton and Oxford and was heir to the 3rd Marquess of Dufferin and Ava, Speaker of the Senate of Northern Ireland. Sheridan was a cousin to both Brinsley Plunket and Maureen.

The name of Sheridan arose from the fact that Brinsley's maternal, and Ava's paternal, great-grandmother, Helen Selena, was a granddaughter of the Dublin-born playwright, Richard Brinsley Sheridan, author of *The School for Scandal*. Indeed, scandal of a quality that would have delighted the famous playwright had attached itself to Helen Selena, a lady much admired by Benjamin Disraeli, who was rumoured to be the father of her son Frederick Temple, the 1st Marquess of Dufferin and Ava. (This was the distinguished 19th-century diplomat who, as Viceroy of India in 1884–8, presided over the annexation of Burma and, on being raised to a marquess, took the Ava of his title from the ancient capital of the kings of Burma.) The Disraeli story seems to have been founded on little more than the olive complexion and rich speaking voice common to the Jewish statesman and Helen Selena's son.[3] It is discounted by Harold Nicolson, in his intimate portrait of his aunt–*Helen's Tower*.[4]

The love match between Maureen and Sheridan was as brilliant and genuine as it was ill-fated. His father–also named Frederick–died in a plane accident while the couple were still on their honeymoon. From then until the outbreak of World War II, the brilliant young marquess and his immensely popular marchioness played host to the social and intellectual élite of Britain and Ireland in their London home or at Clandeboye in co. Down, the beautiful 3,000-acre ancestral estate of the Temple-Blackwood family.

At the start of World War II, Dufferin and Ava was only 30 and had been Under-Secretary of State for the colonies since 1937. What was not general knowledge was the fact that, in common with his illustrious ancestor, the playwright, the Marquess was a heavy drinker, at least to an extent that was causing unhappiness between himself and Maureen. Anglo-Irish and a romantic *au fond* as he was, he saw the war not only as a summons to personal sacrifice but as an opportunity to 'prove himself' to Maureen and his children.

The Japanese invasion of Burma fired his resolve. This was a country linked by history and legend to his family and the title he bore. There was a mission–a dangerous one–for which he felt himself uniquely qualified, and after he had persuaded the War Office to give him the go-ahead he telephoned Maureen–then working in the Belfast naval canteen–and begged her to meet him in London. There, after pledging her to secrecy, he told her of his intention. Together with a Japanese-American, enlisted in San Francisco, he was going into the war zone of the Burmese jungles on an operation aimed at demoralizing the advancing Japanese troops. Keeping constantly on the move and using powerful loudspeaking equipment, they would broadcast in the Japanese language a 'personal message' from the Emperor of Japan urging his troops to leave Burma immediately and return to their Fatherland, where they were badly needed to protect their wives and children.

It was a lonely and perilous mission the young Marquess had

taken on and he made no bones about it. If he returned from it, it would be with 'two DSOs'. If he failed he would at least have given Maureen and his children something to be proud of. He also told her of his wish to spend time, between operations, studying some special-ized subject—he left the choice to her—in which he could return as an authority. Later, after pondering the matter, Maureen arranged to have the volumes of Gibbon's *Decline and Fall of the Roman Empire* sent to her husband through Service channels.

She would never know if he received them. He was ambushed and killed by the Japanese in March 1945 in an area not far from the ancient Kingdom of Ava.

Oonagh, at 19, had married an Englishman, the Hon. Philip Kin-dersley, youngest son of Britain's wartime National Savings chief, Lord Kindersley. A keen horseman and golfer, the tall, dark-haired Philip was also actively involved with his family's interests in the City of London. A son, Gay, and a daughter, Tessa, were born in the first two years of the union but the marriage ended with Philip's falling in love with a young divorcée, Valerie French, whom he married immediately after his divorce from Oonagh in 1936.

That same year, Oonagh married Dominick Browne, the 4th Baron Oranmore and Browne and on the outbreak of World War II she took the Kindersley children to stay with her at Castle McGar-ret, the co. Mayo seat of the Browne family. The children had been made wards of the English Court of Chancery, and Gay had been put down for Eton, but Oonagh wanted to keep him at school in Ireland until the war ended. Kindersley, a captain in the Coldstream Guards, had been wounded and taken prisoner by Rommel's North African army and while in prison in Germany he learned of his ex-wife's intentions for Gay and that she had already made Irish citizens of his two children. There followed a bitter seven-month legal battle, fought by opposing lawyers in the British and Irish courts, before the boy was given to the care of his grandparents, Lord and Lady Kindersley, and put into Eton.

Lady Honor, the eldest of Rupert's daughters, was the fourth of the Guinness girls to get married. She chose a minor American novelist, Henry Channon, who later 'inherited' the House of Com-mons seat held by the Iveaghs. Their wedding was one of the most glittering social events of the season and the list of presents, ranging from the Duke of Marlborough's pig-skin vanity case to Evelyn Waugh's gift of a book, took up half a column of small type in *The Times* of 13 July 1933. But the marriage was a social rather than

spiritual union and ended with divorce in 1945. In that same year
Rupert's youngest daughter, Lady Brigid, married Prince Frederick
of Prussia, a grandson of the former Kaiser.

Only one of these first marriages by the six daughters of Rupert
and Ernest has survived to the present day. This was the union in
1938 between Lady Patricia and the Conservative MP, Alan
Lennox-Boyd (subsequently elevated—if such a term can be applied
to a six-foot-seven lowland Scot—to Lord Boyd of Merton). The
seventh of the 1st Earl of Iveagh's granddaughters, the Hon. Grania
Guinness, delayed marrying until she was 30 when she became the
wife of the 4th Marquess of Normanby, descendant of a Viceroy of
Ireland, seven years after the assassination of her father, Lord
Moyne. By 1965 she had presented her husband with seven children,
the last of whom was born in her 45th year. In this century only her
brother, the 2nd Lord Moyne, has exceeded this Guinness record of
fecundity, with two children by his first wife and nine by his second.

Certain facile, but nonetheless persuasive interpretations can be
put on the fact that five of the Guinness girls accumulated between
them twelve husbands. All of them were born rich and would remain
secure for the rest of their lives from any of the financial hardships
that so often follow in the wake of broken marriages. They had Irish
blood in them—not the most stabilizing of elements—but as Protestants were free of the Catholic Church's ruling against divorce. And
as they reached womanhood, they entered a world that had out-
grown the stigmas and codes of the Victorian society into which their
parents had been born. More, it was a world—especially their
privileged niches of it—in which wealth and status were a passport to
self-indulgence and where temptation in the form of seductive and
'amusing' fortune-hunters was ever-present. There was never any
lack of the latter, for the word was already out that, in his will,
Edward Cecil had stipulated that the trustees could settle up to
£5,000 a year on each of his granddaughters' husbands for so long as
they remained married.

Some or all of these factors would have had an incidental bearing
on the matrimonial sagas of the five 'marrying' Guinness girls. And
as they progressed from one partner to the next the very diversity of
their chosen mates, the colourful spectrum of backgrounds involved,
suggests—with the possible exception of Maureen—a growing disen-
chantment with, and a need to escape from, the milieu that was
theirs by birthright. But the process was gradual, the contributing
circumstances varying from girl to girl. If there had been one constant, from the first dissolution of marriage in 1935 and throughout

the seven further divorce actions to date, it has been the shield of Guinness unity that could always be counted upon to absorb the shocks of unsuitable—and in one case disastrous—liaisons effected over the years.

Lady Patricia, with her 43 years of marriage to one husband, and her thrice-divorced cousin Oonagh represent the two extremes of the spectrum. And it is possibly relevant that whereas Patricia chose a husband 14 years older than herself, her cousin Oonagh married a man only two years her senior. Certainly there was a built-in affinity, from the start, between the politically orientated daughter of Lady Gwendolen, and Alan, the Member of Parliament for mid-Bedfordshire, a seat he had already held for seven years at the time of the marriage in 1938. Under Neville Chamberlain's premiership he had recently been made Parliamentary Secretary to the Ministry of Labour and his capacity for hard work, coupled with an engaging personality, would surely bring him higher political rewards—once he had learnt that discretion in public utterances ought to be the better part of right-wing Tory valour. His admiration of Generalissimo Franco had already made him the *bête noire* of the Left, a label he bore with almost exhibitionistic glee.

Born of a modestly wealthy family of minor Scots lairds, he won a scholarship from Sherborne School to Christ Church, Oxford, where he served a term as President of the Union while reading law. But he had not yet been called to the Bar when he met and married Patricia and was living on his MP's salary, supplemented by a relatively small private income. His union with Guinness wealth now permitted him a splendid residence in Chapel Street, Belgravia (formerly Duff Cooper's), where he and his wife could entertain in style. To this would be added a 53-ton yacht and, on his being made a viscount in 1960, the imposing Ince Castle at Saltash, in Cornwall.

Lennox-Boyd's formidable energies found their outlet in public service and in 1954 he won the appointment on which he had always set his heart when Winston Churchill made him Secretary of State for the Colonies. Under the previous Labour Government, Britain's colonies had been set on the path to self-rule and it seemed almost provocative of Churchill to have chosen, as the imperial nanny to these 'babies', a right-winger whom Michael Foot had described as 'a real Tory, without prefix, suffix, qualification or mitigation'. It was a misjudgement by his critics. With Patricia, Lennox-Boyd had travelled widely throughout the Empire, was totally devoid of colour prejudice, and with his special capacity for enjoyment and hearty laughter would endear himself to the simple folk of such colonies as Kenya, where his towering height won him the affectionate nickname of 'Bwana Kilimanjaro'.

Patricia's husband turned out to be at least as good a Colonial Secretary as any other choice during those years of post-colonial turbulence would have been, and he earned the viscountcy bestowed upon him after his resignation from the Government in 1959 to join the board of Arthur Guinness Son & Co. as an executive director. Before the death in 1967 of his father-in-law, the 2nd Earl of Iveagh, he and Patricia would represent a block of Guinness shares, personally held or in family trust, exceeded only by those of Iveagh's male heir and his first cousin Maureen. And from 1967 until his retirement from the board in 1979, Viscount Boyd of Merton (the title comes from his ancestral home in Scotland) shared the vice-chairmanship of the brewery with Bryan Walter, the 2nd Lord Moyne, who retired the same year.

Patricia had given birth to three sons between 1939 and 1943. The eldest of them, Simon, who had been working for one of the brewery's subsidiary trading companies, now followed his father on to the board of directors in keeping with the long-established tradition of 'packing' the board with Guinness heirs and heiresses who, in any case, controlled about 25 per cent of the shares. The Guinnesses had always shown more tenacity in their grip on the boardroom seats than was the case with other founding families of comparably great public companies. Thus, while the Marks and Sieff families had just seven members on the 26-strong board of the Marks & Spencer chain in 1979 (and this after only three-quarters of a century of trading), the reshuffle of directors in 1979, 217 years after the brewery's foundation, left no fewer than nine of the Guinness family on the 22-strong board, headed by the 39-year-old 3rd Earl of Iveagh as chairman.

Only three of Rupert's and Ernest's six daughters supplied male offspring to the board of Arthur Guinness Son & Co. Paul, the only son of Lady Honor and 'Chips' Channon, had become a director in 1961 and Maureen's only son, Sheridan, was co-opted upon Paul's resignation in 1979. Lady Brigid's three sons were not yet of age and Aileen had produced only daughters. This left Oonagh, who had one son, now 49, by her first husband Kindersley and two by Oranmore and Browne. That none of these had been invited to join the board was hardly surprising, given the background in which they had been reared.

We have already noted how, on the outbreak of World War II,

Oonagh retreated to Ireland with the Kindersley children, Gay and Tessa, and settled in Castle McGarrett for the duration, together with her new-born, Garech (by Oranmore and Browne). All her childbirths had been by Caesarian section, but her fondness for children amounted almost to an addiction and it took no persuasion for her to add to her wartime 'brood' Aileen's two little daughters, Neelia ('Aileen', spelt backwards) and Doon. And by the end of the war she would give birth to another son, Tara. The problem with Oonagh was that, by temperament, she was too much of a child herself to fit the role of a conventional mother. Marginally the prettiest of the three sisters, her fun-loving, prankish disposition, uncurbed by the birth of her first two children, gave her the reputation of 'London's oldest teenager' well into her late twenties. Friends and lovers put her emotional age at that time in an even lower bracket. It was said, unkindly, that she chose Lord Oranmore and Browne for her second husband so as to enjoy the title of 'Lady' already attached to her three cousins, as well as her sister Maureen. Such a motive was hardly in her character, but even if it had been the question arises, 'Why Oranmore and Browne?' when this beautiful and wealthy 26-year-old had the pick of the unmarried nobility?

The short, stockily built Dominick Geoffrey Edward Browne was recently divorced from his first wife, Mildred Egerton, when he married Oonagh. He was not, by Guinness standards, a man of wealth, and his preference was for Irish country life rather than the sophistications of Mayfair and the London 'season'. His guests for dinner at Castle McGarrett—not really a castle, and the least impressive of the Guinness girls' residences—all too seldom matched his wife's concept of 'fun people'. There was a preponderance of Irish lawyers and politicians and it was not unusual for anything up to two hours to elapse before the gentlemen—well ported—joined the ladies in the drawing-room.

By the summer of 1946 Oonagh's second son by Dominick—Tara—was still a baby-in-arms but Garech, born in 1939, was of an age to romp and giggle with his gamesome mother. It was going to be even more fun when her two children by Kindersley, the 16-year-old Gay and the 14-year-old Tessa, arrived from their schools in England to spend part of their holiday at Castle McGarrett. Tessa, like her brother, was an exceptionally good show jumper, with several juvenile equestrian championships already in the bag, and she would be competing in the Royal Dublin Society show shortly after her arrival. In the meantime, she was due for an injection against diphtheria, which the local physician, Dr C. B. Heneghan, would administer.

The injection was given on 2 August after the family had been happily united over dinner. Two and a half hours later, Tessa was dead. At the inquest Dr Heneghan stated that, about fifteen minutes after the diphtheria injection, Tessa went to her mother's room and said she had an attack of asthma. He gave her adrenalin but she showed signs of cardiac failure. He then gave her heart stimulants but she went into a coma. As reported by the *Daily Telegraph* of 6 August 1946: 'The girl's reaction to the injection was rare and unusual but could occur with anybody. The condition of her heart was not good.'

The loss, in such circumstances, of her only daughter had a shattering emotional effect on Oonagh. She had the child's body taken from Castle McGarrett and buried by the lakeside at Luggala, her estate deep in the Wicklow mountains south of Dublin. Over the grave she erected a shrine in the form of a delicate white obelisk that can be seen from the lake-facing windows of the Gothic house, set in a valley dominated by towering black granite cliffs. And there was another, and even more poignant, manifestation of her grief. Several friends of hers, including the actress Hermione Baddeley, noted that for a while after the death of Tessa the 36-year-old Oonagh would sometimes appear dressed 'uncannily like Tessa' as if to assert, in her own person, the survival of her daughter. Over the next three years she and her second husband became increasingly estranged and the marriage ended in the divorce courts in 1950. Dominick went on to marry the glamorous British film actress, Sally Gray, but eight more years would elapse before Oonagh took a third husband.

She and her children were already beneficiaries of the multi-million-pound trusts set up by the 1st Earl of Iveagh, and her father, Ernest Guinness, had settled almost £1,000,000 on each of his three daughters, out of his personal estate, before his death in 1949. Thrift—as virtue or vice—was foreign to Oonagh's make-up and her son Tara would later confide to a friend that his mother's overdraft had peaked at somewhere around £650,000 during the 14 years of her second marriage. All of this, and more, was of course secured by income from the family trusts and, since there was no need for Oonagh herself to provide trust funds for her own children, she was now free to indulge her own whims and preferences as a glamorous divorcée and hostess. In particular she could *in principle* choose her own house guests, with a bias towards the younger generation of 'fun people', writers and assorted cosmopolitan eccentrics.

The qualification concerns her butler, the self-willed and rather 'choosy' Michael, who would often take it upon himself to invite people from his own preferred list of guests, with or without consulting his ever-tolerant mistress. It was one of Michael's proud duties to circulate among the house-guests, before lunch, with a silver tray bearing beakers of foaming Guinness. There was of course no obligation to partake of the dark brew but a certain softening of the butler's regard would reward those who did so and would count in their favour when he drew up his next personal list of invitees.

Oonagh's playgrounds were London, Dublin, New York, Paris, Venice and the Côte d'Azur but there would always be house parties at Luggala for Christmas and by all accounts these were as boisterous as a well-stocked cellar and a spirited *châtelaine* could make them.

The regular presence of the hard-drinking Brendan Behan was a mixed blessing for the rest of the guests, however easy-going their natures. But he lent himself to one incident that redounded to the credit of a person not otherwise held in esteem by Oonagh's kinfolk. An American journalist, assigned to write a descriptive account of the Irish writer's Christmas tomfooleries, was a witness to 'the one story I couldn't print at the time.' Behan, well in his cups, had been caught manifesting unwonted affection for Oonagh's good-looking young son, Tara Browne. Invited by one of the guests to step outside onto the front terrace, the writer was laid out with a punch to the jaw and then solicitously covered with a blanket. The discipline had been meted out by the least likely of Luggala's guests–a New York dress designer named Miguel Ferreras.

This was the man who had skilfully courted Oonagh during one of her visits to America and whom she would secretly marry in New York in 1958. A Cuban, much ornamented with gold rings, bracelets and pendants, Ferreras became Oonagh's third husband when she was 47 and he still in his thirties. It was a marriage that dismayed those of the Guinness clan closest to Oonagh, not least her uncle, the Earl of Iveagh. To cap everything, Ferreras was a devout Roman Catholic and this, had there been any prospect of issue from the marriage, would surely have caused Oonagh's grandparents to turn in their graves.

All too aware, from the start, that most of her friends and practically all her kinfolk were 'uncomfortable' in Ferreras's company, Oonagh bought a villa in Antibes and spent the greater part of the short-lived marriage there, or in Italy or in her commodious flat in Paris, at 52 rue de Université. Gay Kindersley was now well launched upon his extraordinary career as an amateur steeplechase jockey and was married to Margaret, daughter of the actor Hugh Wakefield. Tara was still at school and Garech, on the brink of inheriting Luggala, was making his first impact in Dublin and London as a young Casanova in search of cultural, as well as amorous, fulfilment. The difference in years between Garech and Tara on the one hand, and Gay on the other, added to the fact that most of his first cousins were female, had obliged the gregarious young Garech to seek companionship beyond the immediate family circle, especially since he had ceased to be an amusing playmate for his child-loving mother. His holidays during his teens had been divided between Castle McGarrett and whichever of her European residences his mother found herself in. But as often as not he was left to his own devices. One of Oonagh's friends recalls finding the 12-year-old boy alone in the Paris flat with just the French house-keeper for company. The only instructions she had had from Oonagh were to make sure Garech had cornflakes for breakfast. '*Pas une vie pour un jeune homme,*' she muttered to the visitor.

Life with the socially ambitious Ferreras soon lost its enchant-ment for Oonagh, who was equally at home with the British aristoc-racy and the Dublin roustabouts. She thrived on the iconoclastic banter of such Dubliners as the painter Sean O'Sullivan who on one occasion in the bar of the Shelbourne Hotel expressed, after staring intently at the lithe figure of the Guinness heiress, a wish to paint her. To Oonagh's query, 'Why?' he retorted, 'Because you have an arse on you like an orang-utan.'

The marriage to the dress designer was dissolved in 1965 and Oonagh reassumed the title of Lady Oranmore and Browne. She had meanwhile adopted two Mexican boys and her hopes—if indeed she entertained any—of seeing a son of hers on the board of the family brewery rested on Tara. Gay was totally absorbed in horses, and Garech was not particularly partial even to the taste of Guinness. But Tara, alas, was already proving to be closer in temperament to his mother than to his down-to-earth and rather sober-sided father. At 19 he had secretly married Noreen Macsherry, the 22-year-old daughter of an Irish farmer whom he had met in Chelsea while she was working as a clerk at the Bank of England. It was a genuine love match between Nicky—as she was known—and the handsome, fair-haired young man with the beautiful speaking voice who, at 25, would receive close to £1,000,000 from his mother's fortune. They set up home in a delightful Belgravia mews house, with garage space for Tara's beloved sports cars, and by the time of Oonagh's divorce from Ferreras, Nicky had given birth to two children, Dorian and Julian.

There are conflicting views as to the cause of the marriage's breakdown, but no dispute that in October 1966 Tara left his Belgravia home, purportedly to join the children at Luggala where they were spending a brief holiday with Oonagh, and that he, the children and their grandmother then went into hiding somewhere in Ireland. The children were made wards of court after a fruitless flight to Ireland by Nicky in search of them, and a battle for custody ensued between lawyers on both sides. Meanwhile, Tara left the children in the care of his mother and returned to London, living apart from Nicky. Later that year, the divorce proceedings in court were interrupted by Tara's counsel. His client would be making no further appearance in the case. He had crashed his sports car in Chelsea the night before and was dead of his injuries.

Custody of the children—with legal access to Nicky—was given to Oonagh who by now had more or less abandoned Britain and Ireland for her homes in France. She had bought a beautiful villa, 'La Jolie' on Cap d'Antibes, and was seldom without a houseful of her own and her relatives' children—entertained in the Irish manner, with gaiety and lavish generosity. Her entire domestic staff was Irish. Musicians were flown out from Dublin, and 'Dosha' Young, the wife of film director Terence Young who owned a nearby villa, recalls parties thrown by Oonagh when a mob of guests ('including half the Irish Cabinet') were led by the pipers and their hostess in prancing, singing 'crocodiles' throughout every room of the villa. 'She was a sparkling, wildly generous and totally lovable person who on one occasion, when I invited her to lunch, asked if she might bring "a few friends" and turned up with about fourteen.' 'La Jolie' was a treasure house for what must have been one of the world's greatest collections of Staffordshire china figurines. She lavished expensive presents and surprises on her own and her adopted children while at the same time never shirking her—to them—less agreeable duties as a mother. They in turn treated her with affectionate irreverence, almost as a chum. One of them, overhearing an adult discussion as to whether their mother preferred to be known by the Oranmore and Browne, rather than the Ferreras, surname, piped up: '*We* call her "Mrs Bloody!"'

As the children came of school age she put them into the exclusive Aiglon College in Switzerland and bought a spacious apartment in the Résidence Rosiez at Pully so as to be near them during term time. Today, at the age of 71, she is foster-mother and grandmother to four young males approaching manhood, all of whose upbringing she has overseen with unstinting maternal love. Her personal wealth now greatly reduced, she has chosen tax exile and found peace in her Bermuda villa, 'Whispering Palms', overlooking Bailey's Bay, and her visits to old friends in Europe become fewer and farther between. But the spark is still there and by all accounts the ironic wit is hardly diminished. At a recent dinner party, another septuagenarian woman guest, in nostalgic vein, was recalling how 'one used to feel so *uncomfortable* about a man who tried to sleep with one on one's first date'. Oonagh took a sip of wine, touched her napkin to her lips,

'I still do, darling,' she murmured.

13

A Miscellany of Husbands

1

Clandeboye in Northern Ireland, the ancient castle and estate of the great O'Neills, was stolen from them in the early 17th century by the Hamilton family of Scotland who had been given *carte blanche* by James I to pillage the properties of the rebellious Irish chieftains of co. Down. The theft was mourned by Sir Walter Scott, as from the lips of an O'Neill:

> Ah Clandeboye! thy friendly floor
> Slieve-Donard's oak shall light no more...
> The mantling brambles hide thy hearth,
> Centre of hospitable mirth,
> All undistinguish'd in the glade,
> My sires' grand home is prostrate laid...
> And now the stranger's sons enjoy
> The lovely woods of Clandeboye.

Nearly two centuries later, Frederick Hamilton-Temple-Blackwood, the 1st Marquess of Dufferin and Ava, sold off most of his ancestors' ill-gotten estates for £370,000, retaining only the Clandeboye mansion and its vast acreage, upon which he excavated a series of great lakes, laid out undulating parklands and woods, built a two-and-a-half-mile avenue connecting Clandeboye to the sea, and erected the famous Helen's Tower as a monument to the mother (granddaughter of R. B. Sheridan) whom he worshipped all his life with an Oedipal intensity.

Something of the magic of Clandeboye is captured in a passage from *Helen's Tower*[1] by its author, Harold Nicolson, whose father married the 1st Marquess's wife's sister, Mary Hamilton, and who spent much of his childhood on the estate.

From the roof bastion of Helen's Tower there is a sweep of sky around the battlements and the rush of the winds from Scotland. Below, tumble the green fields and white cottages of Ulster and at one's feet the woods and lakes of the Clandeboye demesne. To the north, across Belfast Lough, rise the hills of Antrim; to the south, shine the wide waters of Strangford and the line of the Mourne Mountains. While to the East, across the North Channel, opens the whole panorama of Scotland, from the Mull of Kintyre to the hills of Carrick and Ayr.

Today, Clandeboye is the property of the 43-year-old Sheridan, 5th Marquess of Dufferin and Ava, Maureen's son. The 4th Marquess, in his will, had left 'the demesne of Clandeboye' to Maureen until Sheridan reached the age of 21. But it was discovered, after his death in Burma, that he had heavily mortgaged his home to a Belfast lawyer as security for the settlement of his many gambling debts. A dispute then arose between Maureen and the lawyer (who, with Maureen and Bernard Norfolk, the Managing Trustee of the Iveagh fortunes at home and abroad, had been one of Dufferin's three trustees) as to the precise intention of her husband's use of the word 'demesne'. Apart from Clandeboye itself and the lake, parkland and woods within its walls, the Dufferin family owned immense lands and properties beyond the walls, including the town of Crawfordsburn, the seaside resort of Helen's Bay and one half of Killyleagh. It was Maureen's conviction that the least her husband intended by the use of the word 'demesne' were the lands within the boundaries of the estate. The trustees, on the other hand, maintained—and were supported by this in legal opinion—that the term embraced only Clandeboye House and the gravel pathway immediately surrounding the mansion. In effect this would have meant that while Maureen would be entitled to no rents or profits from the estate she would be personally responsible for the maintenance of the mansion, for the tied cottages on the estate and for the wages of most of the servant-tenants.

She therefore presented an ultimatum to the trustees. She would either abandon Clandeboye completely and buy herself a country home in England, or she would ask the court's permission to buy from the trustees the mansion and all the lands within the demesne. The courts consented to the second option; Maureen bought the estate for £192,000 and it was vested by the trustees in the Clandeboye Estate Company. At the same time it was stipulated by Maureen that her son—then only 12 years old—should be allowed, if he so wished, to buy the estate back at the age of 40. At the same age, Sheridan would inherit the large fortune from the Iveagh Trust made over to him by his mother. In the meanwhile, Maureen would take a lease from the Clandeboye Estate Company, thereby preserving Clandeboye as a home for Sheridan and his two sisters, Lady Caroline and Lady Perdita.

In the event, Sheridan came into possession at the age of 29 when, upon his marriage to his cousin Serena Belinda ('Lindy'), the only daughter of Loel Guinness by his marriage to Lady Isabel, Maureen made him a wedding present of Clandeboye together with a gift of £50,000. As she put it at the time, 'It was very sad leaving Clandeboye, but as my son has married such a charming wife I felt it would be better if they started to make their home there now.'

The sadness was shared by everyone who had enjoyed the fun-filled hospitality at Clandeboye during the era of Maureen's occupation, even by those who had been the victims of her predilection for practical jokes. One of these is the screenwriter and playwright Michael Pertwee, whose account to the present writer of a weekend spent at Clandeboye nicely evokes the style and techniques of the prank-loving hostess in her mischievous prime. The year was 1941. Michael was then a young lieutenant in the Intelligence Corps and had only recently met Maureen who, with her hospitable nature and faculty for taking an instant liking to certain people, had promptly invited him and his wife as house guests at the mansion. It was Michael's first encounter with the domestic life-style of the affluent landed gentry and, as he recalls, 'I was deeply impressed by the vastness of the house and absolutely terrified of the butler, who eyed new guests as if they were German invaders. I had arrived from Belfast in my army uniform and my "luggage" consisted of pyjamas, slippers, dressing-gown and sponge bag. These were taken off me on arrival and were nowhere to be seen when we mounted to our huge bedroom. After a fruitless search I summoned the butler and told him of my predicament.'

Raising one eyebrow, the butler informed him the 'luggage' was 'in your *dressing*-room, sir'. And there of course it was, in another area adjoining the bedroom, where the few items had been 'carefully distributed around what looked like half of Victoria Station'.

His initiation into the Maureen manner of keeping *ennui* at bay began when he descended for pre-dinner drinks, leaving his wife to complete her dressing. He joined Maureen and two other guests in the library, one a very pretty girl friend of his hostess, named Phoebe, the other an American officer who, like himself, had responded to a spontaneous invitation. Maureen, 'in brilliant deadpan style', introduced Michael as Phoebe's husband, adding that he and Phoebe were on their honeymoon and deeply in love. 'She also mentioned in passing that the American's date for the evening was a very nice spinster friend of hers who simply couldn't get herself a man. This of course was my wife, Betty, who on joining us was introduced, to her amazement, as "Mavis Wibley" or some such name.

'The fiction was maintained by Maureen, with superb disingenuousness, all evening. How sad it was that Phoebe and I, so newly married and so much in love, should so soon be torn apart by this horrible war! The sentiment really got to the American, who produced snapshots of his family back home and at one point actually shed a tear for Phoebe and myself. Or perhaps it was for my real-life wife, who had to sit with downcast eyes while Maureen discussed her unfortunate state of spinsterhood and the mystery of why she could not find a husband. By the time we retired for the night, the joke had gone so far, and so successfully, that there was no way we could tell the American the truth, and thus the deception had to continue for so long as he remained under the roof, to the considerable chagrin of my wife.

'The following morning I was made aware that the taste for practical jokes had been inherited by the children of the house when I was awakened to a jug of cold water, poured over my head by one of Maureen's small daughters.

'Later that weekend Maureen perpetrated another practical joke of a less cruel nature. She herself was a passably good tennis player but among the guests for the day was a young Inspector of the Royal Ulster Constabulary, Desmond Cramsie, who was a first-class player. Also about to turn up were two more American officers, who apparently fancied themselves as tennis players and were a little boring on the subject. It so happened that Cramsie was not only young and good-looking but also endowed with the fresh peaches-and-cream complexion of the fair sex. Under Maureen's direction, he was made-up and costumed like a girl, even to a magnificent pair of boobs, and when the Americans arrived he was introduced as Maureen's friend "Patricia".

'Maureen then proposed that she and "Patricia" should take the two Americans on, at tennis. They pooh-poohed the idea. Two girls could be no match for them; much better they should split up for a mixed doubles. Maureen refused. She and "Patricia" always played together and, anyway, who cared who won in a friendly game? Still protesting, the Americans were dragged onto the court where, for the first couple of games, Maureen and "Patricia" lost practically every point. Again, the Americans proposed splitting up. "Well, let's try one more game," Maureen sighed.

'I shall never forget the face of one of the Americans when Patricia's first serve whined past him. From then on it was slaughter—and the joke was carried through to the end, with no hint given that "Patricia" was anything else than a big-boobed girl with a cannonball service and a paralysing smash.'

To Maureen's imaginative gift for practical jokes was added a natural talent for voice and character impersonation, coupled with the ability to keep a straight face when others around her, in the know, were ready to burst. A friend, giving a dinner party for some pompous business tycoons and their wives, could be persuaded to allow Maureen to disguise herself as a homely Irish housemaid, charged with taking the guests' coats on arrival. Later, it would be her friend's turn to keep a straight face as she received one of her head-shaking guests in the library or the drawing-room. For Maureen would have drawn the guest aside as he arrived and in an authentic working-class Irish accent hissed at him:

'D'ye want to *go*, surr?'

To the perplexed retort, 'Go where?' she would hiss again, with conspiratorial impatience: 'To *go*, surr! Or d'ye want to be gettin' up from the table in there, in the middle of the meal loike, to *go*? Better you should go now, surr, than be havin' to go when you can't, y'know, *hold it in* any more. Here, let me show you where to *go*, surr. Ah, ye'll be so much the more *comfortable* for it!'

In her own home she kept an impressive collection of trick objects for allocation among her dinner guests, such as wine glasses with holes bored below the rims, forks that bent double under pressure, false cheese that was impossible to cut into. Where other hostesses might be fussing anxiously around the dining-room before the guests arrived, she would be calmly instructing the servants: 'Lord X gets the fork, his wife gets the wineglass and, let me see now…'

She had begun to captivate London society from the time of her coming-out ball, given by her father Ernest in his Grosvenor Place mansion. Illness prevented her mother Cloe from being present on that occasion or to chaperone her petite and attractive débutante daughter to the 1925–6 season of balls in the great town houses of the capital. It was a brilliant season for the Guinness family. Earlier, Benjamin Seymour had thrown a ball at Carlton House Terrace for his daughters Meraud and Tanis, attended by the Prince of Wales and Princess Helena Victoria; Prime Minister Stanley Baldwin had been the guest of honour at a dinner party given by Maureen's uncle,

Walter Edward, and in May of that year George V and his queen had been driven the few hundred yards separating Buckingham Palace from Walter's house to dine with the Guinnesses' rising political star.

Aileen had been 'launched' a year earlier by her ageing grandfather the Earl of Iveagh, with royalty among the guests, and was on the brink of romance with her future husband, the Hon. Brinsley Plunket. But at the outset Maureen, so recently arrived from Ireland, was not yet part of the 'London set' and, as she now puts it, 'I wasn't exactly a wallflower, but I did get to familiarize myself totally with the décor of the ladies' lavatories in all the stately houses of London.' In fact, over the next few years preceding her marriage to the young Earl of Ava, the fey young beauty with the heart-shaped face and wide blue eyes was probably the most photographed of all the Guinness heiresses and the most favoured by society hostesses for her sparkle and uninhibited sense of humour.

Most psychiatrists could advance theories as to why the personable and extroverted Maureen should have chosen, three years after the death of Ava, the likeable but unexciting Major Desmond Buchanan for her second husband. The fact of the matter was, she had fallen in love with the handsome Grenadier Guards officer, some years younger than she was, and was radiantly happy to be 'given away' by her ten-year-old son, the 5th Marquess, at the village church of Little Braxted, Essex, in September 1948. (Her 72-year-old father, Ernest, was ekeing out the last months of his life on his Irish estate.) It was a short-lived union, and a childless one. The Major was almost totally dependent on his wife so far as life-style and amusement were concerned and he raised no objection to her decision to continue to be addressed as the Marchioness of Dufferin and Ava, rather than Mrs Buchanan.

Upon Ernest Guinness's death, six months after Maureen's second marriage, she and her cousin Lady Patricia became the first women ever to sit on the board of the brewery. Patricia's husband, Alan Lennox-Boyd, was already installed there, but there was never any move to find a place for Buchanan at the directors' long table in the magnificent luncheon room at Park Royal, where a sherry-tasting ceremony always preceded the meal and a silver tankard holding half a pint of Guinness was by tradition set at every place.

In the best of gentlemanly traditions, Buchanan allowed himself to be divorced in 1954 for 'committing misconduct at a West End hotel with a woman whose name was not revealed in court'. Meanwhile, Maureen had fallen in love for the third time. The man in

question was the 54-year-old John Cyril Maude who had turned
from a distinguished career as a barrister to sit as a judge at the Old
Bailey. Again, it seemed a somewhat less than inspired choice of
husband by the still spirited and fun-seeking 'Guinness girl'. The son
of the celebrated actor Cyril Maude,[2] Judge Maude brought to the
marriage, and into Maureen's life, elements of prudence and of quiet
authority not conspicuous in either of her former husbands, but also
a certain prudery out of tune with her own nature. Despite this, they
are still husband and wife at the time of writing, though the marriage
ceased to be meaningful in a conjugal sense several years ago and
they live their own lives, apart. As the retired judge put it, when
asked why he had not been present at the lavish Savoy Hotel party to
celebrate Maureen's 70th birthday, 'I don't care much about social
life, you know. We're on quite good terms, but as you get older and if
your interests differ it's better not to be together the whole time'
(*Daily Express*, 21 April 1977). This eminently sensible, if somewhat
sad reflection is powerfully highlighted by the difference in life-styles
between wife and husband, after a quarter of a century of marriage.
For whereas Maureen divides her time between an imposing London town house, a cottage in Kent, a villa in Sardinia and a small
place in Jamaica, her husband's home for the past five years has been
a modest but comfortable apartment at Maytham Hall, a Lutyens
house now run as a retirement residence close to Maureen's country
place. Clearly, it is an arrangement that suits them both, freeing the
former judge from the gregariousness of life with Maureen and
leaving her the space and time to pursue her own interests, which are
divided between her still-heavy social responsibilities and the home
for arthritics she set up in 1967.

Of the three daughters of Ernest Guinness it is Maureen who has
most emulated her grandfather, the 1st Earl of Iveagh, in counter-
balancing the enjoyment of wealth with its employment for charitable purposes—and this with no beckoning titles as the reward. The
same Guinness girl who in her late teens had ferried hot meals to the
slums of Paddington started her work for arthritics in 1958 after she
had made numerous visits to the homes of the more elderly and
poorly-off victims of this ailment and was dismayed by their help-
lessness and the paucity of therapeutic facilities available. Over the
next seven years she raised £50,000 for the building of the Horder
Centre for Arthritics as well as donating 30 acres of land at Crow-
borough, Sussex, as the site for the centre. A disagreement over the
timing of the official opening, in which she was backed by twelve

other members of the fund-raising committee, caused her resignation from the centre shortly before the opening ceremony, conducted by her close friend Princess Margaret. As a consequence, the charity committee was deprived of its most effective chairman. ('For Lady Dufferin to resign,' said Sir Tom O'Brien, reported in the *Daily Mail* of 17 September 1966, 'is like taking the bottom out of a bucket.') Happily for the cause she was so wedded to, Maureen had both the money and the enthusiasm to organize a new facility on her Kent estate in the form of her own holiday home for arthritics, known as Maureen's Oast House, to which she still devotes much of her time and energies.

As a businesswoman, in the handling of her own inheritance, she has had to deal, not always smoothly, with the Iveagh trustees headed by Bernard Norfolk, in whom her grandfather vested great discretionary powers over the administration of his trust.

In 1963, Maureen and John Maude took a holiday in Venice, staying at the luxurious Hotel Cipriani, built five years earlier by her cousins, Patricia, Honor and Brigid, in partnership with Giuseppe Cipriani, the owner of Harry's Bar, at a cost of over a million dollars. Following the lead of the Aga Khan, Maureen had already bought some land on the northern coast of Sardinia, an island earmarked for rapid development as a summer resort for the European rich. The land included three picturesque little bays and she was still pondering where to build her villa when Cipriani offered to help her choose the site. On arrival in Sardinia, the proprietor of the hotel where they were staying told her about another piece of land, cheaper and far more beautiful than the piece she had bought at Porto Rafael. With Cipriani acting as interpreter, Maureen met the peasant proprietors of the land and a price of 300 lire a square metre was asked. It seemed to Maureen to be a fair enough price at the time and a good investment, provided the necessary funds could be released for the purpose from her Canadian company, Bangor Investments Ltd, which had been formed by Bernard Norfolk and over which he had complete trustee control.

After flying to Italy to inspect the property, Norfolk proposed the formation of two Italian companies, one to own the villa she would build, the other to own the land. He and Maureen would be directors, together with Cipriani and another Italian gentleman engaged in business.

At her next meeting with Cipriani, Maureen was told that, alas, some rich Belgians were now bidding for the land and if she wanted to clinch the deal she would have to pay the peasants 650 lire a square metre. She agreed to this. A year or so later, a shattered Bernard Norfolk informed Maureen's lawyers that the businessman, in an effort to hide a discrepancy in the books of the Hotel Cipriani, had helped himself to £6,000 out of Maureen's Italian companies' funds. It could have been worse. As the companies were constructed, the businessman—who went to prison for two years—could, on his signature alone, have cleaned out the funds provided by the Canadian company.

A final twist of the stiletto came about a year later when Maureen learnt, via her architect, that the peasant proprietors of her land had never in fact asked for a price higher than 300 lire a square metre, and that in any case the highest price being paid for comparable land by the Aga Khan or anyone else was no more than 80 lire a square metre.

She is unhappy today about the results of her investments. In 1930 she bought her large town house in Hans Crescent for £8,000 and furnished it with some beautiful antiques and paintings from her father's collection, which she paid for out of her own money. Twenty-five years later, the Managing Trustee of the Iveagh Trust made a proposal to her. Why not let the trustees buy up her house, furniture and paintings—as they were permitted to do under the terms of her grandfather's will—leaving her to continue enjoying these for the rest of her life. Delighted by the prospect of raising extra funds to meet the mounting expenses of running Maureen's Oast House for Arthritics, she sold out to the trustees, lock stock and barrel, for more or less the amount of her investment 25 years earlier. She received, for example, only £9,000 for her house in Hans Crescent, representing an appreciation over 25 years of this valuable property of a mere £1,000. It was suggested that she could do likewise with the smaller house and properties she had bought in Kent, in some cases specifically as investments against, as she put it, 'a rainy day'. What she had not appreciated was that any subsequent increase in value of any of these properties would, upon resale, go not to her but directly into the trust fund she had already set up for her children.

The extent of her generosity, over the years, in settlements upon her children out of her one-third share in her father's will was reflected in the 1980 accounts of the Iveagh Trust. These show that whereas each of her children received an income of £17,030, her own portion had shrunk to £1,638 for the year. So she is now living in a house that is far too big for her, from the sale of which she cannot profit, packed with valuables bought originally as sound investments, from which she can no longer reap any benefit. Fortunately, however, she enjoys a substantial income from other investments and properties outside the Iveagh Trust.

To meet the 73-year-old Maureen in person is to be magicked by the chemistry of the occasion back in time to the 1930s and 1940s when an invitation to her home in Hans Crescent was one of the most 'in' things that could happen to a débutante and her socially aspiring escort. A white-coated manservant answers the door and ushers you into a spacious hallway where you are greeted by Maureen's secretary, as impressive a functionary as one might encounter at the portals of a Whitehall minister's private office. You are led up the grand stairway to a first-floor library where, while awaiting the Marchioness, you have time to note the Reynolds and the Gainsborough, the framed photograph of the Queen with its inscription 'to Maureen' and the informal group shot of the Royal Family.

There is a shock, almost, of recognition when the slim and petite figure enters the room wearing an elegant black gown with gossamer tulle sleeves and brushing that errant forelock—so familiar to two generations of *Tatler* readers—from the left side of her small heart-shaped face with its heavily-lipsticked mouth. The once fair hair is now a beautifully coiffeured grey bob, but the eyes still dance with the prospect of amusement. Her femininity is absolute, from her attention to your glass ('Isn't it looking rather sad?') to her pleasure in tugging family photograph albums from their shelves and turning the pages for you.

Down in the spacious ground-floor drawing-room she chuckles as she tells you about the giant Boucher canvas depicting a tableau of naked goddesses and nubile nymphs. 'We dug it out of a cellar at Clandeboye and had it restored. Can you believe that some frightful prude of an Irish ancestor had covered up all those heavenly torsos with black paint!' You move on to the other pictures and she challenges you, with another toss of that lock, to guess what she was holding in her lap as she sat for her 1960 portrait by Annigoni ('the first blonde he had ever painted'). The object in question is rectangular but otherwise undefined by the artist. 'A book?' you hazard. Not so. 'It's a portable wireless, tuned in to "Mrs Dale's Diary". Well, my dear, if you sit in silence the painter starts thinking you're bored, which of course you are, and if you try chattering they complain you're moving your lips.'

By now, having come to accept that your interest in her is genuine, she invites you upstairs to her bedroom to view, through the miracle

of the A-V cassette, a TV interview with the Marchioness, conducted by the actor Derek Nimmo. The TV set is near the foot of the
white satin-covered bed upon which you are invited to perch while
she draws up a chair and manipulates the controls. She proves to be
superb material for this lighthearted interview, generating gusts of
laughter from the studio audience as she recalls the highlights and
lowlights of her first London season. She even resurrects, with
disingenuous coyness, the old story—which she hangs on one of her
girl friends—of the débutante aroused from sleep during a country-
house weekend by urgent rappings on the door and the voice of a
lecherous but unfavoured suitor, pleading entry.

'Go away!'

'Darling, if you knew what I was knocking with I'm sure you'd let
me right in!'

As you descend from the bedroom you pat your pockets, unsure of
your notebook's whereabouts. Her concern...then the roguish
smile. 'I do hope you've left nothing incriminating in my bedroom.'

And your unchecked response to this svelte and scented septuagenarian—'Alas, no'—is close indeed to being heartfelt.

All three of Ernest Guinness's daughters started by marrying the
sons of United Kingdom peers. All three subsequently took husbands from lower ranks in the social order and all three, today, are
husbandless, either *de jure* or *de facto*. Alone of the three, the first-born
Aileen has been unblessed by a son but has two daughters, Neelia
and Doon. (A third, Marcia, died aged three.) It is wry commentary
on the volatility of this line that whereas Doon's one and only husband
is the 5th Earl of Granville, Neelia, thrice married to husbands of
little distinction, now lives out her life in the unstylish, cosmopolitan
'white bourgeois ghetto' of Guadaranque, on Spain's Costa del Sol—
otherwise known by the late Kenneth Tynan's apposite term, 'the
Costa del Sots'. In 1961, at the age of 32, she declared her intention
to convert to Roman Catholicism, making her the second of the
brewery line—after Lady Honor (see below, p. 171)—to defect from
the staunchly Protestant family tradition.

Between Aileen's divorce from Brinsley Plunket in 1940 and her
second marriage, she devoted most of her time to the upbringing of
her young daughters and to entertaining her friends in Luttrellstown Castle, with its parklands ranging as far as the eye can see.
There was little she could do about the rather bogus exterior of the
castle but she engaged Felix Harbord, one of London's top interior
decorators, to turn the interior into a superb model of an 18th-

century mini-palace. The ballroom was brilliantly restructured, with the original Adam mouldings preserved and blended into graceful archways. Before dinner, her guests would assemble for drinks in the Grisaille Room created by Harbord and featuring plaster-work murals offering clever *trompe l'oeil* effects.

Unlike her sister Oonagh, whose house-guests often leaned towards the picaresque, Aileen favoured the more glamorous, or celebrated, members of the international set, personalities such as the Aga Khan, Prince and Princess Rainier, the Maharaja of Jaipur and film stars Ursula Andress and Jean-Paul Belmondo. Black tie was mandatory wear for dinner, formally served by her butler, Cran, and half a dozen liveried servants headed by the footman, Jerry, at a circular table that could be expanded to accommodate anything up to thirty guests.

There was nothing stuffy, however, about the hospitality at Luttrellstown. The author and drama critic, Milton Shulman, recalls that his hostess preferred light-hearted gossip and banter to high-brow conversation at the dinner table. Afterwards, guests were encouraged to let their hair down in Aileen's 'playroom', a discothèque created in the cellars of the castle. Aileen also shared her younger sister Maureen's partiality to practical jokes and the jolly japes practised on unwary guests might include a bowl of artificial vomit placed at their bedside or a realistic stuffed dummy 'asleep' between their sheets.

Aileen was now in her late forties and, apart from Oonagh who had just divorced Oranmore and Browne, she was the only one of the seven granddaughters of the 1st Earl of Iveagh without a husband. Her daughters were already grown up (one of them, Neelia, was now married to the first of her three husbands, Captain Basil de las Casas of the Irish Hussars). She was rich, still attractive and the owner of one of Ireland's most beautiful estates. The quest for diversion from her role as the merry and open-handed widow of Luttrellstown took her more and more to the United States and, early in 1956, in New York, she met and was captivated by an interior decorator, the dark-haired, slightly built Valerian Stux-Rybar, born in Yugoslavia of Austro-Hungarian parents. They were married later that year but divorced after seven years, after Aileen had invested a fair amount of time and money in the marriage. As one of the family friends put it to me: 'The 1st Lord Iveagh, friend and host to three British monarchs, structured the family trusts pretty tightly. If he had known his granddaughters would bring a Cuban dress designer and a Yugoslavian interior decorator into the family he'd have cut them off with a penny.' (A prejudice shared by innumerable Grandfathers about their grandchildren's marriages.)

Aileen's living standards were fractionally affected by the short-sightedness of her father who, despite family pressure, delayed making the settlements on his three daughters in time to avoid punishing death duties. The transfer of trust capital to his daughters during his lifetime had wisely been made from his British estate, with the aim of avoiding a 75 per cent death-duty rate, as against the Eire rate of 41.6 per cent. But his death in 1949 came within the retroactive number of years, short of which both nations could claim duty, and it led to a protracted battle between the respective revenue authorities. His estate in England, after the settlement on his daughters and their children, was proved at only £158,552 gross. The Eire estate came to £3,193,275 and the sum of £229,719, 'elsewhere', was brought in for tax purposes. But it was decided that the settlements on his daughters prior to his death should also be liable to death duties, payable from his estate. The result was a shortfall of £300,000 in the funds available for carrying out his bequests to the family, including his nephews, the 3rd Earl of Iveagh and the 2nd Lord Moyne. The issue was finally resolved in 1951 by a cut of one-sixth from all the legacies, including £200,000 willed to Oonagh's son, Gay Kindersley, who had to make do with an inheritance at 25 of around £167,000.

Today, by Guinness standards, Aileen is no longer a wealthy woman. She lives on in her beloved Luttrellstown but the discothèque she constructed no longer echoes to boisterous laughter and the popping of champagne corks. Sycophants are not corrected when they address her as the Hon. Mrs Aileen Plunket rather than Mrs Stux-Rybar. At the time of writing she was under pressure from the trustees of the Iveagh fortune to put the Luttrellstown estate on the market. With Clandeboye gone from Maureen and Luggala from Oonagh, this would–if, in fact, it happens–symbolize the end of the stately era of Ernest Guinness's three 'Golden Girls'. But decidedly not their social status. As this book was going to press Maureen was busy planning a private dinner party at Hans Crescent for twenty people, with the Queen Mother as her guest of honour.

2

It would be remarkable if any seven girls, descended from the same grandfather and grandmother, turned out to be alike in any way other than (perhaps) their looks and–at a stretch–their place in society. The nature of their own intervening parentage, together with early differing environmental factors, would alone work against any similarity in character and temperament, given the hypothesis that all seven were cousins linked by seven different sets of parents.

The principle needs to be modified in the case of the seven Guinness Girls with their common grandparents, the 1st Earl of Iveagh and his own cousin-wife, Adelaide. For between them they shared only three different sets of parents and, in essence, only two differing environments during the formative years. Aileen, Maureen and Oonagh, as we have seen, were the daughters of the 'most Irish' of Lord Iveagh's sons, Ernest Guinness, the intrepid yachtsman and aviator, and his wife Cloe, descendant of a famous Gunning beauty. Grania's father, the 1st Lord Moyne, had been a British statesman *par excellence*, married to the daughter of a 14th earl. Honor, Patricia and Brigid were the children of the 2nd Earl of Iveagh and his consummately political wife, Lady Gwendolen, and were the 'least Irish' in upbringing of all seven girls. It should follow–though not inevitably–that the two trios of sisters should be distinguishable, one set from the other, by certain affinities in nature and values, and such would certainly seem to be the truth emerging from any study of their life patterns.

We can start, perhaps superficially, with the fact that whereas Ernest Guinness's daughters chalked up between them a score of 8 husbands and 5 divorces, the comparable tally of their three cousins was 5 and 2. An equally illuminating contrast–the 90 years of formally married life put in to date by Aileen, Maureen and Oonagh, against the 128 years totalled by their cousins–takes on extra force from the fact that all of Ernest's daughters married their first husbands several years before Rupert's took their maiden (and, in Patricia's case, only) trip to the altar.

When Lady Honor died in 1976, she had been married to her second husband, Frantisek ('Frankie') Svejdar for 30 years. She had fallen in love with the RAF flight-lieutenant–who had fled Czechoslovakia after its annexation by Hitler–during the dying years of her marriage to 'Chips' Channon, and her happily married life with this unassuming and attentive husband was everything that her years with 'Chips' had not been.

She had married the Chicago-born Channon when she was 24 and he 36. Four years at Christ Church, Oxford, had opened for the American an entrée to British society and an obsession to become an 'English gentleman' that probably finds no parallel in the recorded aspirations of any other American male. As he himself noted, at the age of 30, 'I have put my whole life's work into my anglicization, in ignoring my early life.'[4] At that time he was working in London on his first and only published novel, *Joan Kennedy*, and living on an income of £800 a year, from a settlement of $90,000 made on him by his father, Henry Channon II. That same year (1927) he inherited a further $85,000 from the estate of his grandfather, Henry Channon I, who had founded the family's firm of ships' chandlers. He was able to note in his diary for 3 May that he now belonged 'definitely to the order of those that HAVE—and through no effort of my own, which is such a joy'. By 1935, two years after his marriage to the vastly more wealthy eldest daughter of the 2nd Earl of Iveagh, his joy at now being a super-HAVE expressed itself in terms of almost sickening smugness: 'It is very difficult to spend less than £200 a morning when one goes out shopping.'[5] At that time the purchasing power of £200 would be about the equal of today's £2,500.

With his marriage into the Iveagh line of the Guinness family, Channon was to realize everything that his snobbish and essentially bourgeois nature aspired to and his own limited intellectual powers would have denied him. King George of Greece and 'half of Debrett' turned out for the wedding in St Margaret's, Westminster, between the short-statured, brown-eyed, flat-footed American and his bride, whose passable looks were only slightly marred by the affliction of one 'wall' eye.

From their honeymoon, they set up home first at 21 St James's Place and then at 5 Belgrave Square, in a mansion bought and furnished with Guinness money and next door to the London home of the Duke and Duchess of Kent. It was a house that would become famous for the hospitality lavished on the famous until World War II and it was given a rather grudging accolade by Harold Nicolson in his diary entry for 19 February 1936.[6]

Oh my God, how rich and powerful Lord [used ironically] Channon has become…The house is all Regency upstairs with very carefully draped curtains and Madame Recamier sofas and wall-paintings. Then the dining-room is entered through an orange lobby and discloses itself suddenly as a copy of the blue room at the Amalienburg near Munich—baroque and rococo and what-ho and oh-no-no and all that. Very fine indeed.

It was a glittering showcase for Channon, whose ambitions encompassed a brilliant career in British politics and who had been handed the constituency of Southend on a plate, as it were, by his mother-in-law in 1935 (as described in Chapter 5). Alas for that gifted parliamentary lady and her politically-minded daughter (who had taken a course at the London School of Economics before her marriage), Channon's career in the House of Commons did scant justice to the impressive trappings provided for his assault on the Palace of Westminster. For one thing, the attraction to him of the House of Commons was that of an exclusive and privileged club rather than a legislative chamber. ('I like the male society. It reminds me of Oxford or perhaps of the private school to which I never went.'[7]) For another, he was not, in anything more than an opportunist sense, a 'political animal'. In his diary entry for 10 December 1935 he wrote: 'Most of the day at the House of Commons. Today for the first time I really like it...But I wish I sometimes *understood* what I was voting for, and what against.' And eleven months later (18 November 1936), after an all-night sitting in the House: 'How I scatter my forces! I should have been employed supping with all the royals, as in society I am a power, and here at the House of Commons I am a nonentity. At 7 a.m. I went home in my new Rolls...'[8]

During the whole of his 23 years as the sitting Member for Southend, Channon made only four speeches in the House, totalling 21 minutes, and asked only 18 parliamentary questions. He was, of course, occupying–*grâce aux* Guinnesses–one of the safest Conservative seats in the Commons and his hopes of political preferment rested less on his parliamentary performance than on his social links with the upper echelons of the ruling political party. These he sought diligently to forge while, at the same time, allowing himself to be sidetracked by dreams of (to him) even greater grandeur. In 1937, two years after the birth of his one child by Honor–christened Henry Paul–he persuaded her to buy the country mansion in Essex known as Kelvedon Hall. While they were awaiting acceptance of their offer he mused, for his diary, 'Will I now be a country squire?' And, on its acceptance five days later, 'So now I am a Squire of Essex and shall probably gravitate more and more towards a country life.'[9] It was the eve of the coronation in Westminster Abbey of George VI, to which he, as an MP, was invited with Honor. He records:

At 5.30 the Lord and Lady of Kelvedon woke, thrilled and eager to get to the Abbey, and as I dressed I thought, not only of the approaching ceremony but of Kelvedon: Shall I one day take its name? Lord Westover [his mother's maiden surname] of Kelvedon? Ten years in the Whips' Office might do it, I think...[10]

The last line of his entry for that day, following a rhapsodical description of the pomp and ceremony, reads: 'I must really try and be a Peer before the next Coronation.'[11]

But meanwhile the fascist dictators of Europe were on the march and the great debate as to Britain's options was dividing the ruling Tory Party between the appeasers and the pro-Churchill faction. Channon's own position, and that of Honor's, was what one would have expected of most members of their class. They had met Mussolini in person in July 1935 and were totally captivated by the Bullfrog of the Pontine Marshes. ('It gave me more of a thrill than my interview with the Pope.')[12] Channon was an ardent supporter of Generalissimo Franco and his Falangist insurgents and took the view that Adolf Hitler was the best thing that had happened for Germany and Europe. ('We should let gallant little Germany glut her fill of the Reds in the East and keep decadent France quiet while she does so. Otherwise we shall have not only Reds in the West but bombs in London, Kelvedon and Southend.')[13] Both he and Honor had cultivated the friendship of Hitler's ambassador to Britain, the nauseous ex-champagne-salesman Ribbentrop, and they accepted 'gleefully' an invitation to be Hitler's guests at the 1936 Olympic Games, against the disapproval of more politically fastidious friends such as the Duff Coopers, Harold Nicolson and Philip Sassoon. They were eager guests at the lavish parties thrown in Berlin by Goering and Goebbels and, once again, Channon measured his feelings at seeing Hitler in the flesh against the yardstick of his meeting with the Pope. ('I was more excited than when I met Mussolini...and more stimulated, I am sorry to say, than when I was blessed by the Pope in 1920.')[14]

More than ever, now, Channon saw himself as especially suited for a role in the Government of Neville Chamberlain in which he could exert his influence in favour of the 'stability' of a Europe dominated by a Tory Britain and the three fascist dictators. His chances of preferment were less than slim whilst Anthony Eden was at the Foreign Office, but his hopes began to soar when Eden resigned in 1938 in protest against Chamberlain's policy of appeasement and was replaced by R. A. ('Rab') Butler. Channon had first met Butler socially in 1935 when he was Under-Secretary for India and 'Chips' only a fledgling backbencher. Two days after Butler's appointment, the new Foreign Minister was chatting to a colleague, Harold Balfour, in the Members' Lobby when Channon stepped up, offered his hand, and declared that 'Europe is to be congratulated'.[15] Balfour told Channon, later, that he and Butler had discussed the eligibility of 'Chips' for the post of Parliamentary

Private Secretary to the Foreign Minister and the prospect of becoming a PPS—the lowliest rung on the ladder to the Front Bench—put Channon into a state of anguished euphoria. ('Will my star lead me there? It cannot happen.')[16] Four days later, Butler offered him this (unpaid) post of parliamentary messenger-boy. ('My heart throbbed, and I felt exhilarated, as I said he was voicing my life's dream.')[17]

It was said for Channon, in the undefended divorce action he brought against Honor in February 1945, that his wife had become 'indifferent' to him after the birth of their son, ten years earlier. Presumably, this applied only to their sexual relationship, for they continued to live together and to entertain the high and mighty at 5 Belgrave Square and at Kelvedon Hall until October 1940 when, shortly before Channon's departure overseas on a private visit to his friend Prince Paul, the Regent of Yugoslavia, Honor told him she was 'tired of married life' and wanted a divorce. The *Blitzkrieg* against England had already been launched by Hitler's *Luftwaffe* but little Paul Channon had been evacuated to the United States and when his father returned from the Balkan trip he found that Honor had moved out of their homes, leaving no forwarding address.

Their divorce was allowed on the grounds of Honor's desertion, but there was a sense in which she had in fact been deserted by Channon from the date of his appointment as PPS to 'Rab' Butler. Honor, with her roots in British politics, could not be expected to be wildly impressed by her husband's appointment, any more than she was by his parliamentary performance to date. He, on the other hand, saw it as 'a position of power, great power...' and 'beyond belief exciting'[18] and until Churchill, who held Channon in contempt, took over the wartime National Government, the Chicago-born PPS served his new gods, Neville Chamberlain and 'Rab' Butler, with a dedication that excluded almost all matrimonial intercourse with Honor, save in her role as hostess to the great ones of Whitehall and Fleet Street.

He was badly shaken by Honor's defection at the end of 1940. Everything he had acquired—his 'squireship' of Kelvedon, his mansion in Belgravia, his inexhaustible pocket-book, his job at the Foreign Office—he owed directly or indirectly to the Guinnesses. In 1937 he had been elected to the board of the brewery ('a great honour and a position of power and prestige')[19] where, with her, he represented one of the major holdings of shares in trust for the family. The last thing in the world he needed now was the loss of the Earl of Iveagh's eldest daughter, and the prospect dismayed and depressed him.

In the event, he emerged from the situation in better shape than he had a right to expect, thanks to the good-will of the Iveaghs, who liked him as a person, and the impatience of Honor to marry her Czech lover, Frankie Svejdar, six years her junior. Channon was given the custody of his son Paul, whom he adored. He kept Kelvedon and the Belgrave mansion, he was retained on the board of the brewery until 1953 and continued to live the life of an English gentleman he had coveted so passionately in his youth. The peerage he had dared to hope for on the dissolution of the wartime Government never came but he received a knighthood in the New Year Honours of 1957, less than two years before his death from a heart attack at the age of 61. He would have been pleased by the turn-out for the memorial service at St Margaret's, Westminster, attended by the Duchess of Kent, Prince Paul of Yugoslavia, the Speaker of the House of Commons and a crowded congregation of diplomats, Government ministers and members of both Houses of Parliament. (Lady Honor was 'unable' to attend.) He left an estate in Great Britain valued, after payment of £40,677 in death duties, at £73,646 from which £1,000 was to be set aside for binding and calendarizing the Channon diaries already deposited for posterity in the British Museum. His stipulation that the diaries should not even be examined until 50 years after his death was not acceptable to the museum's trustees but a heavily edited version of them, covering the period 1934–53, was published nine years after his death by arrangement with his son.

Channon's personal holding of Guinness shares was worth only about £20,000 before his death, but his son Paul became a beneficiary, through Honor, of shares valued at around £2,000,000 in 1969 as well as having 'inherited' the Southend West constituency from his father. He is married to Ingrid, the divorced first wife of his cousin by marriage, the Hon. Jonathan Guinness (see below, p. 197), is stepfather to her three children by Jonathan and has fathered three of his own by Ingrid. Between them, these six children, ranging in age from 11 to 29 at the time of writing, are heirs to two separate Guinness fortunes, that of the Earl of Iveagh and that of the Barons Moyne.

Paul, who inherited his parents' homes in London and Essex, lacks the social panache of his father but has more than compensated for this by his solid success as a parliamentarian with a highly civilized and politically moderate stance on most issues, domestic and European. He became a Junior Minister under the premiership of Edward Heath and again under Margaret Thatcher, but he is not a Thatcherite in politics and his future as a Tory front-bencher, promising though it is, may have to await the 'Iron Lady's' political eclipse.

From the time Honor first met Frantisek Svejdar, at a wartime village dance in Hampshire ('It was love at first sight,' she said later), her whole personality and way of life underwent a radical change. They were married as soon as the divorce from Channon became final, and upon 'Frankie's' release from the RAF they moved to Ireland, setting up home on the Phibblestown estate at Clonsilla in co. Dublin inherited by Honor from her father, where they spent eight months of the year farming and breeding racehorses and the other four on the island of Mustique, where Honor built the splendid villa now passed on to her son Paul. She brought 'Frankie's' mother, his brother Jarda and his family from Czechoslovakia to Ireland, set them up in business in Dublin and became in 1961 the first of the brewery line to convert to Roman Catholicism. She was also the first of Edward Cecil's granddaughters to die—in Dublin in 1976, from cancer. Frankie followed her six months later, at the age of 61. Present at the requiem mass in London for Lady Honor was the only Guinness in history who, while totally unrelated to the family chronicled in this book, has added a unique lustre to the name. In a generous gesture, from one who has been plagued throughout his lifetime with the ever-recurring query: 'Are you one of the—er—?', Sir Alec Guinness read the lessons to the congregation.

Honor's youngest sister, Brigid, was the least interested of all three girls in the glamour of Mayfair or the high politics of Belgravia and Westminster. She married a dashing Hohenzollern prince of the once all-powerful Prussian empire and a great-great-grandson of Queen Victoria and Albert, Prince of Saxe-Coburg-Gotha. By this marriage, which caused a sensation at the time, came children whose Guinness blood is genetically mingled with that of the British royal family.

Prince Friedrich Georg Wilhelm Christoph of Prussia was born in Berlin in 1911, the youngest son of Crown Prince Wilhelm, whose father was then Kaiser Wilhelm II of Germany. After the defeat of Germany in 1918, Friedrich's father joined the deposed Kaiser in exile in Holland, but he returned to the Hohenzollerns' ancestral seat at Hechingen in 1923 and subsequently he and all his four sons became members of the Nazi Party. Clearly, they had nothing in common with the upstart Austrian corporal, Adolf Hitler, but he had deigned to visit them at Hechingen, where he had spoken in vague terms of restoring the German monarchy after his 'mission' in Europe had been accomplished.

After studying law at Berlin University, Friedrich, or 'Fritzi' as he was known to all his peers, came to England as an undergraduate at Cambridge, and during Cowes Week in 1934 he became the first male Hohenzollern to be received by George V since the start of World War I. The elderly monarch had forgotten he was godfather to the six-foot, flaxen-haired and strikingly handsome young prince, and when he was reminded of the fact he presented Fritzi with a pair of cuff-links that would figure, 32 years later, in a drama that made headlines all over the world. Two years later the prince represented his family at the funeral of George V and again, later, for the coronation of George VI. He had been working meanwhile at a bank in Bremen and in December 1937 he took an unpaid job at Schroder's bank in London. This was at a time when the Munich crisis had caused the British Home Secretary to cut down on work permits for German citizens in Britain and questions were raised in the House of Commons as to the wisdom of bending the rules for Fritzi. The fact of the matter was that the prince had become—in private at least—a dissident from the Nazi regime. Nevertheless, he returned to Germany in July 1938 upon being recalled for six weeks' military training in the Wehrmacht, but was back in England immediately afterwards to take a job with the London agency of the German potash syndicate.

Most of the Hohenzollerns' vast revenues from their estates in Germany and German East Africa had dried up with the Kaiser's exile, and what remained had to be apportioned among a large family, including Fritzi's three elder brothers. In true Hohenzollern manner he therefore sought an alliance with a suitable—i.e. wealthy—wife who would not be averse to the title of 'Princess of Prussia'. He would have made an ideal 'catch' for the Woolworth heiress, the late Barbara Hutton, who had installed herself in Winfield House, Regent's Park (later the residence of the US ambassadors) where, during his undergraduate years, Fritzi was a regular and affectionately welcomed guest. But Barbara was then married to the second of her long string of husbands, Count von Reventlow, who after a while became so concerned by the growing intimacy between his wife (a mere countess) and the man who could possibly, one day, make her an Empress that he complained to Fritzi's father, who came at once to London and ordered his son to stay away from Reventlow's cabbage patch.

'Chips' Channon and Honor had met Fritzi by now and they met again when the Channons were invited to lunch with his mother, the Crown Princess, during the 1936 Olympic Games in Berlin. The prince was then 25 and Channon's unmarried sister-in-law, Lady Brigid Guinness, only 16. But the prospect of having a Hohenzollern prince, and a relation of the British royal family, as a future brother-in-law would hardly have distressed the Germanophile Chips and from then until the outbreak of World War II he took steps to bring Brigid and Fritzi together as often as possible, at Belgrave Square and Kelvedon.

Fritzi chose to stay on in England rather than fight with the Germans but any romance between him and Brigid was nipped in the bud in 1940 when, with the threat of invasion by Hitler, he was detained under Regulation 18b and sent to an internment camp in Canada for potential fifth columnists. Released in January 1941, under pressure from Queen Mary who was said to 'dote' on him, Fritzi returned to England and, after serving for a while in the Pioneer Corps, clearing up bomb-damage rubble in London, he quietly took up farm work in Hertfordshire under the alias of 'George Mansfield'. He kept in touch with the Guinnesses, mainly through Channon, and when he was injured in an accident involving a tractor it was Lady Brigid—then a wartime nursing auxiliary—who came to look after him.

In July 1945 he and Brigid were married in the church of St Cecilia in the village of Little Hadham, Hertfordshire, where the prince, for the past eighteen months, had been studying estate management. It was intended that the wedding should be kept strictly secret. The horrors perpetrated by the defeated Nazi regime had only recently bludgeoned the conscience of the world. Fritzi was still a German citizen. His eldest brother, Wilhelm, had been killed while fighting with the Wehrmacht during the invasion of France and his cousin Prince Oskar had died earlier, in Hitler's rape of Poland. No one in the village knew the true identity of the bridegroom, 'George Mansfield', and Brigid's father Lord Iveagh was concerned to keep it that way so far as the rest of the public was concerned, at least until the nation's disgust with Germany had abated. He sought the cooperation of the Home Office and, as a result, a police superintendent from Bishop's Stortford called on the rector of Little Hadham several weeks before the wedding to ask that there should be no publicity and, especially, that no one should be allowed to inspect the marriage register which, of course, would have let the cat out of the bag. The Guinness family characteristically underestimated the resources and skills of the British press, and the story of the marriage of the Kaiser's favourite grandson to the Earl of Iveagh's youngest daughter was splashed in the newspapers the next day.

By her marriage, Brigid lost her British nationality, but it was restored by the Home Secretary a year later when Fritzi applied for naturalization, giving notice that he would renounce his German title. He was granted citizenship. Four years later, by deed poll, he reverted to the name Friedrich George Wilhelm Christoph von Preussen. Disingenuously, he explained, as the *Daily Telegraph* of 11 September 1951 reported: 'Instead of George Mansfield, I wish to be known as von Preussen. There are many people who know me as Prince Friedrich, and will continue to call me by that name. Others will, no doubt, address me as "Mr von Preussen".'

The real reason for dropping 'Mansfield' was the death of Fritzi's father, the ex-Crown Prince Wilhelm, a few weeks earlier.[20] (The Kaiser had died in 1941.) This made the eldest surviving son, Prince Louis, the official Pretender to the throne of Germany and the inheritor of his father's still considerable estates. At some time, possibly in the near future, it was going to suit Fritzi to seek the restoration of his German citizenship as a Hohenzollern prince.

Meanwhile, he and Brigid had bought the 350-acre property, Patmore Hall, at Little Hadham, which he would develop into a model farm by acquiring adjoining acreage as well as extending and improving, with Teutonic thoroughness, what had once been a rather modest country house. A modernized wing housed the offices of the Prince, his male secretary, and those of the farm manager and his clerk. A loud-speaker system was installed throughout the house, and a tutor for the 17-year-old Nicholas von Preussen recalls waiting alone in the drawing-room for his first lunchtime interview, and being startled by a disembodied voice announcing, 'Luncheon is served, Your Highness!' By then it was *de rigueur* to address the couple as 'Prince and Princess Friedrich' and, lest there was any ignorance as to their credentials, a portrait of the Kaiser was on conspicuous display together with one of Iveagh in his ceremonial robes as a Knight of the Garter.

Behind the façade of a successful marriage a basic incompatibility of character began to make itself felt after the birth of the third child, Victoria, in 1952. Brigid was the prettiest of the Iveagh daughters but by temperament the most unassuming of the three. London society held little attraction for her; she was happiest with the country life, her children, her horses, the beautiful gardens she had laid down at Patmore. By contrast, Fritzi was a dynamo of energy and gregariousness, never happier than when leaping into a jeep to tour his model farm, into a plane for a trip to his large sheep farm in West Africa or to Rheinhartshausen Castle, the family seat on the Rhine near Wiesbaden, converted after the war into an hotel. Wherever his restless travelling took him he expected to tread the red carpet–literally or figuratively–proper to the Kaiser's favourite grandson, and he thrived on the attentions of beautiful and complaisant females. Undoubtedly, it was a source of irritation to him, and another stress upon the marriage, that he, brought up in the court of the all-powerful Kaiser, should be almost totally dependent, in Britain at least, upon the fortune inherited by Brigid from her father.

In 1953 he resumed his German nationality as a duel citizen of both countries because, as the *Daily Telegraph* of 21 February reported, 'of legal requirements in connection with his properties and estates in Germany'.

Over the next three years the marriage deteriorated sadly, although 'normal' appearances were kept up so far as the children and the staff at Patmore Hall were concerned. Brigid had found companionship in a divorced neighbour, Major Patrick Ness, and Fritzi had renewed his friendship with the wealthy Franco-German aristocrat, the Princess Antoinette von Croy. It was arranged between Brigid and Fritzi that their marriage should be dissolved on grounds of incompatibility in an action brought by Brigid, with the minimum of publicity, in the Frankfurt court where divorce proceedings were not publishable in the press. Instead, the stage was set, on 19 April 1966, for a drama that would not only expose the impending divorce action but would fill columns of the German and British press over the next two weeks.

Fritzi was staying in the luxurious apartment permanently set aside from him in the Schloss Rheinhartshausen. Shortly before midnight he walked out of the hotel, empty-handed and without a word to any of the staff. He never returned.

Over the next few days, search parties of the German police, using helicopters, bloodhounds and patrol boats, combed the area and the reaches of the Rhine for a trace of the missing prince. Suicide was discounted after the police had drawn a blank. Detectives then took over and Interpol was brought in. Six days after Fritzi's mysterious disappearance, Brigid flew in, together with her 19-year-old son Andrew. As her brother-in-law Lord Boyd of Merton put it, and as the *Daily Express* of 26 April 1966 reported, 'Princess Friedrich did not wish to alarm her younger children about their father's disappearance until it became inevitable.' In fact she flew in to be interviewed by the German police and returned to England shortly afterwards.

While the search went on, the authorities strove to find a motive for the prince's disappearance.

The first hearing of Brigid's divorce action had been scheduled for 3 May, but this had been an amicable arrangement and had not prevented Fritzi from enjoying a deep-sea-fishing holiday in the West Indies immediately prior to his arrival at the schloss.

It was established that he had come to Rheinhartshausen to discuss 'problems of inheritance' regarding the Hohenzollern estates and that his brother Prince Louis had telephoned him earlier on the evening of his disappearance to say he would be arriving at the schloss the following day.

That same day there had been a meeting between Fritzi and the widow of his brother Hubertus.

Just before the prince walked out of the schloss for the last time he received a telephone call from Princess Antoinette. According to her, 'We agreed to meet at the weekend.'

On the morning of 1 May, 12 days after his disappearance, pedestrians on the banks of the Rhine near Bingen, ten miles downstream from the schloss, sighted a body floating in the river. The police brought it ashore and the corpse was identified by a member of the Rheinhartshausen staff as that of Prince Friedrich. Still in place were the cuff-links given to him by his godfather George V.

A post-mortem ruled out any question of foul play and the obvious assumption was that Fritzi had committed suicide, but the motivation for it has never been publicly revealed. His brother Louis, who throughout the search for Fritzi had totally discounted the possibility of suicide, now declared, as *The Times* of 2 May reported, that the prince had been 'suffering from nervous depression', caused by circumstances of which he did not want to give details. Princess Antoinette had gone into hiding on 26 April and a joint statement issued by Prince Louis and Brigid after the body was found declared that, 'In view of the publicity that Princess Antoinette von Croy has received, Prince Friedrich's brother, Prince Louis Ferdinand of Prussia, and Princess Friedrich wish to state that Princess Antoinette was in no way involved in the divorce proceedings.'

To this day there are those who insist on the unlikelihood that Fritzi–an excellent swimmer in superb physical condition–would choose suicide by plunging into the Rhine, and there are others who hint darkly (but with no apparent logic) at intrigues revolving around the issue of the restoration of the German monarchy.

His estate in England, valued at £14,504 before tax, had been willed to his wife. Brigid was left with her five completely anglicized children, the princes Nicholas, Andrew and Rupert and the princesses Victoria and Antonia (the twin of Rupert). At the time of writing, three of them are married: Nicholas to the daughter of the 2nd Baron Mancroft; Antonia to the Marquess of Douro, the son and heir of the 8th Duke of Wellington; and Victoria—whom Nicholas's tutor recalls as 'rather a pain in the neck' as a teenager—to Philip Alphonse Ache-Ache.

After the death of Fritzi, both Brigid and her neighbour Major Patrick Ness were at pains to deny, publicly, that they were romantically involved in any way. But a year later the widowed Guinness lady was quietly married to the tall, handsome ex-Hussar with whom she had long shared so many interests, notably in horses, and whose temperament differed so greatly from Fritzi's. They live happily today in the privacy of Patmore Hall, protected by its woods, separated from the public highway by a mile-long drive that once bore a blond Hohenzollern prince, in his glittering white Mercedes, to the pleasure spots of the world. It is a long way, in time and distance, from the castle of Rheinhartshausen and the river of legends whose dark waters parted for Fritzi, that April night in 1966.

14

Of Poets, Horses and Dusky Nymphs

If one is to define tragedy in a family as the loss of one of its loved ones in youth through sudden death from external causes or by personal design, then it is hard to escape the impression that the grandchildren of Edward Cecil, the 1st Earl of Iveagh, have suffered perhaps more than an actuarial share of misfortune. To infer from this—as an article in the *Sunday Times*, headed 'From Greek Gods to the Guinnesses', did on 3 September 1978—that there might be some kind of a curse on Iveagh's descendants is absurd. What is a fact is that tragedy, as defined, has struck at five out of the nine separate family units of this seventh generation of the brewery line.

There is a corner of England, a Guinness enclave not hitherto mentioned in this narrative, where the grandchildren and great-grandchildren of Edward Cecil can escape to, either for weekend rest or to shake off the press, or to console one another in times of adversity. It is the picturesque little village of Bosham on the southern coast of England, near Chichester. The village and much of the hinterland was acquired by the 1st Lord Iveagh precisely for these purposes as well as to provide 'grace and favour' accommodation for the family's retired servants. He built the yacht club here, and also a landing stage for the Guinnesses' boats, giving immediate access, through a garden, to one of the several houses set aside for the use of the family. Later, he and his grandson—who had inherited the courtesy title of Viscount Elveden from his soldier-father—developed part of Bosham manor into a luxury estate of thirty-three houses; but in 1962, when the Bosham parish council suggested naming one of the roads on the new estate as either Iveagh or Elveden Road, the proposal was immediately squashed by the head of the family and his heir. None of the telephone numbers of the Guinnesses' houses is listed in any directory or reference book. The permanent domestic staffs are all either old retainers or the offspring of parents whose lives were spent in the great Guinness mansions, and the villagers, as a whole, will protect the privacy of the family from all outsiders. Only among themselves, when they speak of the young 'masters' and 'misses' they knew, and can no longer serve, is there a shaking of a grey head, a sigh or two...

There were, altogether, ten grandchildren of Edward Cecil, four by his eldest son Rupert Edward, three by the Hon. Ernest Guinness and three more by the assassinated Lord Moyne.

Tragedy struck thrice at Rupert Edward's family. His first-born son lived for only two days. His second son, Arthur, was killed in action towards the end of World War II. His granddaughter, Henrietta, who committed suicide three years ago, is the subject, with her cousin Natalya, of the last chapter in this book.

Of Rupert Edward's three daughters—Honor, Patricia, and Brigid—only the latter, as we have seen, has had to face tragedy, with the suicide of her children's father, Prince Friedrich. It is when we turn to her cousins Maureen and Oonagh that the drama of sudden death takes a particularly poignant toll of the Iveagh descendants. Each of these 'golden Guinness Girls' has been smitten twice by tragedy. As we have seen, Oonagh lost her only daughter, Tessa, at the age of 14 and her son Tara at 21. The jungles of Burma claimed Maureen's first husband, Basil Sheridan, and her much-loved granddaughter, Natalya, became a heroin addict by the age of 18.

All these tragedies, shattering as they were to this generation of Guinnesses, must be put into the perspective of a very large family of siblings and first cousins, the great majority of whom are happily married today and have produced a lively seventh generation of Guinnesses to perpetuate the line from the 1st Earl of Iveagh. It is a generation that has produced two MPs for the House of Commons, a pop singer, a painter, a champion amateur jockey, a topless model for Andy Warhol, and two professional authors. In the latter category—and outstandingly the most talented writer thrown up by the whole of the Guinness clan—is Lady Caroline Blackwood, the eldest child of Maureen Guinness.

Caroline was a late starter, for although she had earlier shown literary promise with, for example, a critique of film director Ingmar Bergmann for *Encounter* magazine, she was already into her early forties before her first book was published. This was a combination of ironic short stories and straight reportage entitled *For All That I Found There*.[1] A close friend of hers recalls that from being 'rather fetchingly disorganized' in her thirties she suddenly emerged as 'not only a perversely discerning but also–more surprisingly to her friends–a highly disciplined writer'.

This change was probably influenced by her close friendship with Robert Silvers of the *New York Review of Books* and it was subsequently reinforced during her love affair with, and ultimate marriage to, the prolific and doomed American poet Robert Lowell.

Neither of Caroline's two previous husbands would seem to have provided the right 'vibes' for an aspiring author. With the first, the abstract portrait painter Lucien Freud, she was caught up in an egocentric orbit of party-giving and -going and unpredictable changes in mood. (His many nude studies of Caroline, two of which are among his works in the Tate Gallery, are said to be a record of a man falling out of love with his subject.) From Freud to a semi-ordered life with her second husband, the Russo-American composer Israel Citkowitz, must have been somewhat of a relief and produced three children: Natalya, Eugenia and Ivana. But where Freud sought distraction and contributed little to Caroline's self-enhancement, Citkowitz, for all his supportive warmth, was basically a creature of convention with no special claim to literary perception.

To have been born to one of the glamorous Guinness sisters would surely have brought problems enough to a girl who as a child was rather plain and pudgy. To have lost her father when she was 14 could only have compounded the insecurities, so that even today this gifted writer remains a singularly private person, shunning the limelight and exorcizing her ghosts (one hopes) through her work, much of which is clearly autobiographical with 'a talent for the truly gruesome, for the image that haunts the mind like a glimpsed skull'.[2] (It was reported, in the *Daily Telegraph* of 1 December 1976, that on one of her rare appearances on a public occasion–the award of the David Higham Prize for her short novel, *The Stepdaughter*–'She was shaking as she mounted the staircase at the National Book League in Mayfair and just managed a "thank you".')

In Robert Lowell, fourteen years her senior, she found a lover, mentor and–despite or because of the emotional stresses afflicting their years together–a soulmate whose tormented personality called poignantly to her own.

Regarded by many critics as one of the best English-language poets of his generation, Lowell had won a Pulitzer Prize in 1947 for his *Lord Weary's Castle* when Caroline was only 16 and his first marriage to the brilliant American fiction-writer, Jean Stafford, was breaking up. Two years later he married another writer, Elizabeth Hardwick, by whom he had a daughter, Harriet.

Probably his first awareness of the Guinness family came in 1959 when he shared with W. H. Auden and Edith Sitwell the Guinness Poetry Award for his *Life Studies*. This annual award had been initiated two years earlier by the 2nd Lord Moyne and, whether or not the 28-year-old Caroline was present on this occasion, she would not have met Lowell, who at the time was being treated for his manic-depression as an out-patient of the Massachusetts General Hospital's psychiatric unit.

They met for the first time in 1966 while Caroline was living with her children in the large house she had bought in New York's Greenwich Village. They met again four years later, when Lowell came to England, first as a Visiting Fellow at All Souls College, Oxford, then as Professor of English Literature at Essex University. This time the result was an 'explosion of emotion' on Lowell's part.

The couple set up housekeeping almost immediately, first in London at his flat in Redcliffe Square, and then at Milgate, the ancient Blackwood estate in Kent...It was here, in the spacious old house, that Caroline gave birth in August 1971—while Lowell was still legally married to Hardwick—to the poet's second child, a son, Robert Sheridan Lowell.[3]

The baby was born after twelve hours of labour by his 40-year-old mother and another year would elapse before the poet obtained a divorce in the Dominican Republic ('a barracuda settlement') from Elizabeth Hardwick.

It is in Caroline's character that she has never written about her relationship with the poet, and for insights into this one must turn to the unrhymed iambic pentameters of his volume *The Dolphin*, dedicated 'For Caroline'.[4]

Virtually the whole of this 78-page work is an intimate record of their meeting, their love, quarrels, separations, misunderstandings and anguishes—to an extent that one American critic, Marjorie Perloff, found 'embarrassingly personal'.[5]

In the stanza 'Mermaid', written before their marriage, he celebrates (?) the duality of Caroline's character.

I see you as a baby killer whale,
free to walk the seven seas for game,
warm-hearted with an undercoat of ice,
a nerve-wrung back...all muscle, youth, intention...

Your stamina as *inside-right* at school
spilled the topheavy boys, and keeps you pure.

> Will money drown you? Poverty, though now
> in fashion, debases women as much as wealth.
> You use no scent, dab brow and lash with shoeblack,
> willing to face the world without more face.

He is deeply in love, perhaps more with the challenge of it than with its flesh-and-blood recipient, and as Caroline, with two wrecked marriages behind her, holds back:

> you will not marry, though disloyal to woman
> in your airy seizures of submission,
> preferring to have your body broken to being
> unbreakable in this breaking life.

(From 'Marriage')

Then, under 'Knowing':

> ...We have our child,
> our bastard, easily fathered, hard to name...

followed by a 14-line stanza to Robert Sheridan Lowell.

His verse vacillates, neurotically, between ecstasy and a self-pitying anguish.

> After fifty so much joy has come.
> I hardly want to hide my nakedness—
> The shine and stiffness of a new suit, a feeling,
> not wholly happy, of having been reborn.
> (From 'Flight to New York, 1')

But from a holiday in America with his daughter Harriet and her mother Elizabeth, he writes: 'I despair of letters. You say I wrote H. isn't interested in the thing happening to you now. So what? A fantastic untruth, misprint, something; I meant the London scene's no big concern, just you...'

The tides of the marriage ebbed and flowed with the poet's manic-depressive bouts and with Caroline's demeanour in the wake of them. And between periodic admissions to hospital, and semesters spent at Harvard teaching literature, the erosion was setting in. *En route*, alone, from London to New York, Lowell cries:

> If I have had hysterical drunken seizures,
> it's from loving you too much. It makes me wild,
> *I fear*...

(From 'Flight to New York, 2')

And again:

> If I cannot love myself, can you?...
> Born twenty years later, I might have been prepared
> to alternate with cooking, and wash the baby–
> I am a vacation-father...no plum–
>
> (From 'Flight to New York, 4')

Towards the end, the estrangements and reconciliations became more and more spaced out and on 12 September 1977, returning from an abortive effort at reconciliation with Caroline in Ireland, Lowell suffered a massive coronary in a New York taxi.

The funeral took place on 16 September at the Church of the Advent in Boston, Lowell's birthplace, and the 600 mourners included Saul Bellow, Susan Sontag, William Styron, Richard Wilbur, Elizabeth Hardwick and her daughter Harriet. Caroline flew from Ireland with Robert Sheridan and her three daughters, and was reported, in the *New York Times* of 17 September 1977, as 'looking worn and distraught'.

Caroline's third book, *Great Granny Webster* (Duckworth, 1977), had just been published in Britain. Presented as fiction, narrated in the first person singular, it is in fact a model of autobiographic licence with abundant clues to the real-life identities of several of the characters, notably 'Great Granny Webster'.

We meet the narrator as a girl of 14 sent to convalesce in the seaside house of her paternal great-grandmother, the wealthy widow of an Anglo-Irish aristocrat who had died when the narrator was 'quite young'. The house was at Hove, on the south coast of England, where Caroline's real life great-grandmother, the widowed Cecilia Woodhouse, did in fact live.

The first chapter of the book is taken up with a witty and beautifully observed account of the tedium, to a young schoolgirl, of her daily existence in a big gloomy house with a mirthless old dragon who would sit erect and silent for hours on end 'in one of the most horribly uncomfortable Victorian gothic chairs I have ever seen...a chair that appeared never to have been designed for human use'.

In the third chapter we are given a brilliantly evocative picture of life on the Ulster estate of the narrator's grandfather, 'Sir Robert Dunmartin'. He is described as the son of a former Governor-General of Canada (Caroline's paternal great-grandfather, the 3rd Marquess of Dufferin and Ava, was a Governor-General of Canada). 'Sir Robert' had inherited 'Dunmartin Hall' and had died when the narrator was still 'very young'. (Dufferin and Ava died when Caroline was 14.) And, like Caroline's real grandfather, 'Sir Robert' had a son, educated at Eton and Oxford, who died in Burma in 1945. So the author has now led us to Clandeboye, the co. Down seat of the Dufferin and Ava family. But her description of 'Dunmartin Hall' is probably a pastiche of other Irish country houses she had known.

It is when the narrator lets us in on private sessions at the Mayfair home of her 'Aunt Lavinia' that the story begins to exude the special flavour and style of the period and the effervescent ambience in which the Dufferin and Ava and Guinness ladies lived. In fact, while 'Aunt Lavinia' has been judged by some to be a pastiche of Maureen, Oonagh and Aileen, she more vividly reflects the personality of Caroline's aunt, Lady Veronica Blackwood.

'Lavinia', famous for her beautiful legs, is dedicated to fun 'as though it were a state of grace', addresses all her peers as 'darling', lavishes kisses on her poodle Poo Poo and devotes hours every day to chatting on the telephone with her male and female chums while she washes away last night's hangover with a huge mug of Guinness laced with vintage champagne. She entertains her friends and lovers on a recklessly generous scale (though continuously on the verge of going broke). As she recounts her latest 'adventure' in a Mayfair idiom peppered with 'divine', 'ghastly', 'wretched', 'heavenly' and 'deeply' this-and-that, she is stroking her silky auburn hair with a silver-backed Cartier hairbrush, or applying a perfect Cupid's bow to her lips, or manicuring her long scarlet fingernails as she reclines on the gleaming white satin cover of her large Hollywood bed. Her spoken prose, tumbling from the Cupid lips in breathless periods, is a charming cascade of amused self-pity and hyperbole, as when she entertains her 'niece' with the story (a little classic of humorous writing by Lady Caroline) of her near-rape by 'Dr Kronin' whilst recovering from her botched attempt at suicide by razor. ('I had it all perfectly planned, darling. It couldn't have been more Roman...')

'It was absolutely typical. Just when I was writhing in the abyss, a wreck of a woman with no make-up and dirty clotted hospital hair, that most hated figure of all, the head psychiatrist, developed the most unwelcome and fatal crush on me. I really had quite a ghastly time with him, darling.'

Lady Veronica died in 1951 at the age of 53. The present writer is assured that anyone who knew her would identify her at once as 'Lavinia'. A *jolie laide*, with a superb figure and a wicked wit, she indulged her chief pleasures—men and alcohol—to excess, would borrow money 'to pay the rent' and spend it forthwith at Asprey or Cartier on presents for her current men friends.

She and her brother Basil Sheridan were frequent house guests at Cecilia's home in Hove, where the old lady put up with Veronica's drinking and her mischief-making for the sake of her brother, whom Cecilia adored. But Basil was not so tolerant of his sister and would find excuses to prevent her ever re-visiting her childhood home, Clandeboye. A friend of the family recalls that, after World War II, Basil's widow Maureen, encouraged by the news that Veronica had 'taken the cure', invited her to stay at Clandeboye. 'It was disastrous. She took to drinking again and to seducing the male guests, one of whom was found in her bedroom by the maid, bringing early-morning tea.'

Maureen's impressionable young children–Lady Caroline, the 5th Marquess, Sheridan, and Lady Perdita–were of course captivated by their attractive and witty aunt and eagerly swallowed the amusingly malicious stories she concocted about their great-grandmother Woodhouse. Granny Woodhouse became an object half of awe, half of ridicule, to the schoolgirl Caroline, and the portrait of 'Great-Grandmother Webster' has to be read in this light. It is a vastly amusing character study but it belongs mainly in the realm of Veronica-inspired fiction. Her contemporaries remember the real Granny Woodhouse as a sweet and harmless–even lovable–old lady.

In October 1980, shortly after it was announced that Lady Caroline had embarked on a biography of the Duchess of Windsor, the reclusive 49-year-old novelist, now living in England, had her privacy rudely shattered by a news story that made headlines on both sides of the Atlantic.

Some years earlier she had rented out her four-storey house at 250 West 12th Street, New York City. What she did not know was that the premises were being used as a sado-masochistic bordello–known as 'The Mansion'–by a team of five prostitutes who specialized in flagellation, bondage and other sophisticated devices for the humiliation of their wealthy clientele, including mock crucifixions. When the story of the goings-on in 'The Mansion' broke in the New York press, the professional dominatrices fled their den of vice and by the time the outraged Caroline arrived on the scene, vandals had broken in and caused £25,000-worth of damage by making bonfires of the black leather harnesses, whips and birches.

Back in England, Lady Caroline had to face the good-humoured quips of her friends and family, including her pretty 16-year-old daughter Eugenia's allusions to the house she had been partly reared in as 'Mummy's Brothel'.

In 1964, Maureen's son, Sheridan, by marrying his cousin Serena Belinda ('Lindy'), effected a third matrimonial union between the brewery and the banking line of the family.[6] Two distinct Guinness fortunes therefore flow to this marriage and a common interest in the visual arts is shared by the tall, slim Sheridan and his attractive marchioness. With Sheridan it has taken the form of patronage and the financing of London art galleries. Lindy is a serious painter—recently of scenes in Venice and India—with two exhibitions behind her up to the time of writing. But friends of the couple discount the likelihood of an heir to the 5th Marquess.

Maureen's youngest daughter, Lady Perdita Blackwood, received a lavish launching in 1952, when Maureen gave a ball at the Hurlingham Club to celebrate the 18-year-old Perdita's birthday and her sister Caroline's coming-of-age. The humdrum décor of the spacious premises was festively transformed for the biggest private party given in the club since the end of World War II, with 500 guests headed by Princess Margaret and the Duchess of Kent. But the interests of the younger belle of the ball were already focused on thoroughbred horses rather than blue-blooded bachelors and while she awaited her own coming-of-age, and the trust funds this would release to her, she supplemented her allowance from her mother by working for a period as a waitress in a Park Lane café.

Her ambition was to acquire her own stables for the breeding and training of show-jumpers and she realized this, while still in her twenties, by buying a small farm close to the Clandeboye estate in co. Down. Her uncle Bryan Walter, the 2nd Lord Moyne, started her off with the present of a prize stallion from his own stud of Arab horses and from then on her life became devoted to her Irish bloodstock. Today, at 47, she would stand by the statement she made when she turned her back on Mayfair, more than twenty years ago, and reported in the *Daily Express* of 11 August 1960: 'I don't miss London and I'm sure it doesn't miss me.'

Only one other Guinness of her generation outshone Perdita in enthusiasm for horseflesh, and this was her first cousin Gay Kindersley.

From Eton, and National Service in the 7th Hussars, Gay went up to Oxford to study agriculture. He would inherit around £167,000 at the age of 25, but he would need all of that for his life's ambition, which was to excel as a steeplechase jockey and trainer. Combining a profitable farm with training stables was one way to go about this and when he came of age he took over the farm in co. Dublin bequeathed to him by his Guinness grandfather, bought his own first racehorses and began his remarkable career as an amateur jockey.

His marriage, at 25, to Margaret Wakefield was conducted in such secrecy at a London register office that neither of their fathers were told about it, though Oonagh and the bride's mother were present at the ceremony. The couple set up home first at the Manor House in Cuckfield, Essex and then on an 80-acre farm in Surrey. In 1961, a year after the fearless Gay had won the title of Britain's leading amateur jockey under National Hunt rules, he bought for £135,000 a 1,000-acre farm, at Lambourn, in the heart of the training country, where he set up his own training and breeding stables. He now owned his own string of twelve steeplechasers and his one remaining ambition as a jockey was to ride in the Grand National at Aintree.

He had already suffered a fracture of the spine, broken collarbones and dislocated shoulders before he mounted his horse 'Eric Star' for the two-mile February chase at Hurst Park in 1962. Three fences from home he was thrown heavily and kicked in the back as his mount struggled to its feet. Once again his spine was fractured, wrecking his hopes of entering the National that year, and his doctors warned him against racing again. But it was like ordering the small and lean—almost fragile—jockey to give up breathing. Over the next three years, his spine braced by a steel corset and steel pins holding his shoulder-bones in place, he continued to ride as an amateur, suffering another bad fall when his horse threw him in Ireland and three following horses stumbled over his body, badly bruising his ribs and arm.

In March 1965 the indomitable Gay—by now one of the most charismatic of figures at British race meetings—mounted his horse 'Ronald's Boy' and, wearing his own colours of green and mauve, rode in the Grand National for the first and only time in his sixteen years as a jockey. His mount fell at the third fence of this gruelling course and though he continued for several years to ride in the 'flats' his career as a steeplechase jockey was over.

Ironically, the nearest he came to death was not on a racecourse but in accepting a flippant challenge during a Thames-side party given in 1963 by BBC producer John Irwin. The December night was cold and frosty, but when Irwin suddenly cried, '£100 to the first man across the river' the only guest to respond was Gay who, shedding his jacket and shoes, plunged immediately into the icy river. On reaching the far bank, 162 yards away, he called back to the party, 'I've done it!' On his way back he developed cramp and would have been swept away on the tidal flow had not two of the younger guests plunged in to rescue him.

On retiring as a jockey, Gay disposed of his own string of racehorses and concentrated on the breeding and training of blood-stock for sale. Neither his standard of living nor his chosen avocation had been conducive to the amassing of a fortune and, early in 1975, with the aim of establishing domicile for tax purposes outside of England, his wife Margaret took their children to Antibes to stay at her mother-in-law Oonagh's villa while she house-hunted on the Côte d'Azur. The family's home on the farm at Lambourn was closed down and Gay's intention was to spend the weekdays training his horses, flying out at weekends to be with his wife and children. Meanwhile, he moved into a cottage near the big house.

But by June of that year his 20-year-long marriage to Margaret was in trouble. He confessed to her that he had fallen in love with Philippa Harper, 17 years his junior, and he begged his anguished wife not to rush back to England since, as the *Daily Express* of 30 October reported, 'his love for this woman would soon burn itself out'. Four months later she did in fact return, only to find the affair with Philippa still burning strongly. She divorced Gay the following year and married another Lambourn trainer, Anthony Johnson, three weeks before Gay's marriage to Philippa.

A droll reflection on the so-called 'generation gap' came in the autumn of 1979 when the 50-year-old Gay received a transatlantic call from a 36-year-old Harrovian, Robert Millbourn, then based in New York. Millbourn had renewed an old acquaintanceship with Gay's daughter, the 21-year-old Catheryn—arguably the most beautiful of Ernest Guinness's great-granddaughters—when she came to New York to watch her brother Robin run in the City Marathon. He was now calling to ask Gay for his daughter Catheryn's hand in marriage. It was the first time Gay had spoken to his future son-in-law and he was deeply impressed. As he told the *Daily Express* of 13 September, 'Most courteous of him, don't you think?'

It would be tempting, but trite, to equate Gay Kindersley's passion for horses with his half-brother Garech's partiality to exotic females. It would also be salutary to note that the two surviving sons of Oonagh Guinness had, apart from horses and women, devoted at least part of their time to the interests of the brewery from which their portions of the Guinness fortune flow. Conveniently for the world of steeplechasing and gossip-column journalism, this has not been the case. And it would be remarkable—given the nature of their mother and the backgrounds of their respective fathers—had it been so. Instead, they represent two of the most colourful of those of the seventh generation from Richard of Celbridge who have eschewed their birthright to a career in the brewery in order to pursue their own interests.

Garech is of the same generation as his cousin Arthur Francis Benjamin, the present Earl of Iveagh and chairman of Arthur Guinness Son & Co. They were born within two years of each other; they both live in Ireland and their common ancestor was the First Arthur. And there any resemblance between them ends. Compared with his tall, bespectacled, publicity-shy cousin, Garech is a cross between Brendan Behan and Cyrano de Bergerac. His Irishness comes out in his addiction to the gregariousness of tavern life; his gallantry in the fact that he is at his best, even in those predominantly male preserves, with a stunning female at his side. And whether it be in the smart cocktail lounge of Dublin's Shelbourne Hotel, at the long bar of Neary's, in Chatham Street, or at the York Minster in London's Soho, the most animated group of tipplers will be found gathered around the short stocky figure with its Yeats-style beard, its fair hair ribbon-tied into a pigtail, its amused blue eyes complementing the soft dreamy smile of an Eastern guru. His friend Gloria MacGowran, widow of the great Irish actor, has written:

People call his friends sycophants, his circus, his court. Outsiders see him as a palish man...frittering away his time on licensed premises, his own court jester. The puritanical see him as the living source of the seven deadly sins, a self-indulgent reprobate. The pompous see him as a traitor to his class. Few see the man who has revitalized Celtic art and music, realize the passion, and notice the razor mind—even when it's their own face that is being nicked.[7]

The fact of the matter is that Garech Browne is, and has always been, his own man—on a 'take me or leave me' basis. That he has had the wealth, since coming of age, conducive to this attitude is not, of course, an irrelevance. What is more to the point, however, is that rich or poor there is in his nature a romanticism, a nostalgia for the eras of minstrels, chivalry and carousel that could never have been chained to a desk job. His first romance was with a housemaid in his mother's service at Luggala and it led to his temporary banishment from that brooding lakeside estate which is now his kingdom. Several years later, having been separated from the sum of £6,000 by one of his many mistresses, he not only shrugged it off but made a point of bestowing exactly £6,000 on the estranged lady's daughter, as a birthday present.

Meanwhile, and characteristically, he made a decision to put traditional Irish folk music on the commercial map at a time when the 'pop' groups were dominant and virtually no one was interested in the pipers, the fiddlers and the goatskin drums. He set up a recording company in Dublin, assembled his own group of musicians selected from one of the few remaining traditional orchestras, the Sean O Riada Ceoltoiri Cualann, and created The Chieftains, whose recordings are now distributed worldwide. Simultaneously he was recording Irish poets reading their own works and adding to his unique collection of Irish horse-drawn carriages (which finally totalled about sixty and are in constant demand by film producers and for festive Irish events).

At the time of writing, it would seem that Garech, now 42, is about to embark on the one venture most of his friends would have put beyond him: matrimony. The girl in question is the lovely 27-year-old Princess Purna whose father, the late Maharaja of Morvi, once ruled over the small princely state north of Bombay. She is British-educated, independently wealthy and she faithfully served her two-year apprenticeship as a saloon-bar companion to her peripatetic lover.

Garech denies that all the women in his life have been dark-eyed Eastern beauties. But if as few as only one in four of them fell into that category—which is his own vague estimate—it confirms his reputation as a Lothario, given the roll-call of the 'few' and the fact that most of his past liaisons were of respectable duration. His odyssey through the scented meadows of exotic nubility began at 25 with a Chinese girl, Chan Ling Fen, then studying medicine in Dublin. From there, the Caribbean called, in the seductive Jamaican shape of Tessa Wellborn, who as the stepdaughter of a former Finance Minister named Prendergast, had appreciably elevated the interest rates of London upon her arrival there in the early fifties. Three and a half years later, Tessa was succeeded by a spirited Eurasian beauty. This was the aptly-named 'Tiger' Cowley, widow of the 5th Earl of Cowley and daughter of an Indian surgeon named Ramiah Doraswamy Algar.

The affair with 'Tiger', who is now married to the Tory MP Piers Dixon, lasted for about five years, taking Garech towards his mid-thirties, and between then and his final response to the siren call of

India, the romantic voyager took on board a dusky Bangladesh maiden named Farida Majid and the sloe-eyed Hiruko, one of the crew of a Japanese film unit on location in Ireland.

The metaphorical 'siren call' takes on added relevance in the light of Garech's navigation towards the landfall of matrimony. For the beautiful Maharanee of Morvi has two daughters and it was the eldest of them, Princess Maya, whose song first turned him from his set bachelor course. In the event, however, it was the younger voice of Princess Purna that sounded the sweeter in his ears, providing a resolution to Garech's enviable dilemma that has been accepted by the senior siren with grace and good humour.

If their marriage is blessed with children, their genetic inheritance will be half 'export' Indian, a quarter Guinness and a quarter Browne, a brew of which their wassailing father can be deservedly proud. His and Purna's friends will continue to be welcome at Woodtown Manor in the Rathfarnam suburb of Dublin, his 'little' house located in Stocking Lane which, as Garech smilingly points out, will also lead one to nearby Mount Venus. And the route laid down for them by their host will of course be keyed to a series of pubs such as 'The Yellow House' and 'The Tuning Fork', indispensable watering places on a drive from the Irish capital that could take as little as twenty minutes or as much as three hours, depending upon one's thirst.

On more festive occasions, such as Christmas, guests of 'Himself' and his princess will make the longer journey to Luggala, where thirst has always been honoured as a state of grace.

15

Bryan Walter, and All the Moynes

Bryan Walter Guinness, who inherited the title Lord Moyne when his father Walter Edward was assassinated in Cairo, is today not only the 'elder statesman' of the family but also, as we have seen, the most prolific of its sixth generation with his eleven children and fifteen grandchildren. One has to go back in the 'Founder's kin', to the First Arthur's son Hosea, to find a slightly more impressive record of fecundity. Of the banking Guinnesses only one, the prolific Henry (born 1829), pips Bryan–by one Guinness head–to the reproductive post.

Bryan got off to a good start in 1929 by marrying Diana Mitford, one of the six daughters of Lord Redesdale, when she was 18 and he only 23. It turned out to be a sprint compared with his second marriage, to Elisabeth Nelson, but it did produce two sons–the Hon. Jonathan Bryan and the Hon. Desmond Walter–before ending with a suit for divorce in 1933. It was fun while it lasted, this union between the slim, dark-haired son of then Minister of Agriculture and the blonde and beautiful Mitford girl. They moved into a house in Buckingham Street, Westminster, and promptly staged the year's most amusing hoax on the art critics and connoisseurs of London by inviting them to an exhibition of the works by the German 'émigré' genius Mr Bruno Hat. The introduction to Hat's catalogue was written by Evelyn Waugh and the critics were considerably impressed by the *avant-garde* style of the canvases and their interpretation, in German, by the mustachioed, dark-spectacled painter and guest of honour. The works were, in fact, pastiches created by a painter friend of the young hosts, Brian Howard, and 'Mr Bruno Hat' was none other than Diana's brother, the Hon. Tom Mitford.

Bryan was studying at Oxford for the Bar when he married. He was an intelligent, 'bookish' young man with a pleasing and unassertive personality but no evident interest in the world of politics to which his father was already so deeply committed. Diana, on the other hand, began after the birth of her second son to be stirred by the forceful demagogy of the ultra-political British fascist leader, Sir Oswald Mosley, and there can be little doubt that her marriage to Bryan foundered on this contrast between the personalities of the two men.

Her secret marriage to Sir Oswald was not publicly revealed until November 1938, and then only as the outcome of a report—which might have been just a *ballon d'essai*—by the press to the effect that she and Mosley had been secretly married in the Führerhaus at Munich on 4 December 1937 in the presence of Adolf Hitler, with whom they afterwards shared a wedding breakfast, presumably also in the company of Diana's sister Unity who by then was a devoted acolyte of the Führer. In a carefully-worded rebuttal of this report, published in the *News Chronicle* of 29 November 1938, Mosley's British Union of Fascists immediately issued a statement declaring that 'Sir Oswald has not been in Germany at all for over two years past. Therefore the alleged marriage document to which publicity has been given in certain papers, either does not exist or is another forgery.'

The next day, Sir Oswald himself made a statement, reported in the *Daily Express* of 1 December, to the effect that his marriage to Diana took place 'just over two years ago' (i.e. sometime in 1936). As for its having happened in Munich, this was a city 'I have not visited for three and a half years.' Curiously, in the light of his concern to shoot down the story of a wedding ceremony in Nazi Germany, he offered no details as to the whereabouts or precise date of his marriage. And he chose to release his prepared statement through the columns of his party newspaper, *Action*, rather than face the kind of grilling he could have expected from the lay press. The truth had to await the publication of Mosley's autobiography 25 years after the end of World War II. In this he admits marrying Diana in Germany, in October 1936. 'Frau Goebbels, who was a friend of Diana's, helped to arrange the marriage and after the ceremony she gave a luncheon for us at her villa near Wansee [a south-west suburb of Berlin]. Hitler was a guest.'[1] Mosley does not mention whether Hermann Goering, who once described Diana as 'one of the most perfect specimens of Aryan womanhood', was also invited.

By the time of his divorce from Diana, the Hon. Bryan Walter Guinness had abandoned the law and embarked on a part-time career as a novelist, poet and playwright, a career which, over the

years, if not exactly prolific, trail-blazing or profitable, has won him
the kind of reviews most dilettantes can comfortably live with. A
novel, *Landscape with Figures*, published after his divorce, was followed a year later by a book of verses entitled *Under the Eyelid* and in
1938 his first play, *The Fragrant Concubine*, was given a Sunday
presentation at the Little Theatre in London.

In 1935 he had nearly added to the roll of Guinness tragedies in a
road accident that injured him badly about the face and required
surgery. But in the following year he married Elisabeth Nelson, the
daughter of a well-known publisher (whose company later published
Sir Oswald Mosley's self-serving autobiography). Elisabeth managed to produce her nine offspring in precisely alternating gen-
ders–girl-boy-girl-boy-girl-boy-girl-boy-girl. The last six were born
with the title 'Honourable'–since their father had succeeded to the
Moyne peerage in 1944–and were brought up on their father's two
estates, Knockmaroon House at Castleknock, co. Dublin, and Biddesden House at Andover, Hampshire, where Bryan Walter, when
not writing poetry, administered a well-run farm and a breeding
stable for Arab horses.

In addition to the major share of his father's great fortune, Bryan
Walter had inherited the 1st Lord Moyne's seat in the House of
Lords; but the broad canvas of national and international politics
held far less fascination for the son than it had for his celebrated
parliamentary father, and his maiden speech, delivered three years
after he had first bowed to the Woolsack, was a plea that Irish
servant girls employed in England should not be prevented by the
Exchange Control Bill from sending money to their relatives in Eire.
'Good in content and persuasively delivered,' the *Daily Telegraph* of
19 February 1947 reported, 'Lord Moyne's speech well deserved the
warm cheers with which it was received.' That same year he published a slim volume of poetry, *Reflexions*, dedicated to his wife
Elisabeth, and over the next 28 years he would add to his canon of
works another play, *Riverside Charade*, which was given a brief exposure at Dublin's Abbey Theatre; four novels; a fairy story entitled *The
Paralysed Princess*; a collection of essays; and a scrapbook of 1925, *The
Giant's Eye*, described by a critic of *The Times* of 14 May 1964 as
'charming', with 'an absurdly idyllic quality. The sun seems to have
shone perpetually on obedient children building sandcastles under
Nanny's eye while elegant parents dash madly off to treasure hunts
and masked balls.'

If much of Bryan Guinness's writings had the ring of fairy tales
spun from his own idyllic childhood, his infrequent interventions in

House of Lords debates were as down to earth as might be expected from a major shareholder in one of the world's greatest breweries. He had been made a director of the company at the age of 30 and in 1949 he was appointed vice-chairman, a position he would hold until his retirement from the board thirty years later. When it was proposed to introduce commercial TV to Britain, he wrote to *The Times* deploring the prospect of commercial TV channels supported by advertising. In his letter, published on 31 July 1953, he considered 'existing channels [the BBC monopoly] entirely adequate and commercial TV an unnecessary and extravagant extension which the snowball effect of competition would oblige all advertisers to use if once it were opened.' The scion of an empire created out of a quasi-mystical devotion to the doctrine of 'healthy' competition through private enterprise vigorously opposed the new TV Bill during its passage through the Lords. He hoped, as *The Times* of 1 July 1954 reported, that 'the commercial circus would never be put on the air'; and he explained his stand, in an earlier press interview (with the *Sunday Graphic* of 27 November 1953), with engaging frankness: 'If we have commercial TV and our competitors—or the soft drink concerns—started advertising, we'd have to consider doing the same. This might force us to raise our prices or reduce our profits...'

In fact, from the date of the advent of commercial TV, until Moyne's retirement as vice-chairman, Guinness's annual net profits soared from £2,387,006 in 1954 to £34,500,000 in 1979, and this without any strain on its advertising budget from the new medium.

Meanwhile, and wearing his other hat as a patron of the arts, Bryan Guinness inaugurated in 1957 the Guinness Poetry Awards whereby the three best English-language poems published in the British Isles would receive every year prizes of £300, £200 and £100 out of the coffers of Arthur Guinness Son & Co. These annual awards were discontinued five years later. Recipients over those years included Louis MacNeice and Robert Graves, as well as Robert Lowell.

Not surprisingly, Lord Moyne has difficulty sometimes remembering the birthdates of his 'football team' of offspring. When a reporter of the *Evening Standard* telephoned to check the age of his ninth child, the seven-year-old Hon. Catriona Rose, his lordship said, as the paper reported, 'I have forgotten. Just a minute, I'll go and ask her.' Up to the time of writing there have been only two marriages among his nine children by his second wife, the youngest of whom, the Hon.

Mirabel, is now 25. The eldest, the pretty dark-haired Hon. Rosaleen, married an Indian businessman based in Bombay, Mr Sudhir Mulji, by whom she has had three children—Sachin Sudhir, Sangita Rosaleen and Kabir Jayantilal—the first Eurasians of half-Guinness stock. The second-born by Elisabeth was the Hon. Diarmid Guinness, director of an overseas branch of the brewery, who died at the age of 39 leaving a net personal estate of £1,168,922 and four children by his wife, Felicity.

Neither of the two sons by Bryan's first wife—the Hon. Jonathan Bryan and the Hon. Desmond Walter—has been actively drawn into the moderate mainstream of Conservative politics favoured by their grandfather Walter Edward and their own father—to the extent that the latter was ever actively involved. In Desmond's case, architecture and the preservation of Anglo-Ireland's Georgian heritage claims most of his time and energy. With Jonathan—born 1930, eighteen months before his brother—we are into a more complex pattern of character and motivation. Both of them went to Eton and then up to Oxford to study languages. Each of them married early, Jonathan at 21 and Desmond at 22, but from then on they went their own ways, the younger brother first into farming, the elder to Reuters news agency where, for part of the time, he was employed as a correspondent in the agency's bureau at Bonn. Neither was especially impressive in looks or stature but they made up for that with a good deal of personal charm and, of course, the easy self-confidence that comes, to some, with the knowledge that they can never be less than rich.

It would be Jonathan's destiny to become, after Enoch Powell, one of the most controversial activists on the right wing of the Tory political camp and to split the ranks of the faithful much as his maverick stepfather, Sir Oswald Mosley, split (for a short while) the front ranks of the Labour Party when he broke away from it in 1931. Jonathan was only six years old when his mother Diana, whom he adored, married Mosley; but later, at Eton, he read his stepfather's seminal work, *The Greater Britain*, and while he could never swallow the whole pill of Mosley's ideological thesis, there were parts of it—particularly its uncompromising hostility to the Soviet Union—that would powerfully influence his own judgements as a politician. He could not have been comfortable working for a news agency such as Reuters that required at least the veneer of objectivity in its reporting of world events and it is doubtful if his strong personal prejudices would have carried him into the agency's hierarchy, had this been his aim. In fact, having inherited his first portion

Lady Patricia's husband, Lord Boyd of Merton (then Alan Lennox-Boyd), at his desk shortly after he joined the board of the brewery in 1959.

Popperfoto

The indomitable amateur jockey, Gay Kindersley, Oonagh's only son by her first marriage, with his first wife, Margaret, at the Oxford University point-to-point in 1959.

S and G Press Agency

Topham

Loel Guinness's son Patrick had only four more years to live when he escorted Tina Onassis to a New Year's party in 1961. Death came in a car crash.

The present Earl of Iveagh (then Viscount Elveden) with his lovely Scots bride, Miranda Smiley. They were married in 1963.

Topham

Topham

An engagement photograph of Loel
Guinness's daughter Serena Belinda
('Lindy') with her fiancé, the 5th Marquess
of Dufferin and Ava. Like his mother
Maureen, the Marquess had fallen in love
with a cousin.

Above Deep in the Wicklow Hills, the lakeside Guinness retreat of Luggala House, now the property of Oonagh's son, Garech, by her second husband, Lord Oranmore and Browne.

Left Castletown House, co. Kildare, showpiece and headquarters of Desmond Guinness's society for the preservation of Ireland's Georgian architecture.

Keystone

The controversial Jonathan
Guinness makes another – and
unsuccessful – bid for Parliament in
the Coventry by-election of 1976.
Tory Party leader, Margaret
Thatcher, helps him out.

Hollywood actress Fiona Guinness,
great-great-granddaughter of
Henry Grattan. She made her
debut as a 'topless' showgirl in Las
Vegas.

Topham

The next queen of England? Back in the summer of 1979 people were betting on Sabrina Guinness, of the Anglo-Irish family's banking line.

Sabrina's father, banker James Edward Rundell Guinness. His great-great-grandfather, Robert Rundell Guinness, founded the banking branch of the family in 1836.

Camera Press

The tragic Lady Henrietta Guinness, sister of the present Earl of Iveagh. Her rebellion against 'the rich man's viewpoint' ended in suicide.

of the Guinness fortune while still at Reuters, he left after only three years in order to go into merchant banking and to prepare himself for an assault on the Westminster corridors of power.

His first marriage had been to the 20-year-old Ingrid Wyndham, who had studied acting at the Royal Academy of Dramatic Art. It lasted eleven years, during which Ingrid presented Jonathan with three children, Catherine, Jasper and Valentine, before divorcing him on the grounds of adultery. (She subsequently married Jonathan's cousin, Paul Channon.) No third party was named in this undefended action, which gave custody of the children to Ingrid. Jonathan later married Suzanne Phillips, recently divorced from the artist Timothy Phillips.

During the last year or so of the Phillipses' marriage, Timothy had bought, for their home in Spain, a seventeenth-century former monastery perched on a hill above the bay of Cadaques, the secluded summer resort of artists and writers from Cataluña and nearby France. He disposed of the property, privately, to an agent after splitting with Suzanne and was 'staggered'—as the *Daily Express* of 28 August 1964 reported—to learn, almost immediately, that it had been re-sold to Jonathan Guinness. It was a perfect wedding present for Suzanne, who had loved the place, and it was a tribute to the self-confidence of her new husband that he could dismiss whatever 'ghosts' might dare to persist from the previous marriage.

Jonathan was now 34 and embarked on a career as a merchant banker that would take him, in 1962, to the board of the prestigious Leopold Joseph & Sons, Ltd. as well as a directorship of the family brewery. But this was the grandson of a distinguished parliamentarian, the stepson of a radical politician and a person who, as a young man, had spent an apprenticeship with Reuters at the centre of world affairs. Politics were in his veins and in the air he breathed, especially the politics of confrontation with what he conceived to be an international Communist conspiracy to take over the world. His anguish in this context reflected the 'Reds-under-the-bed' fervour of the American Legion rather than the pragmatism of European politics—as when it was reported (in the *Daily Mail* of 16 May 1968) that he had joined Mrs Mary Whitehouse's 'Clean up TV and Radio' campaign after hearing a religious sermon over his car radio. It was, he declared, 'straight Communism'. And giving play to his taste for the emotive phrase he denounced the clergymen broadcasters as 'Marxists in surplices'.

It was around this time that he joined the Monday Club, which had been formed in 1968 by a group of right-wing Conservative MPs whose blood pressure had been put up by Harold Macmillan's 'Winds of Change' speech, moving away from the traditional Tory position on Black nationalism in Africa. The original idea was that members of the club, which could include influential Tories outside the House of Commons, should hobnob over a good lunch on Mondays and act as a right-wing ginger group inside the party which, in the opinion of club members, was in danger of changing its political colour from true-blue to pale-pink. Over the next few years its membership increased, both in the House and in the constituency associations nationwide, until it could claim some 3,000 members supportive of its policies and concerned to ensure that the 'right' type of candidate, in both senses of the word, was returned to Parliament at election times. Inevitably, the club attracted most of what Bernard Levin described in *The Times* of 4 June 1972 as 'the lunatic fringe of the right', including MPs like Geoffrey Stewart-Smith, who identified pornography as a subversive Communist plot, and George Young, who wanted to 'scare the pants off those pansies at Broadcasting House'.

Jonathan lined himself up, from the start, with the Tory backwoodsmen by co-authoring a Monday Club pamphlet entitled *Ireland—Our Cuba* that raised the sombre spectre of the Red Terror over the situation in Northern Ireland. Claiming, for this purpose, to give 'an Irishman's view' he wrote, as *The Times* of 1 December 1970 reported: 'We must speak to Orange supporters as fellow Conservatives and fellow patriots, to convince them that the danger does not come from the Pope or the Irish Republic but is a common European danger, a world danger. It is a Communist revolution, the anarchy that leads to a dangerous atheistic tyranny.'

On a more serious level the Monday Club was generally opposed to Britain's joining the EEC, wanted to lift the sanctions against Rhodesia, favoured corporal and capital punishment and the repatriation of coloured immigrants. Its position on relations with the Soviet Union was simply that it did not want any.

Jonathan had already unsuccessfully sought nomination as a prospective Tory candidate for Parliament and he no doubt viewed the club as a possible springboard to a seat in the House. In principle, he supported most of its policies, though he personally favoured Britain's entry into the Common Market. He was with Enoch Powell in the latter's prediction of a Britain torn by civil war between blacks and whites, and in one of his more eccentric moods he advocated leaving razor blades in the cells of convicted murderers (for a purpose other than shaving) and declared, as the *Daily Mail* of 2 April

1973 reported, that he would be willing personally to execute criminals 'if it was my duty to do so'. By then he had secured for himself the chairmanship of the Monday Club by defeating his rival, the more moderate MP Richard Body, with a healthy margin of 676 votes to Body's 223, and his victory helped to win him the official Tory candidature in the Lincoln by-election. He fought a vigorous campaign but ended up a poor third, collecting only 6,616 votes, against the 15,340 votes polled for the Tory candidate in the previous election at Lincoln.

To their credit, the executives of the brewery of which Jonathan Guinness was now a director were scrupulous in avoiding partisanship during the campaign. All the posters commending Guinness as being 'good for you' were replaced by posters advertising another of the company's beverages—Harp lager.

Rejected though he had been by the Lincoln electorate, Jonathan retained his power base as chairman of the Monday Club, a job he described as 'like riding a tiger'. The reference was to the fact that the club was already split into a 'right' and a 'left' wing—terms that made sense only within the convoluted politics of its warring members.

Those on the 'right' favoured confrontation with the Tory leader, Prime Minister Edward Heath, who in their view was leading the party down the road to socialism. As a first step they wanted their hero, the anti-marketeer Enoch Powell, brought back into the Cabinet. The 'left', uncomfortably led by Jonathan, who on most issues was a hardline Tory, was opposed to splitting the party by outright confrontation on such issues as the EEC and immigration. Members should fight for the soul of the party from within rather than without its corporate conscience. 'We are,' he declared in a statement published by the *Sunday Times* on 4 June 1972, 'much more analogous to an Arsenal supporter who is on his team's side...even if someone in it commits a foul.' Further complicating matters was the position of Richard Body, MP, and his supporters. Body was a staunch anti-marketeer but considered to be 'soft' on such issues, precious to Jonathan and both wings of the club, as ending immigration, backing Smith's Rhodesia and restoring capital punishment.

During the months following Jonathan's defeat at Lincoln, the bitter struggle waged between these factions—both internally, for control of the club's 25-strong executive council, and on public platforms—led to the resignation of a dozen of its 35 MPs, the expulsion of some key members and, finally, a full-scale row over Jonathan's continued chairmanship. His re-election in April 1973 by the narrower margin, this time, of 624 votes against the 455 balloted for his 'right-wing' opponent, George Young, only aggravated the split in the club and from there onwards its days as an influential ginger group were numbered. Later, with hindsight, Bernard Levin was to write in *The Times* of 23 August 1973 that 'A single glance at the membership of the Monday Club must have made it clear that it could not survive as a single body, ranging as it did from a decent and harmless old bonehead like Sir Victor Raikes to some of the nastiest political creatures ever to be found crawling on our body politic.' But by then six more members of the executive council had either resigned or been expelled and an unsuccessful campaign to oust Jonathan from the chairmanship had led to the purging of a hundred other 'rebels'. Their resentment of this 'thoroughly un-democratic' purge was expressed in a letter from one of the re-signed officers, S. M. Swerling, to the *Daily Telegraph* on 24 August 1963:

Mr Guinness may or may not resign. What is quite apparent is that a very substantial proportion of the membership feels that the present troubles are the product of such poor leadership that a change of chairman is essential, a view which I myself, a former club officer and recently resigned executive member, have arrived at after many long hours working for reconciliation.

After a special meeting of 300 members—who had voted over-whelmingly for the resignation of the club's chairman—were told by Jonathan that he had no intention of standing down, a group of them met to discuss forming a Tuesday club. Consequently some much-needed lighter relief was provided by a letter from Beryl M. Gold-smith (published in the *Daily Telegraph* of 23 August 1973), who wrote: 'I am considering forming a Wednesday Club. Its purpose will be swiftly to find something to squabble about so that a Thurs-day Club may then emerge. By this means it will not be too long before we are back to the Monday Club—Mark II of course.'

Jonathan, refusing to acknowledge the validity of the vote, flew back to join his wife in their monastery house at Cadaques. Two months later his position as chairman was upheld at another special general meeting and his opponents, the so-called 'Powellites', re-signed *en masse*. It was a pyrrhic victory that spelt the end of the Monday Club as a credible influence inside the party, and almost immediately Jonathan was dropped by the Lincoln Conservative Association as their Parliamentary candidate for the forthcoming general election.

To his credit, and for all of his own ultra-right—often eccentric—views on many issues, Jonathan Guinness had been concerned to prevent the club from being taken over by the 'wild and woolly' political neanderthals of the Tory party. His failure to achieve a consensus sprang from his impatience with opponents and his authoritarian reaction to dissent, qualities that had led his otherwise brilliant stepfather Sir Oswald Mosley into the wilderness of British politics.

He was given one more crack at proving himself as a candidate for Parliament by fighting, as the official Tory choice, the by-election at Coventry North-West caused by the death in 1976 of the sitting Labour member, Maurice Edelman. He had unsuccessfully contested this Labour seat as a Heath man at the previous general election that had toppled the Conservative Government and led to Margaret Thatcher's succession as leader of the party. This time he presented himself as a good Thatcher man, laid off razor-blades for criminals and the expulsion of non-European immigrants and made the most of a favourite theme—the threat to Britain of the red peril of Communist tyranny. In the event, he lost to the Labour Party candidate though he increased his own vote from 11,717 to 13,424. But the mood of the country was then against the Government in power and the favourable swing of 5 per cent achieved by Jonathan was not considered particularly impressive. He had retired two years earlier as chairman of the Monday Club, whose membership had fallen by then to 2,000. But he continued, thereafter, to take up political issues with letters to the press from his town house or his Warwickshire mansion, Osbaston Hall, and in punchy articles for political weeklies. But he wisely decided against writing a biography of his aunt Unity Mitford (Hitler's follower) although all her papers had been entrusted to him in her mother's will.

He shared, however, the common interest in Nazi history and it was this, rather than any past family connection with the regime, that caused him unwittingly to embarrass his Tory colleagues and perhaps to reduce his chances of future selection as a candidate by any of the party's constituencies. In November 1977, as part of the promotion of a new book in praise of Himmler's Waffen SS, a former adjutant of Hitler, the SS Colonel Richard Schultze-Kossens, came to England and was a guest for several days in Jonathan's London house. The book had already been attacked by the Tory frontbencher, Airey Neave, as 'whitewash propaganda' for the notorious SS, and a consequent public outcry led to the expulsion from Britain of the former SS colonel and two fellow-officers who had accompanied him. When it was revealed that the colonel had been put up at Jonathan's house, the 48-year-old heir to Lord Moyne said he had welcomed this as 'a wonderful opportunity of talking to someone who had seen history'. That was probably fair enough, but the colonel's host did little to disarm his outraged critics by describing his guest as 'a very pleasant person to talk to' (the *Guardian*, 19 November), and a '...dignified, clearly highly respectable middle-class German sort of character, well informed, quiet and modest...His line was that no doubt the SS atrocities happened, but he didn't directly see it' (*Evening Standard*, 18 November). Later, in a letter to *The Times*, he managed, not very adroitly, to turn the subject of his hospitality to the colonel into a side-swipe at the Soviet Union, whose civilians were among the worst victims of the SS action squads. His letter concluded: 'To divert attention from the pressing Communist danger to a fictitious Nazi one is to play into the hands of a powerful and ruthless enemy.'

It is possible, but not very likely, that the Hon. Jonathan Guinness could again enter the hustings and secure a seat in the House of Commons where his grandfather, the 1st Lord Moyne, once brought distinction to the Guinness name. But at 51, and with no ministerial experience behind him, he could hardly expect advancement, even if the leaders of his party were willing to risk the indiscretions of this intelligent but headstrong right-winger. The day will come, however, when he inherits the peerage of his father Bryan Walter (76 at the time of writing), takes his seat in the House of Lords and contributes his unique brand of fireworks to the proceedings of that august body.

His eldest daughter, the 29-year-old Catherine Ingrid, is totally apolitical and displayed more diverting attributes with her bare-breasted pose for Andy Warhol's latest book of photographs, entitled *Exposures*. His second son, Valentine Guy, after graduating from Oxford with history and economics degrees, recently signed a contract with Mickey Most, a record promoter, and is now launched on a career as the lead singer of a group called The Panic. Clearly, neither his political father nor his MP stepfather, Paul Channon, have had much influence on his choice of vocations. 'I dislike politics intensely,' he declared during his final year at Christ Church, reported in the *Evening News* of 30 June 1980. 'I want to be rich, I want to be famous, I want to be respected.'

The first of these three wishes is virtually assured; the other two, as Professor Joad would have put it, depend upon what you mean by 'famous' and 'respected'. Conceivably, Valentine's last two wishes could be nudged towards realization by his uncle, the Hon. Desmond Guinness, a close friend of Mick Jagger and who, from time to time, opens up the grounds of Leixlip Castle, in co. Kildare, to the massed fans of such pop groups as The Boomtown Rats, The Police and Squeeze. Desmond is no more of a political animal than his nephew Valentine, though there was a time, earlier on, when he contemplated a career as a diplomat and in fact sat for the entrance examination to the Foreign Office. This was during his language studies at Oxford in the early fifties, where the then 22-year-old undergraduate–a great dandy of his generation–was famed for the style of the parties he threw and for his sartorial idiosyncracies. (It was said that his brown shoes were polished daily with brandy and white of egg, and he would appear at some of the more informal parties clad in leopard-skin trousers and a fancifully embroidered sweater.)

He did not pursue his interest in diplomacy. He had already become involved, while still at Oxford, with his own foreign affair in the person of a young German princess, Marie-Gabrielle von Urach, Countess of Württemberg. Their marriage in 1954 at Christ Church Cathedral established a second Guinness link with the British royal family since the Urach-Württembergs, like the Hohenzollerns, were related to the House of Hanover.

From languages and thoughts of diplomacy, Desmond turned to the study of agriculture and for a while actually farmed the Moyne estates in Ireland. But in 1958, with his purchase of Leixlip Castle, the seeds were sown of a new vocation that would absorb both him and his wife over the next twenty years.

The existing owner of the castle–a 12th-century Norman pile on a hill overlooking the little village of Leixlip and the river Liffey–was reluctant to move out even after selling the property. According to Marie-Gabrielle–or 'Mariga', as she prefers to be known–in an interview with the *Evening Standard* published on 20 November 1969, 'He said there was room for all of us and we said we had quite enough uncles, thank you. We had to besiege him with bonfires for six months till he got out.' (The new owners later found themselves on the receiving end of the bonfire treatment. Their first-born, Patrick Desmond, a 23-year-old law student, observed two teenage boys at large in the grounds of the castle. He opened fire on them with a shotgun, peppering them both with pellets, and only escaped going to jail by paying generous compensation to the lads. As the *Daily Telegraph* of 19 July 1980 reported, on being arrested he told the police his family had been troubled by trespassers and there had been 'many hay fires' on the estate.)

The dark-haired and voluptuously built Mariga speaks her precipitate and fluent English in an accent that might be described as part 'country', part 'Hampstead-chic'. Her Edwardian 'orfs' and 'gels' spatter a mannered, ceaseless torrent of acute 'throw-away' observations and rapid anecdotage, all delivered with a deadpan assumption that her audience is as informed as she is on the subject dearest to her German heart: the Irish Georgian Society. The society was formed–or rather refounded–by Desmond and Mariga in 1958 with the object of preserving for posterity as much as possible of the Georgian architecture threatened by decay or by property developers. Initially, the idea was to enlist public support for the creation, by the Irish Government, of the equivalent of the English National Trust.

Aesthetically, their crusade was probably irreproachable. What it failed to take into account was the historical and social fact that the fine buildings and residential terraces of Dublin were a memorial to the Protestant Ascendancy in Ireland and the bases from which a cruel, corrupt and tyrannical élite tried to crush the national and republican spirit out of the Irish Catholic majority. The Irish did not at once flock in their thousands to sign up as saviours of these relics of an imperial past, which probably goes to prove that aesthetics make a poor substitute for a national political conscience. Nor did the Government in the Dail evince any enthusiasm for the Guinnesses' crusade. But the Hon. Desmond and his energetic German princess were not downhearted. During a tour of America shortly after their marriage, when Desmond lectured on 'Irish Castles and Plastered Ceilings', he found audiences enthusiastic about preserving the outward symbols of a regime from which their own Irish ancestors had been forced to flee. And his beautiful and regal wife, then afflicted with a mild form of yellow jaundice, was only faintly discouraged by being referred to, throughout one of the tour-promoting dinner parties, as the daughter of Emperor Hirohito of Japan–though this may have confused some of the blue-rinsed matrons uncertain of the historic connection between Nippon and the Emerald Isle. American memberships of and contributions to the Irish Georgian Society would later do much to sustain the crusade, stimulated by regular appearances of Desmond on the cultural US lecture circuit and the active support of no less a 'Georgian' than Mrs Joseph Kennedy, mother of the assassinated President.

Their first target, while they were 'Georgianizing' the interior of

Leixlip Castle, was a down-at-heel, half-demolished square in Dublin, thirteen of whose remaining Georgian houses had been bought by property developers for reconstruction as an office block. Desmond snookered the philistines by buying one of the Mountjoy Square houses, slap in the middle of the developers' property, and by raising over the next two years, through the Society, the wherewithal to save the neighbouring houses from destruction. Bank loans were raised. Individual members of the Society were cajoled by the personable Desmond and his untiring wife into buying a house here, another there, and a whole batch of five crumbling structures were bought by an American *aficionado* named Carroll Cavanagh, the proprietor of Cavanagh Hats, a gentleman obviously impervious to the prospect of being dubbed the Mad Hatter.

The year 1967 saw the publication of Desmond's first book, *A Portrait of Dublin*,[2] as well as his single greatest *coup* for the Irish Georgian Society. Castletown House, in Celbridge, co. Kildare—three miles away from Leixlip—was build in 1722 for a Speaker of the Irish House of Commons, the flamboyant William Connolly, to the design of the Italian architect, Alessandro Galilei. It was Ireland's largest and most magnificent private house and it remained in the Connolly family until 1965 when it was sold to a property developer, together with 800 acres, by Connolly's descendant Lord Carew. The property went for £166,000 but the developer was only interested in the land and the stately house remained empty and was vandalized over the next two years.

There could obviously be no better showcase for the Irish Georgian Society and in 1967, with the help of a loan from his father, Desmond was able to acquire Castletown House, together with 120 acres of surrounding parkland for £93,000. He had already decided to have the great house furnished, decorated and opened to the public as a Georgian museum and a centre for the 18th-century arts of Ireland and he set off almost at once to 'sell' the Castletown project to American well-wishers. Over the years since then he has realized his dream of restoring Castletown House and making it one of the major tourist attractions for visitors to Ireland and a Mecca for the members of his Society. 'As an act of preservation,' wrote a diarist of *The Times* on 17 June 1973, 'it was the most dramatic thing that has happened to Ireland.'

In that same year an estrangement began between Desmond and his wife who had laboured so long and so unstintingly for the Society and who, in the eyes of many of its members, was the 'heart' to Desmond's 'head'. Into her husband's heart had now come an

attractive blonde ten years younger than Mariga: Penny Cuthbert-
son, granddaughter of the Dutch artist Nico Jungman. Penny's nude
figure had been celebrated in several of the paintings by Lucien
Freud. Over the next eighteen months, while Mariga moved out of
her beloved Leixlip, Penny took her place as hostess of the castle.
However, Mariga moved right back early in 1975 when Desmond
took Penny off with him on another lecture tour of America. Upon
the couple's return all three shared the same battlements, occupying
different wings of the castle, and even appeared as an apparently
amicable trio at Georgian Society happenings, to the confusion of its
more conventional members. As Mariga put it at the time, in the
Daily Mail of 3 March 1975, 'My husband and I really get on quite
well, in a disagreeable kind of way.'

In 1978 Mariga moved out again. By then her 21-year-old son
Patrick had moved into a cottage on his father's estate together with
his mistress, a local colleen named Liz Casey, and their two-year-old
child Jasmin; Mariga's other child, the 20-year-old Marina, had
made some money selling—according to her mother—'either Belgian
potatoes to the Irish, or vice versa', and was off to the USA with a girl
friend and a scheme to breed California chickens for sale to New
Yorkers. This enterprise folded because 'the dear girl didn't realize
her chickens had to be kosher-killed', whereupon Marina tried her
hand as a second-hand car dealer and, when last contacted by the
present writer, was looking after some dogs—or vice versa—in the
clapboard Los Angeles suburb of Venice.

By the spring of 1980, the indomitable Mariga was back in Leixlip
Castle, but the atmosphere therein was closer to that of Siberia than
of 18th-century Georgian frivolity. When I drove out to the castle in
May 1980 it was at once obvious that I could interview Mariga or I
could interview Desmond, but not the two of them together. While
her husband and 'his friends' picnicked beside the nearby swimming
pool, Mariga took me on a tour of the castle's interior, leading me
from room to room only after first cautiously checking they were
without occupants and, at one point, hustling me through a door-
way, finger to lips, when footsteps sounded from one of the stairways.
She showed me her own room, with its great four-poster bed, her
husband's, with its even grander four-poster, the tower room where
Marianne Faithfull would stay 'when she wanted to get away from it
all', the dining-room where they had entertained Princess Margaret
and Lord Snowdon in happier times. And all the while her antennae
were out for the sound of voices or footsteps heralding the approach
of her cohabitants. It was as if the ghost of the woman who created all

this had materialized for this one visitor and would fade again into the Georgian shadows upon my departure.

An Irish friend of the couple shook his head sombrely. 'I'll tell you one thing: You'll never catch me in that old castle, alone at the dead of night, not for love or money.'

16

A Dynasty Secured

From the First Arthur Guinness, down through the generations, chairmanship of the great brewery–even after it went public–was by tradition handed from father to son, except for the short interregnum at the turn of the century when the 1st Earl of Iveagh's cousin, Reginald Robert, stood in for him for a few years. Otherwise, the tradition remained unbroken until 1945 when Arthur Onslow Guinness, great-great-great grandson of the founder and the heir to the 2nd Earl of Iveagh, was killed on active service in Holland. He was 33 at the time of his death and could obviously have expected to take over the chairmanship from his elderly father while still in the prime of his life. His own son, Arthur Francis Benjamin, was then only eight years old. Thus, Arthur Onslow's death threatened the first break, after six generations, in the father-to-son tradition.

Had the 2nd Earl's own death occurred anywhere within the normal span of life, the chairmanship would presumably have gone to his brother, Bryan Walter, or to his son-in-law Alan Lennox-Boyd, if only as 'regents' holding the family fort until the young Arthur Francis Benjamin (who had inherited the courtesy title of Viscount Elveden from his father) was judged capable of heading the Guinness board. But two circumstances–both abnormal–came to the aid of family tradition. One was the longevity of the 2nd Earl of Iveagh, who lived to the ripe old age of 93. The other was the early maturing of Viscount Elveden who was able to step into his grandfather's shoes upon the latter's retirement at 88, when Ben, as he is known to his family and friends, was only 24.

He would probably have qualified for inclusion, as the youngest-ever chairman of a great public company, in a work of reference that by now was carrying the family name into the four corners of the earth. Eight years earlier the managing director of the brewery, Sir

Hugh Beaver, having badly missed a golden plover that had rock-eted out of cover, sought compensation in the conjecture that the bird in question belonged to the fastest-in-flight species of game bird. When the standard encyclopedias failed to produce any data bearing on this, Sir Hugh fell to wondering where one could turn to for a completely comprehensive guide to superlatives. He discussed the subject with a member of his staff at the Park Royal brewery, the athlete Chris Chataway who was then the holder of the world's three-mile track record. Chataway put him in touch with the 29-year-old McWhirter twins, Norris and Ross, two London journalists whose agency specialized in digging out obscure factual data for the press. As a result, the McWhirters were commissioned to compile a book of records that would fill the gap left by the encyclopedias by listing such recondite facts as the weight of the world's fattest woman, the slowest traffic lights, the longest aria, the lengthiest published letter ever sent to the editor of *The Times*, etc. The out-come, after nine months of intensive research, was the publication in 1955 of the first *Guinness Book of Records*.

It became, after a sluggish start, a publishing phenomenon. By 1970, five million copies of the annual publication had been sold. By 1980 it was being published in 23 languages and, with 41 million copies sold, had achieved its own record with the largest sales of any copyright book in history. It is also, of course, a public relations triumph, establishing the name Guinness as a household word among millions who have never tasted the product of the brewery. Today, Guinness Superlatives Ltd, the publishing company set up with Guinness money, puts out, annually, 45 other high quality reference works on subjects ranging from car facts and feats to astronomy, from steeplechasing to soccer, etc., etc. Norris McWhir-ter still heads the empire. His twin brother Ross met his death tragically in 1975, murdered by the IRA.

The young Viscount Elveden, as we have noted, was eight years old at the time of his father's death and was living with his mother, Lady Elizabeth, and his two younger sisters, Elizabeth and Henrietta, on the Elveden estate. He had started at a private school four miles away in Thetford, but petrol rationing had obliged his parents to put him into the free village school built by the Guinnesses in the village of Elveden, separated only by the highway from the great gates leading to the Hall. Here, so long as the petrol shortage persisted, 'Benjy'—as he was then called—took his lessons with the farm-workers' children under the eye of the lanky schoolmistress, Miss

Marie Manning, swopped stamps and conkers and showed off the prize possession of his overstuffed pockets, a particularly impressive pocket-knife. Two years before he entered Eton, his widowed mother married Rory More O'Ferrall, of the celebrated family of Irish blood-stock breeders and trainers. From then on, Benjy and his sisters divided their time, when not in Ireland, between the Old Rectory on the Elveden estate and the handsome town house at Regent's Park–Gloucester Lodge–that the 2nd Earl had turned over to his daughter-in-law.

Rupert Edward now had nine grandsons by his daughters Honor, Patricia and Brigid. He loved them all and they would all benefit from the great fortune passed down to him by his own father and grandfather. But Ben, heir to the Iveagh title, was the apple of his eye and would in time be entrusted with the future of the Elveden estate and farms to which the old earl had devoted so much of his life. His one fear was that he might die inside the five-year period when death duties could be levied on the vast estate, which might have to be broken up to meet them; and so, in his 74th year, he surrendered his life interests in the 23,000-acre estate, including the £400,000 endowment fund created by his father, plus all his other Irish properties, to the Iveagh trustees against the coming-of-age of the then 10-year-old Benjy.

Contemporaries at Eton of the young Viscount Elveden–already, on paper, one of the richest boys in Europe–remember him as a 'good chap', fairly intelligent at studies and completely without 'side'. He would round off his education at Trinity, Cambridge, with six months at Grenoble University betweenwhiles, improving his French. And to please his grandfather his main subject at Trinity would be agriculture. In the event, as he told the *Eastern Daily Press* of 21 May 1958, he found 'the scientific side was too much for me' and after the first year he turned instead to History. The fact of the matter was that Ben, deprived of his father at eight, brotherless, with an aged grandfather and a sporty stepfather as the chief influences on his early development, was already settled in his mind as to his role in life, which would be divided between his duties as chairman of the family brewery and–the Turf.

Neither politics nor the sybaritic attractions of Mayfair held much fascination for him, but at the age of 19 he had got off to a not very auspicious start as a racehorse owner by buying for £5 one leg in the then yearling, 'Guitarist' (influenced, perhaps, by his own modest proficiency as a banjo player). After a couple of unpromising out-ings, 'Guitarist' landed a gamble in a two-year-old seller at Leicester and was bought at the auction by a Newmarket trainer. To the chagrin of his former owners, the horse went on to win ten more races.

Ben would do a lot better than that in the future. Meanwhile he prepared himself for his major role in life by working industriously at the brewery during the long vacations from Cambridge. His coming-of-age party at Elveden in 1958, attended by 1,500 Guinness employees, including planeloads from the family farms in Canada and his aunts' hotel in Venice, commemorated not only his 21st birthday but his appointment as a director of Arthur Guinness Son & Co. and his partnership with grandfather Rupert Edward in the Elveden estate.

Ben was now immensely wealthy in his own right and generally regarded as Britain's most eligible young bachelor. It was not in his nature, nor would it be prudent, for the only heir to the Iveagh earldom to rush into marriage, however much his grandfather must have hoped to see the male succession assured before his death. Instead, the young viscount devoted his working hours to his job as assistant managing director of the breweries at Park Royal and James's Gate and most of his leisure time to the racecourse. He already owned his own small stable of thoroughbreds but his eyes were on the famous Kildangan Stud in co. Kildare whose owner, Roderic More O'Ferrall, had acquired the share held by his former partner, Sir Percy Lorraine, after the latter's death. In November 1961 it was announced that the share had been sold to Lord Elveden, who thus became a partner in more than 20 mares and two dozen yearlings and foals worth somewhere between £150,000 and £200,000.

Five months later, upon Iveagh's retirement, his grandson became chairman of an empire with a stock market value at that time of £87,000,000. He was not the youngest of the family ever to have occupied the Guinness 'throne', for his great-grandfather Edward Cecil had sat on it from the age of 21. But he had been groomed to it, from his childhood, almost as fastidiously as the heir to any royal family. A year later he got married.

He had met his 22-year-old bride four years earlier, as Miranda Daphne Jane Smiley, daughter of a gentleman-farmer, Major Michael Smiley, of Castle Fraser, Aberdeenshire. There was immediate mutual attraction between the Guinness heir and the tall, dark-haired and very lovely young débutante, and from then on the romance developed quietly but progressively until Ben felt ready to make his commitment with an announcement of their engagement in December 1962. Rupert Edward was probably the most contented of all the 110 Guinnesses who witnessed the ceremony in St Bartholomew-the-Great in the City of London, culminating with a reception for 800 guests afterwards in the ballroom of Claridges. As a writer for the *Daily Express* of 13 March 1963, reporting the ceremony, put it:

It was a distinctly Irish occasion. Nothing you could actually put your finger on. More that feeling you have in Dublin that everything in sight is slightly out of tune with the universe.

The Irish girls looked magnificent, tall, dark-eyed and lissom, clothed with a wild elegance that set off the formal modishness of the bride's Givenchy gown. One, in a black, low-crowned trilby and flaming red coat, looked as if she had just ridden in from the hills of Andalusia.

Stirring shamrock greens abounded. The women wore hats of it. The page boys wore sashes of it. The bridesmaids carried bouquets of it…The entire dynasty looked in splendid form.

And, inescapably, he ended his report with, 'Guinness, it was plain to see, was good for them.'

With impeccable precision, the Countess Miranda gave birth to her first child exactly nine months later. It was a daughter, Emma. A second daughter, Louisa, was born in 1967, in the last year of Rupert Edward's life. Two years later she presented her husband, now the 3rd Earl of Iveagh, with a male heir. There had been an 'Arthur' in every generation of Guinnesses from Richard of Celbridge, father of the brewery's founder. 'Benjamin' had been the second most persistent Christian name, followed by 'Edward'. The name 'Rory' had no antecedents in the Guinness pedigree but it was the first name of Ben's stepfather and turfside companion. With wonted modesty he named his son, the new Viscount Elveden, as Arthur Edward Rory Guinness.

The baby and his sister Louisa had been the first of the Iveaghs to be born at the family's Dublin seat, Farmleigh, since the children's great-great-grandfather bought the estate in the 1870s. That same year, Ben had presented himself at Buckingham Palace to deliver up to Queen Elizabeth the Order of the Garter she had bestowed upon his father in 1955. The monarch did not, on this occasion, express the hope that Iveagh would keep up the shoots at Elveden, as her own grandfather, George V, had when Rupert Edward delivered up the Order of St Patrick conferred upon his own deceased father. Elveden Hall had remained unused as a Guinness residence since 1939. Ben, after becoming chairman of the brewery, had talked about his 'dream' of opening up the great house again but had got no further than restoring one room as a study for himself. Indeed, he applied for, and was granted, Irish citizenship in 1967, and his intention at that time was to spend part of the year in Ireland and part in England, either at his house in Regent's Park or the flat he had furnished in Upper Cheyne Walk in Chelsea. He would of course be saddled with income tax in both countries, but this did not seriously depress his life-style and the problem of future death duties was not even on the horizon for the robust and healthy 3rd Earl.

All this would change after 1974, when the British Labour Party was returned to power and legislation was drafted for the imposition of a wealth tax on the rich. At that time he was holding, in his own interest, 1,093,958 units of Ordinary 25p shares in the brewery, another 1,815,297 units under 'family beneficial interests' and 4,117,649 units under 'other interests' (i.e. holdings in trusts not directly beneficial to Ben and his immediate family)–a juicy taxable plum for a Labour Chancellor of the Exchequer to get his teeth into. And this apart from the capital value of his land and other properties in the United Kingdom.

To sympathetic murmurs from shareholders at the 1975 Annual General meeting at Park Royal, Ben announced that he was exiling himself from Britain for tax reasons and would therefore have to give up his sole chairmanship of the Guinness group, incorporated in England, since he would be unable 'for several years' to attend the annual meetings. He would remain joint chairman of the Guinness holding company, without salary, and would continue as chairman of Arthur Guinness Son and Co. (Dublin). The tax men had told him that if he set foot only once in the United Kingdom they would jump on him; but after three years of enforced, if not exactly cruel exile, during which he had to give up his London residences in Regent's Park and Chelsea, the officials of the Inland Revenue gave him permission to make limited annual visits to Britain. He thereupon resumed his group chairmanship, which had been kept warm for him by the managing director, Robert McNeile, and sat once again in the impressive wood-panelled office at Park Royal, with the portraits of former Guinness chairmen looking down on him.

Meanwhile, the handling of the family trust fortunes and the activities of the brewery group were referred for approval to Ben's office at James's Gate or to his home at Farmleigh. Back in 1968, the year following Rupert Edward's death, the trustees had acquired the beautiful Warter Estate in East Yorkshire in a deal that at the time had been described (in the *Daily Telegraph* of 12 December) as 'possibly the biggest sale of agricultural land in England'. For around £4,000,000 they bought up 14,400 acres, including about 1,000 acres of woodlands, a 16th-century manor house, 22 farmhouses, 35 cottages and the entire village of Warter. The estate had been put on the market after the death of its owner, Mr George Vestey, the last surviving son of the 1st Baron Vestey of Kingswood, founder of another remarkable family of traders whose empire—greater even than that of the Guinnesses—had enriched its heirs at an expense to the British exchequer that made Ben's self-exile in Ireland look almost like an act of patriotism. The money for Warter had come out of the trust set up by the 1st Earl of Iveagh for his descendants and the beneficiaries of this deal would be the seven children born over the years 1954–65 to Lord Moyne's sister Grania and her husband, the Marquess of Normanby.

Four years after the Warter acquisition, details were announced of a scheme for the development of the 1,400-acre Pyrford Court estate at Woking, Surrey, where Rupert Edward had devoted so many years of his life to agricultural research and invention. Management of Pyrford had been vested in another Guinness trust company, Burhill Estates, and the plan for its development as a residential complex and leisure centre was in the best tradition of Ben's ancestor, the 1st Lord Iveagh and his brother Lord Ardilaun: namely the public benefit. A wooded area of what was then one of the finest private residential estates in Britain would be set aside for low-rental retirement homes. There would be two public golf courses, tennis and squash courts, children's play areas and riverside walkways. The fine mansion of Pyrford Court itself would become a cultural centre modelled on lines similar to an existing one in Denmark, and the rest of the estate's farmland would remain intact, after extensive reorganization. The whole scheme had Ben's enthusiastic endorsement and, had it gone through, would have redounded to his credit as an Iveagh just as Ken Wood had to his great-grandfather and St Stephen's Green, Dublin, to his great-uncle. But while he was making the best of his exile in Ireland the efforts by the Burhill Estate agent to win planning approval from the local and county authorities ran into one hitch after another and by the time Ben was allowed back in England, most of the more ambitious aspects of the project had to be abandoned. What was left was permission to build a public golf course, a driving range and a club house. Meanwhile the mansion of Pyrford Court became a residence for elderly gentlefolk, and a one-time servants' house on the estate. 'The Bothy', provides residential qualification for the Euro-MP representing that part of Surrey, the Marquess of Douro, son-in-law of Lady Brigid.

The modest and self-effacing Ben was now, at 42, the head of a worldwide trading group with an annual turnover of £650,000,000, and between himself and his nine relatives on the board of Arthur Guinness Son & Co. Ltd, the family totally outclassed the other directors with their holdings of Ordinary stock. There were Guinness breweries either wholly owned or operating under licence in 19 different countries of the world and being imported into another 120. Only the United States, with the biggest beer consumption in the world, remained stubbornly intractable over the years to the merits of the 'good-for-you' stout.[1] Various efforts, before and after World War II, had been made to break into this rich market and some modest progress had been made in New York, with its large Irish-American community. One of the problems had been the cost of shipping across the Atlantic the heavy kegs of draught Guinness preferred by many New Yorkers to the bottled product. An ingenious way around this has since been found by the supply of a special bottled brew which, after being poured into a glass, is put into a box and bombarded with sound waves to agitate the drink and produce the desired creamy 'head'. The system was installed in 200 New York bars in 1980, but the ingrained national taste for 'near-beer', together with the enormous promotional investment required to compete in this tough market, remains an obstacle to Guinness and its American associates.

Under Rupert Edward's chairmanship the group had begun to diversify into non-brewing interests such as confectionary and plastic products and the process was speeded up by his grandson until, in the late seventies, Guinness's empire of subsidiary companies embraced pharmaceuticals, auto engineering, a chain of over 300 retail shops, hauliers, soft-drinks, flower-growing, meat processing and a dozen other unrelated enterprises. Miscellaneous factories were acquired by a property company under the chairmanship of Jonathan Guinness. A fleet of 165 holiday motor-cruisers was put on the Shannon by a wholly-owned subsidiary, the Emerald Star Line, and an 80 per cent interest was bought in America's leading manufacturer of infant accessories, Glenco Infant Items, Inc. Departing from his ancestors' policy of not owning their own pubs, Ben gave the nod to the purchase of several such institutions through a subsidiary company of the group.

Diversification continued apace. Full-page magazine advertisements, featuring nubile model girls, urged male and female readers to step into the Guinness 'both' robe, a garment described as 'Something very special for when you've not got much on'—an invitation that would surely have brought a blush to the cheeks of the brewery's founder, back in the 18th century. 'Pour yourself into a Guinness' was a neat switch of slogan for the subsidiary marketing woollen sweaters. An anti-coagulant, Arvin, was developed from the venom of the Malaysian pit viper and marketed worldwide by a laboratory jointly owned with Knoll AG. And in 1978 Guinness became a force in the movie industry by acquiring a majority interest in Hollywood's Film Finance Group, headed by Richard St Johns. Guinness money has not yet produced a blockbusting box-office hit, but made it possible for cinema-goers to get another eyeful of the naked charms of the delectable Bo Derek in her second movie, *A Change of Seasons*—another use of Guinness funds that might not have commended itself to the ancestors of the 3rd Earl of Iveagh.

Not all of the group's ventures into non-brewing activities proved successful, but by 1978 they were accounting for some 32 per cent of its trading profits. Meanwhile—and starting two years before Ben became chairman—the directors had taken a sniff at the wind of change in drinking habits and, with a faint shudder, had committed the ultimate but well-advised heresy of launching upon the market their own brand of lager beer. They started by hiring a German brewmaster, Dr Hermann Muender, and by testing the public reaction to their pale amber product first in Ireland, with considerable success. From there they spread to Scotland and England and by 1970 Iveagh was able to report that Harp Lager was also, and predictably, 'doing well' in the USA, where its dark brown elder brother was still being generally cold-shouldered.

From a diminutive 2 per cent share of the UK beer market in 1962, when the Guinness–Harp consortium opened the first of its new breweries at Dundalk, co. Louth, lager beer of all brands had climbed by 1980 to over 29 per cent of the market, largely boosted by the demands of the younger pub-drinkers. Other brewers were by now flooding the market with their own lager beers but Harp remained the brand leader, proving that it *was* possible to teach an old dog new tricks. Cecil Edward Guinness, of the separate line of Guinnesses founded by Samuel the goldbeater in the 18th century (which had 'cross-fertilized' with the marriage of his great-aunt Adelaide to her cousin the 1st Earl of Iveagh), is the chairman of Harp Lager Ltd. But profits from the Guinness group's 70 per cent holding flow to the descendants 'of Founder's kin' and in large measure to Lady Brigid's eldest son, Prince Nicholas, through a settlement arranged by Rupert Edward before his death.

Meanwhile, a gentle decline in the sales of Guinness stout on the home market during 1977 and 1978 was arrested and even turned upwards in the following year, aided by a vigorous advertising campaign. And, as always, the advertising space bought by the brewer was handsomely supplemented that year by the free editorial coverage given to a name that was already a household word when the cavalry officer, wounded in the Battle of Waterloo, wrote his testimony to the recuperative powers of 'a glass of Guinness' (see above, p. 19). On 25 August 1979, almost a full page of Britain's biggest-selling tabloid daily paper, the *Sun*, was devoted, under the banner headline 'ALE AND HEARTY!', to the picture-story of a 52-year-old heart transplant patient, Keith Castle, who, on recovering from the operation, asked for 'just what he fancied...a drop of the [Guinness] dark stuff'. That same year, Ben was able to report to the shareholders' meeting an increase in after-tax profits, to £34,500,000.

Arthur Guinness Son & Co. Ltd has been a public company from 1886, since when the Guinness family has been a minority shareholder in the ever-growing capital structure of the great enterprise. But only after the new Company's Act of 1967 came into effect was it possible to assess the total market value of the 3rd Earl of Iveagh's holding both in his personal interest and as a trustee for his future descendants. This was then shown to be a little in excess of £10,000,000. The most recent director's report at the time of writing (year to September 1980) showed the chairman's holding of Ordinary Stock, in his own, his family's and 'other interests', at 9,776,180 units of 25p, with a market value of around £9,250,000. But the annual disclosure of Guinness directors' shareholdings tells only part of the story of the family's beneficial interest in the brewing group. Major shareholders include the Iveagh Trustees whose present managing director, Mr I. S. S. Ferris, was shown, in the company report for 1980, to be 'interested in holdings of 11,014,200 Ordinary Stock units'. These are not great fortunes compared with the sums personally amassed by Ben's ancestors, in particular the 1st Earl of Iveagh. But they take no account of Ben's inheritance of securities, art treasures, farms and other real estate properties in the United Kingdom and abroad, the total value of which is probably incalculable.

The First and Second Arthur Guinnesses were tradesmen, pure and simple. Their successor, Sir Benjamin Lee Guinness, significantly raised his family's social status by virtue of his public benefactions and private life-style. The next in line, first of the 20th-century earls of Iveagh, rooted his family in the British

Establishment, and his son Rupert Edward powerfully nourished these roots not only through his own person but also through his daughters' political and royal marriages. But Ben grew up in a post-war world that had changed, radically, from the one in which his ancestors had lived. Elveden was not the first, nor the last, of the great country houses to reach the end of their glory in his lifetime. The social and economic revolution ushered in by World War II and carried forward by successive Labour Governments was a death-knell to the London season of glittering balls, débuts at Buckingham Palace, royal garden parties where 'everyone' knew virtually 'everyone'. In any case, inflation, coupled with the burden of taxes, had made it not only impractical but illegal for part-time exiles such as Ben, and so many of his social peers, to maintain their families' impressive London residences.

As it happens, none of this is of consequence to the present Earl of Iveagh. He cannot rise any higher in the social hierarchy. His ambitions have never included politics or the entertainment of the great ones of the land and he is happiest at home with his family in beloved Farmleigh or watching one of his racehorses pipping the rest of the field at the winning-post. Elveden rarely sees him these days. One of its glories, the great dairy herd of Friesian and Guernsey cows built up by his grandfather and amounting to 2,300 head in 1962, was down to 1,800 head in 1980, and these were subsequently sold off as part of an EEC scheme for ending the over-production of milk.

Certainly he deserved inclusion, as 'the archetype of a young Irish country gentleman', in an article published by *Fortune* in November 1966 under the heading 'The Elegant Life of the Business Aristocrats':

They combine their 20th-century duties as business executives with a style of living of a bygone era, steeped in an elegance unmatched anywhere else in the world. They do their 'commuting' between sumptuous mansions and palatial country villas, hunt on their own preserves, relax amid art treasures that were collected long before collecting became the vogue among successful businessmen.

In all respects, Arthur Francis Benjamin has worn with grace the mantle passed down to him by the First Arthur Guinness and has kept bright the silver salver bequeathed, as a symbol of continuity, to 'the Eldest Male Branch of my Family...who shall be in the Brewing Trade'. He plays his part as chairman of a great commercial empire with the wisdom and unflappability of one born to the dynastic role. In his dealings with the lesser ranks he is—to quote the old retainer

Jim Speed—'a gentleman to his fingertips'. He has a male heir, aged 12 at the time of writing, who will be educated and tutored to become the Fifth Arthur Guinness at the head of the firm. No breath of scandal has ever touched him.

To the low-profiled, publicity-shy Ben, all seemed to be for the best, in the best of all possible worlds. Until the morning of 3 May 1978 . . .

17

Postscript

On a spring day in 1978, Henrietta Marinori took her own life at the age of 35 by plunging 225 feet from an aqueduct in the central Italian town of Spoleto, 75 miles north of Rome. She was well-off, happily married to a young Italian and the mother of a seven-month-old daughter.

Seven weeks later, in the early hours of 22 June, Natalya Citkowitz, in the act of injecting herself with heroin, slumped head-first from her seat on the toilet into a filled bathtub and died of postural asphyxia. This attractive and popular 18-year-old had, for the past year and a half, been spending most of her £100-a-week allowance on the drug, which she injected into her veins at least once a day.

The common factor between these two tragic females was their Guinness blood. Henrietta was the younger of the 3rd Earl of Iveagh's sisters. Natalya was a granddaughter of Maureen, one of the 'golden Guinness Girls'.

They had little else in common. Both, of course, had been born to wealth: Henrietta was the beneficiary of around £5,000,000 of the Iveagh trust fortune; Natalya would inherit part of the fortune passed down to her mother, Lady Caroline. Otherwise, and apart from both of them having been drawn into the 'Chelsea scene', there were few similarities in their backgrounds. They were born a generation apart. Lady Henrietta had been educated mainly in England and brought up on the great estates of her grandfather, the 2nd Earl of Iveagh. Natalya, offspring of the marriage between her novelist mother and the composer Israel Citkowitz, had been schooled in France and America. Though they both belonged to the brewery line of Guinnesses, with a common ancestor in the First Arthur, their branches of this line rarely intertwined socially except on such formal 'Guinness occasions' as a wedding or funeral in the great family.

For the purposes of popular Press headlines they both were categorized as 'Poor Little Rich Girls', a saccharine cliché designed to console the less-privileged readers by underlining the mixed blessings of inherited wealth. Still, the cliché wraps a truism; and Scott Fitzgerald's dictum about the rich being 'different from us' deserves better than Hemingway's 'Yes–they have more money'. Inherited wealth on the scale enjoyed by so many of the Guinness family not only sets them apart from ordinary mortals in terms of received, and perceived, values: in individual cases it alienates them brutally from the very values they might be expected to endorse. In drug addiction Natalya, granddaughter of a marchioness, sought escape from her heritage years before it could possibly weigh upon her. Her cousin Henrietta chose another route...

Henrietta Guinness was barely two and a half years old when her father, Viscount Elveden, was killed in action during World War II. She and her elder sister Elizabeth were brought up with their brother Ben by their widowed mother. Their wartime and post-war childhood homes were the estates of their grandfather–Elveden and Pyrford in England, Farmleigh in Ireland. Permanent staffs of servants at all three places were at their beck and call, and although the children were neither cosseted nor spoilt there was no way of disguising from them the fact that they were 'different' from the vast majority of other kids, out there beyond the boundaries of the estates.

By the age of 19, with schooling and 'finishing' behind her, Henrietta was ready–perhaps all too ready–to switch from the country mansions to the classless Chelsea environment of the early sixties, in which the children of the aristocracy were rubbing shoulders in an endless round of parties and 'happenings', with the new 'elite' of working-class painters and photographers, Cockney model girls and trendy hairdressers. Henrietta was no beauty. She had the blonde, bland, blue-eyed Guinness looks and was short in stature with a tendency to plumpness. But she gave off a sparkle, a zest for living and a generosity of spirit that was all the more endearing to her new Chelsea friends for being totally uncontrived. With it, of course, came a defencelessness against her own youthful ardours, almost tragically exemplified by her runaway affair with the 26-year-old Michael Beeby, and the resultant car crash in the South of France that all but took her life. The effects, mental and physical, kept her in and out of nursing homes and psychiatric clinics over the next two and a half years and undoubtedly accounted for the eccentricities and irrational behaviour that would estrange her more and more from her family over the lifespan left to her.

There is probably no such animal as a 'quintessential Guinness', but so much past intermarriage between cousins, taken together with the centripetal pull of their interlocked wealth, has produced a recognizable Guinness 'style' to which the great majority of the family conform. Friends attest to their being 'almost Oriental about losing face among themselves' and that they 'would do anything rather than admit to another member of the family that they had made a wrong decision'. 'They break a lot of the social conventions periodically but they are basically a hangover from Victorian society. Weddings have to be conducted with the utmost protocol. They'll probably all get blind drunk and take off their clothes at the party afterwards but the affair has to be arranged with almost Victorian propriety.'

And again, and typically: while the Guinnesses have been among the most generous of public benefactors, 'if they find the most minute indiscretion—such as a mistake in the milk bill—they hit the roof.'[1]

Henrietta was a maverick from the Guinness herd. From the time of her near-fatal accident, and between recurring bouts of depression, she found her happiness in the ambience of the King's Road *demi-monde* and a measure, at least, of fulfilment in deploying her wealth for the benefit of her friends. It kept her at constant loggerheads with the Iveagh trustees, headed by her own brother, who out of concern to protect her inheritance had prevailed upon her to sign it all into an unbreakable lifetime trust shortly before her grandfather Iveagh's death in 1967. A portion of it bore regular interest which Henrietta dispersed virtually as soon as—and sometimes before—it reached her bank, either in outright gifts or in hospitality to the mixed company of freeloaders and fairweather friends who, together with the more genuine variety, made up her peripatetic Chelsea 'court'.

One of the most 'in' restaurants of the sixties was the establishment at 124 King's Road run by Alvaro Maccioni, who came to play something of an avuncular role in Henrietta's life. At this period—the most unsettled in her short life—she was smoking pot, like the rest of the gang, and being 'ripped off', as Alvaro put it to me, by most of the other Chelsea restaurateurs, who were happy to 'pad' her nightly bills in compensation for the often outrageous behaviour of her retinue. Alvaro kept the Iveagh trustees more or less happy by restraining Henrietta from inviting strangers off the streets to join her nightly food and wine feasts. He protected her, as far as he could, from the scroungers looking for an 'easy touch' and he was there when she needed comfort and advice in her depressions.

'She fell in love with my sauce chef, Benito Chericato, and wanted to marry him. Nice quiet boy, goodlooking and a hard worker. I tell you, it was something. I couldn't keep her out of the kitchen, washing dishes, glasses—anything to be with Benito. There was another girl in his life, and he had children by her. He just couldn't make up his mind, even after Henrietta went with him to Italy to meet his parents. Even after she became a Catholic. Even after she set him up in his own restaurant in Belgravia. In the end it fizzled out, but they remained friends.'

The restaurant had cost her £28,000. A year later, at a reported cost of £20,000, she set up a salon in Kensington for the man who for years had taken care of her hair. She was now 27, a Lady in her own right (following the death of the 2nd Earl of Iveagh) but still under periodic psychiatric care and more than ever a rebel against the life-style pursued by her brother Benjamin and her sister Eliza, now married to David Nugent. She had expressed herself forcibly, and poignantly, after her trip to Italy with Benito:

'I hate the rich man's viewpoint and his attitude towards life. I am tired of snobbery. I want to be with real people.'[2]

The real people included modern painters as well as sauce chefs and, for a while, Henrietta's enthusiasms switched from the Chelsea bistro scene to London's art galleries and studios. She bought works by David Hockney and Kenneth Nolan and at one point had to be restrained by the Iveagh trustees from buying up the whole of an exhibition by the North Country painter, Norman Stevens. Her prodigal generosity, together with the annual tax burden on her unearned income, ruled out any accumulation of savings and the trustees had clamped down on the release of further capital sums. Italy beckoned her again. The people were 'real', they appreciated good painting and music. She could live happily enough there on her income and, like her brother Benjamin, escape the clutches of the British tax master by establishing residence abroad. She would buy a house, possibly in the area of Rome, where her friends could fly out to join her in exile. The trouble was...

She called on the services of the distinguished lawyer, Lord Chelmer, who had no professional connection with the Guinnesses. Could the trust be broken? Failing that, could the trustees be persuaded to release a lump sum for the purchase of a house abroad? He discussed the situation with the lawyers—Travers, Smith, Braithwaite & Co.–acting for the Iveagh trustees. They were not very hopeful. A property yielding an income–well, maybe. A private residence? That was something else.

Henrietta took off for Rome. A year later, at the annual arts festival in Spoleto, she met and fell in love with an unemployed ex-medical student, Luigi Marinori, seven years her junior. She moved in to live with him in his parents' modest working-class home and they were married a few months after the 35-year-old Henrietta had given birth to a daughter, Sarah.

On the morning of 3 May 1978, precisely three months after marrying Luigi, Henrietta left the office of the Spoleto dentist where she had been having a filling fixed, walked on to the narrow passageway over the Ponte delle Torri aqueduct, put down her handbag and leapt to her death.

It is profitless to speculate on the state of her mind during those minutes before she took the fatal plunge. She had had a nervous breakdown after the birth of her daughter, seven months earlier, and it was suggested that she might have been suffering from puerperal psychosis, a curable mental condition sometimes affecting women after childbirth. Certainly there was nothing to suggest disillusionment with her life in Spoleto. She had bought an old monastery nearby and was planning to renovate it as a home for herself, Luigi and Sarah. And, shortly before her marriage, she had sought legal advice in England as to the formalities for settling part of her property upon her husband. She had apparently been advised that three months would have to elapse, from the date of marriage, before anything could be done about this.

Her mother Lady Elizabeth, her brother Benjamin and her sister Lady Eliza had flown to Spoleto as soon as they heard of her death and it was agreed that Sarah should remain permanently in the care of her Italian father. A trust fund would be set up for her, but the extent of this and the benefits available to Luigi remain a secret, as closely guarded by the Marinoris as it is by Henrietta's own family.

Henrietta was the only Guinness girl, of a clan richly endowed with females, to have taken her own life. It is a safe enough conclusion that she had never fully recovered the balance of her mind after her near-fatal accident at the age of 20. It was also her misfortune to be born at the least vital end of the eight-generation scale measuring the saga of this extraordinary Anglo-Irish family.

The giants among the Guinnesses–whether as brewers, bankers or evangelists–were mostly products of the 3rd, 4th and 5th generations, people like the Second Arthur and his son Benjamin Lee; Richard Seymour and his vigorous, fortune-building offspring, Gerald Seymour, Benjamin Seymour and Richard Sidney; the Rev. Henry Grattan and his adventurous children. They knew exactly what they wanted, they knew what it would cost in terms of single-minded dedication, and they went out and got it. In any one of those generations, the zest for life and boundless energy of the young Henrietta would have found a positive outlet as against the negative one of escape from the social trap into which her own generation of Guinnesses was born.

It is the fate of dynastic commercial families to lose impetus over the years in ratio to the growth of their empires and the thinning of entrepreneurial blood in each succeeding generation. When, as in the case of the brewery Guinnesses, a social ascendancy based on titles is added to accumulated wealth, the process is accelerated. Guinnesses still dominate, numerically, the board of the brewery but the overall administration is the province of a non-Guinness Managing Director backed by a working committee of 13 which includes only two members of Founder's kin. Family representation on the merchant banking empire of the Guinness Peat Group is now confined to James Guinness and one of the grandsons of the famous Samuel–Graham Carleton Greene.

But the charisma of the family name remains undimmed. It is the common reference point for a dozen aristocratic titles that never quite upstage it. ('Yes, well she's actually a Guinness, you know.') It is at once a password to the Royal Enclosure at Ascot and an 'open sesame' at the guarded doors of the latest 'in' discothèque. ('We had *three* Guinnesses in, opening night.') The physical monuments to Guinness philanthropy are still there, from the statues in Dublin to the blocks of working-class flats on the King's Road, Chelsea, where Henrietta once held court. And the spiritual values cherished by the clergymen Guinnesses are upheld by their descendants in a dozen foreign missions as well as in London's East End where Father Jack Clephane Guinness, of the New Zealand branch, returned in 1972 to preside over the Anglican Community of the Resurrection.

Somewhere across the globe, as you read these last lines, another Guinness child is about to be born as a direct descendant of the First Arthur or his brother, Samuel the Goldbeater. By the time he or she grows up, the world will have changed, for the better or the worse. If he cares to, he will seek out this, one man's chronicle of the family history.

Let him read it with pride.

Appendix

Let us examine the 'evidence' for the supposed Magennis–Guinness link in order of its appearance.

In Volume 2 of the *Dictionary of the Landed Gentry of Britain and Ireland* compiled by Sir Bernard Burke and published in 1857 it is stated:

> The Guinnesses descend from the ancient and eminent house of Magennis, in which family vested the Viscountcy of Iveagh. Several members of the Iveagh family lie interred in the churchyard of St Catherine's, Dublin, and in the Parish Register the transition of the name from Magennis to McGuinness or Guinness is clearly traceable.

This statement has been repeated without correction in all subsequent editions of the *Landed Gentry* down to the present day. It is totally without foundation. The registers of St Catherine's, still preserved, record the burials of two Viscounts Magennis of Iveagh in the latter part of the 17th century and the first mention of a Guinness—a century later—is an entry of 10 April 1762, recording the baptism of the eldest child of the First Arthur.

In 1856, a year before the publication of Volume 2 of Sir Bernard's dictionary, Richard Samuel Guinness, a barrister and Member of Parliament for Barnstable, Devon, had responded as follows to a request for information from Sir Bernard: 'My father...was the eldest grandchild of Richard of Celbridge, who died when my father was 8 years old, viz., in 1763 at the age of 83, so he must have been born near 1680. I had always heard that the father of Richard had come into Ireland from Cornwall with Cromwell.'

Sir Bernard accepted for his dictionary the estimated date of 1680 but suppressed the information about Cornwall and Cromwell. It is perhaps pertinent to add that his informant was the son of another barrister, of a line of Guinnesses unconnected with the brewery, whereas the correspondence took place at a time when Benjamin Lee Guinness, father of the 'first' Lord Iveagh, was the immensely wealthy head of Dublin's principal industry and a recent lord mayor of the city.

Between 1888 and 1897–a period spanning the assumption by Edward Cecil of the Iveagh title–two genealogists, John O'Hart and Richard Linn, published works[1] stating that Richard of Celbridge was the great-grandson in male descent of Sir Conn Magennis, second son of Arthur, 1st Viscount Magennis of Iveagh. Neither author produced the slightest evidence to support this claim.

Henry Seymour Guinness, born in 1858, was a great-grandson of the First Arthur's youngest brother, Samuel, a goldbeater by trade and the founder of the banking line of Guinnesses. He was educated at Winchester, trained as an engineer and, after serving with the Public Works Department in India, was appointed High Sheriff of Dublin in 1899. He became a Senator of Southern Ireland at the age of 63 and of the Irish Free State a year later, when he was also appointed Governor of the Bank of Ireland.

From his banker father he had inherited a fine house, Burton Hall in Stillorgan, co. Dublin, but he sold it when his wife Mary, a Durham girl, became 'fed up' with the life of a 'Lady of the Manor'. With the help of professional genealogists he devoted several years of his life to a search for the origins of the Guinness family. He set out on this task with an open mind. If it should lead him to a noble lineage, all to the good: if not, he would at least have the satisfaction of tying up some loose ends and perhaps putting an end to the guesswork going on within the family.

The data given here emerged from his painstaking researches into the Guinness pedigree. They are part of a wealth of documented material uncovered by Henry Seymour and embodied in a volume privately printed in 1924[2] that, until now, has never been put before the public. The book will be found in neither the British Library nor the National Library of Ireland. How it came into my hands is a story I shall perhaps reserve for my own autobiography.

Henry Seymour contested that Sir Conn Magennis was a son of the 1st Viscount Magennis of Iveagh and that Sir Conn had any children other than a daughter, Sarah. And he dismissed the above-mentioned genealogists, O'Hart and Linn, as 'notoriously inaccurate and unreliable'.

He found that the most fanciful of all the documents aimed at establishing a Magennis-Guinness pedigree were the work of the Rev. Thomas Moray Fahy, who seems to have divided his energies between the creation of genealogical fairy stories and the rectorship of Annaduff parish in co. Leitrim.

Fahy starts with a Philip Magennis of co. Down, born *circa* 1590, who married into the house of O'Neill in co. Tyrone. This Philip left one son, Henry, who also married an O'Neill, was killed at the siege of Clonmel in the Cromwellian wars and left two sons, Edward (born 1648) and John (born 1650). Both, according to Fahy, were colonels in the Jacobite army led by the exiled Catholic King James II, and both were killed during the second siege of Athlone in 1691. Edward died unmarried but John 'left two sons, Richard born about 1689 and William born in 1691'. This is the Richard we are asked by Fahy to believe was the father of the First Arthur Guinness, having changed his surname from Magennis to Guinness (and, presumably, his religion, though Fahy makes no mention of this) to be more acceptable to the English Protestant Establishment in Dublin.

At this stage of the narrative—it becomes even more fanciful as Fahy waffles on—let us put his 'evidence' to the test.

There may well have been a Philip Magennis of co. Down who had a son Henry, although this would have been the only occurrence of such a Christian name in the Magennis clan. Fahy makes no mention of Sir Arthur Magennis, who had assumed the title of the 1st Viscount of Iveagh three years after the birth of Fahy's Henry, from which it can be deduced that his Philip Magennis, if he indeed existed, was not in the direct line of Iveaghs. He says that Philip's grandson John, of Jacobite fame, married Ellen Grace, a relative of Oliver Grace, MP, but there is no record of a Magennis marriage to a Grace in the definitive history, *Memoirs of the Family of Grace*, published in 1823 by Sheffield Grace. As for the roles of Colonel John and his colonel-brother Edward at the second siege of Athlone, there were in fact many Magennis officers in the Athlone garrison but curiously no mention of either of these brothers in D'Alton's *King James's Irish Army List* of 1689. Nor do these gentlemen figure in contemporary accounts of the siege published in the *London Gazette* of 13 and 26 July 1691.

The significance of the alleged Grace connection becomes apparent as we pursue Fahy's fiction.

Of the existence of Richard Guinness there is no doubt. His name was recorded in the official pedigree of the family drawn up in 1814 and filed in the Office of Arms, Dublin, and his family were scheduled in the religious census ordered by the Irish Parliament in 1766. The fact that nothing positive is known about his parentage has baffled members of the Guinness family right down to the present generation and it led Henry Seymour to conclude in 1924 that 'his children appear to have deliberately destroyed or suppressed all reference to their father'. These children were, of course, the First Arthur and his brothers.

Theories, nonetheless, abound and we shall examine some of them. But in the meantime–back to the Rev. Mr Fahy.

He tells us that Richard's 'younger' brother William (in fact he was the elder of the two) was brought up by Oliver Grace who placed him in Archdekin's Brewery, Kilkenny, where he learnt the trade, married Maud Archdekin, resumed the name of Magennis and set up a brewery of his own in the town of Loughrea where he was joined by his nephew Arthur (Richard's eldest son and the First Arthur Guinness) and afterwards by his own son Edward, 'all of whom made the brewery a great success'. In fact, as the official pedigree of the Guinness family attests, William was a Dublin gunsmith who married Mary Williby (or Willoughby) and had nothing to do either with the first small brewery leased by his nephew Arthur at Leixlip, 150 miles east of Loughrea, or with the James's Gate brewery that Arthur leased in Dublin three years later. There was in fact an old brewery at Loughrea, but 'no trace of a Magennis ownership can be found, nor among the muniments of the Marquess of Clanricarde, who was Lord of the Soil, and which are preserved at Portumna and Loughrea, has any lease or memorandum whatsoever been discovered connecting a Magennis with Loughrea'.[3]

The Rev. Mr Fahy wraps up his narrative by telling us that William's son, 'Edward Magennis', married Ellen ffrench of Monivea Castle and they had a son John who married Anne Moray. John changed his family surname again, this time to McGuinness, and it was an Anne McGuinness, daughter of John and great-great-aunt of Fahy from whose manuscript notes the reverend gentleman claims to have constructed his narrative, she in turn having been given the history of the family by her grandfather Edward who had brought her up.

It remains to add that the ffrench family of Monivea Castle asserted positively to Henry Seymour that there had been no marriage between a member of their family and a McGuinness. The most painstaking research has uncovered no record of John's marriage to Anne Moray. Anne McGuinness, according to Fahy, lived and died (1869) at Loughrea and was buried at Ballinasloe. Henry Seymour writes: 'Loughrea has been searched, old inhabitants questioned, census returns and parish registers examined and graveyards searched, but no trace of Anne McGuinness can be found.'

Upon being asked, after the publication of his narrative, for a sight of Anne's original notes, the rector of Annaduff regretted that they had been 'destroyed by damp many years ago'.

So much for the efforts made during the lifetimes of Sir Benjamin Lee and Sir Edward Cecil (later Lord Iveagh) to establish a blood line from the Magennis family to the Guinnesses. Turning from fiction to fact, we can now review the documented history of the real Magennises of Iveagh.

On the death in 1629 of the 1st Viscount Magennis of Iveagh he was succeeded by his son Hugh as the 2nd Viscount and on Hugh's death in 1639 the title passed to his eldest son, Arthur. When Arthur died in 1683 his brother Hugh became the 4th Viscount and married Rose O'Neil, leaving three sons—Bryan, Phelim and Roger—upon his own death in 1684. Bryan became the 5th Viscount and, having fought for James II against William of Orange in the war of 1690, when the Irish forces were defeated in the Battle of the Boyne, he was stripped of his peerage by the victorious William and took service in exile under the Austrian crown. Bryan's marriage to Lady Margaret Burke, daughter of the 7th Earl of Clanricarde, did not produce an heir and with his death in 1693 the title of Viscount Magennis of Iveagh became extinct as a peerage of the Kingdom of Ireland. However, since the Jacobites refused to acknowledge William of Orange's sovereignty, Bryan's descendants continued to use the title bestowed on the Magennises by James I. It passed first to Bryan's brother Phelim—as evidenced by a suit in the Commons Plea Court in Ireland dated September 1700 naming Phelim as 'Lord Iveagh'—and thence to his younger brother Roger, described in contemporary documents as 'Lord Viscount of Iveagh'.

In his research into the Iveagh succession, Henry Seymour cites evidence produced in 1885 by Lady Ferguson, wife of Sir Samuel Ferguson, Deputy Keeper of the Records in Ireland; the public archives at Simancas, Spain (Secretariat of the Exchequer, carton No. 966 and Secretariat of War, bundle No. 2593); an article, 'Lord Iveagh and other Irish Officers in France', published in 1901 by the president of the Irish College, Paris, based on Miscellaneous Papers (A.10,816) in the Mazarin Library, Paris, and 'Jacobite Extracts from the Registers of the Parish of St Germain-en-Laye' published by Mr C. E. Lart in 1910. (After his defeat at the Boyne by William of Orange, James II set up his Irish court at St Germain-en-Laye.)

These records attest that Roger Magennis, the 7th Viscount, followed James II to St Germain, married Jane O'Neill in 1701 and had a daughter Mary who died in 1711 aged nine; a son Roger who died aged six weeks; another son, Arthur, born on 22 April 1706, and a daughter Louise Marie, born 31 December 1708. The registers of St Germain show that Mary, the widow of James II, was Mary Magennis's godmother and that Princess Louise Marie was the godmother of her namesake among Roger's children. All entries in the register name the children's father as 'Lord of Iveagh'.

The only surviving son was Arthur, the titular 8th Viscount, who after marrying and fathering two sons took Holy Orders and in 1751 became rector of St Patrick's Church in Madrid. His son Hugh is included in the service books of the Hibernia Regiment of Infantry compiled in Spain in 1772 as 'Captain Hugh Magennis, Count of Iveagh in Ireland and born in 1728'. It states that he was married and still living in Spain in 1772, and although Henry Seymour's own detective work ends at this point, he cites the evidence of the Spanish authoress, Fernan Caballero, writing in 1861, that 'among the many families of Irish descent still living in Spain was that of Magennis, represented by General Magennis, Lord Iveagh, in active service'. Thus the succession of Iveaghs down to the 9th Viscount is clearly established by contemporary records and, as Henry Seymour puts it, 'there is every probability that with further research in Spain a complete pedigree of the family to the present day could be obtained'.

Finally, a word about the claim by O'Hart and Linn that Richard of Celbridge was the great-grandson in male descent of Sir Conn Magennis, second son of Arthur, 1st Viscount of Iveagh. Sir Conn, knighted in Ireland by Viscount Falkland on 21 June 1627, was the owner of Newcastle, co. Down. At the outbreak of the Rebellion of 1614 he seized the town of Newry and held it for 27 weeks until it was recaptured by Lord Conway and General Monro on 1 May 1642, whereupon Sir Conn was outlawed and a price of £600 put upon his head. He married his cousin Evelyn Magennis, daughter of Ever Magennis of Castlewellan, co. Down, and, as affirmed in three of the '1641 Depositions' preserved in Trinity College, Dublin, he died in 1643. The only recorded issue of the marriage was one daughter, Sarah, who married Art Magennis of the clan's Clanconnel branch.

Had there existed any acceptable evidence of Magennis ancestry, it is inconceivable that the Rev. Hosea would not have cited it in his original bid for confirmation of the Magennis arms already—as we have seen—in use by his father the First Arthur Guinness. In theory he might have claimed that Arthur's forebears changed their surname from Magennis to Guinness to escape the penal laws against the Papists. This, however, would have ruled out a lineage connection with the male descendants of the 1st Viscount of Iveagh, all of whom, as we have seen, preserved their family name.

In an article written for *The Times* on 10 November 1959 the 2nd Lord Moyne, grandson of the first Guinness to take the title of Iveagh, skated delicately around the issue—by ignoring it.

The origins of our family are hidden in the mists of a not very remote antiquity. The first Guinness of whom there is an undoubted record is Richard Guinness of Celbridge, county Kildare, who was born about 1690 and was living in Leixlip in 1766. Efforts to trace the origin of the family beyond him have met with no success; conjecture, supported by inconclusive pieces of evidence, have led principally in the direction of the Magennis family of county Down and of the Gennys family of Cornwall.

As it goes, this is a perfectly honest statement. It would have been made totally scrupulous had he noted, for the reader's benefit, the connection between the Magennis family and the ancient title of Iveagh.

It is not impossible that the Guinnesses might have descended from a minor branch of the Magennis family but, as Moyne admits, no reliable evidence of this has ever been uncovered whereas, prior to the birth of Richard of Celbridge, there were many families in Ireland, mostly of English origin and some of the Protestant faith, whose surnames were Guinness or variations of that spelling such as Ginnis, Gennys, Gunnis and Gynes. And if it was the Rev. Hosea's sincere belief that the Guinnesses were a cognate branch of the Magennises, having changed their name and religion somewhere down the line, these would be the only 'descendants' of the Magennises to have done so. (During the lifetime of the 1st—Guinness—Earl of Iveagh, for example, a Charles Donagh Magennis, born a Catholic in the northern Ireland city of Derry in 1867, emigrated as an architect to the United States. There he built schools, churches and colleges, designed the bronze doors of New York's St Patrick's Cathedral, and in 1937 became President of the Institute of Architects.)

Reference has been made to the letter addressed in 1856 to Sir Bernard Burke by Richard Samuel Guinness in which he stated, 'I always heard that the father of Richard [of Celbridge] had come to Ireland from Cornwall with Cromwell.' Writing 40 years later, Richard Samuel's nephew, Richard Seymour, says he remembers his father 'telling me he thought the first [of the family] who appeared in Ireland had come from England as a private soldier in

Cromwell's army of invasion.' Henry Seymour investigated the origins of families, settled in Ireland and using the above-mentioned variations of the Guinness spelling, and he concluded that the most likely possibility was that Richard of Celbridge was one of the sons of Owen Guinneas (*sic*) of Murphystown, afterwards of Simmonscourt, Donnybrook, and the descendant of a Cornish ancestor by the name of Gennys who came to Ireland during the Cromwellian wars. He came to this conclusion after tracing the first of the Gennys family back to the period 1272–1346 in the persons of John de Seintginas, Robert de St Gennis, Symon de St Gennys, etc., all of whom took their surnames, in the varying spellings common at that time, from the Cornish town of St Gennys. His meticulous piecing together of the genealogical clues leading to this judgement is a fascinating essay in detection. It ends in 1726 with the granting of a lease to George Guines (*sic*), dairyman, and his brothers William and Richard, but the piece of the jigsaw covering the period from the birth of Richard, *circa* 1690, up to 1726 remains missing.

All we know is that Richard's first wife, Elizabeth Read, died in 1742 at the age of 44 and was buried in the old churchyard of Oughterard, co. Kildare; but Read family tradition has it that Richard was a groom in their employment before eloping with Elizabeth. Ten years after her death Richard married a widow, Elizabeth Clare, and took lease of a house in Celbridge, believed to have been a coaching inn where, according to local tradition, he acted as the ostler.

Notes

Introduction

1. By Patrick Lynch and John Vaisey (Cambridge University Press, 1960).

Chapter 1

1. *Brendan Bracken*, by Charles Edward Lysaght (Allen Lane, 1979), p. 95.
2. Evelyn Waugh confirmed the 'Carlton-Club' ambience of the house with his diary entry for 10 June 1930: 'Bryan [Walter's son] took me over Grosvenor Place—more unhomely than any marble palace would be.' (*The Diaries of Evelyn Waugh*, edited by Michael Davie, Weidenfeld & Nicolson, 1976.)
3. Lynch and Vaisey, *Guinness's Brewery in the Irish Economy, 1759–1876*, p. 77.

Chapter 2

1. Lynch and Vaisey, *Guinness's Brewery in the Irish Economy, 1759–1876*.
2. This and earlier portraits show him with a decidedly aquiline nose, whereas his father's portrait features a perfectly straight one.
3. *Cox's Irish Magazine*, June 1913. A dig at the English accent.
4. Lynch and Vaisey, op. cit., p. 143.
5. Ibid., p. 107.
6. Ibid., p. 235.
7. Ibid., p. 81.
8. W. F. Monypenny, *Life of Disraeli*, vol. II.
9. *Long Forgotten Days*, by Ethel M. Richardson (Heath Cranton, 1928). More than a century later, a more philosophical tribute would be put in the mouth of a character in Oliver St John Gogarty's *As I Was Going Down Sackville Street*. 'Like dark sleep,' he says of Guinness, 'it knits up the ravelled sleeve of care, and, what is an achievement, it wastes the time that might, if we were not drinking, be devoted to scheming, hypocrisy and money-making.'

Chapter 3

1. *Iveagh House*, by Nicholas Sheaff (Department of Foreign Affairs, Dublin, 1978).

2. The intricate blood transfusion between the Guinnesses on the one hand and, on the other, the great Anglo-Irish families of the Plunkets, the Blackwoods (Dufferin and Ava) and the Hamiltons will be dealt with in a succeeding chapter.

3. *Dublin Daily Express*, 10 June 1865. Quoted by Lynch and Vaisey, *Guinness's Brewery in the Irish Economy, 1759–1876*, p. 181.

Chapter 4

1. Lynch and Vaisey, *Guinness's Brewery in the Irish Economy, 1759–1876*, p. 184.

2. The name was derived from that of an island in one of the lakes of his Ashford estate.

3. Childers was the Irish-born propaganda chief of that faction of the IRA opposing the treaty by which the Irish Free State was set up with dominion status inside the Commonwealth. Captured in November 1922 during the civil war between pro-treaty and anti-treaty forces, he was shot at dawn a week later.

4. *Pantaraxia* (Hutchinson, 1965).

5. Lord Rowton (founder of London's 'Rowton House' hostels for the poor), Mr Ritchie (President of the Local Government Board) and Mr Plunket (First Commissioner of Works).

6. It has now been replaced by an office building, housing the General Accident, Fire & Life Assurance Corporation.

7. *The Times*, 20, 23, 25 October 1928.

8. Lynch and Vaisey, op. cit., p. 188.

9. This rule applied to all the *objets d'art* at Grosvenor Place and, after his death, it was given as an excuse by his son, the 2nd Earl of Iveagh, for not lending some of his father's valuable tapestries for a charity exhibition organized by Blanche, the widow of Lord Algernon Gordon-Lennox. Rupert Edward gave way only after the indefatigable Blanche induced the Queen to intervene on her behalf. See *The Diaries of Lieut.-Col. Sir Robert Bruce Lockhart* (Macmillan, 1973), p. 79.

10. For most of the material concerning Duleep Singh the author has drawn on Michael Alexander's authoritative biography, *Queen Victoria's Maharaja* (Weidenfeld & Nicolson, 1980).

11. Alexander, op. cit., p. 11.

12. Martelli, *The Elveden Enterprise*, p. 49.

Chapter 5

1. *The Recorder*, 3 April 1954.

2. Martelli, *The Elveden Enterprise*, p. 87.

Chapter 6

1. *Anatomy of Britain*, by Anthony Sampson (Hodder & Stoughton, 1962), p. 590.

2. *Time* magazine, 26 March 1951. In the same story readers were reminded of James Joyce's preferred version of the slogan, in *Finnegans Wake*: 'Genghis is ghoon for you'.

3. *The Deed*, by Gerold Frank (Simon & Schuster, 1963). This disgracefully romanticized version of the tragedy honours 'two boys who gave their lives for an idea'.

4. There was no exaggeration here. Churchill had long been a political supporter of Zionism.

Chapter 7

1. Now the Irish seat of the 2nd Lord Moyne, Bryan Walter Guinness.

2. Alex's father, Lord Odo Russell, was a brother of the 9th Duke of Bedford and an eminent ambassador during the latter part of the 19th century to the USA and Germany. Alex's mother, Lady Emily Villiers, was a daughter of the 4th Earl of Clarendon, and his brother, Oliver Arthur Villiers, a one-time Governor of Madras, had married Lady Margaret Lygon, the daughter of the 6th Earl of Beauchamp.

3. *The Rise of a Merchant Bank*, by Ivy F. Jones (A Guinness Mahon Publication, Dublin, 1974).

4. The famous advertising slogan, 'Guinness is good for you', finds its earthier Irish bar-room version in: 'A baby in every bottle'.

5. A barrister at 24, Robert went on to become High Sheriff of Warwickshire at 66 and died at the age of 79.

6. His nephew, the publisher Clarence Paget, recalls wandering into the library at Dorton House as a child and finding his uncle intent on his copy of Burke's Peerage. 'Two things worth living for,' the old man barked at him. 'Finance, and—' banging his fist on Burke's—'this!'

7. Weidenfeld & Nicolson, 1961, p. 117.

8. The great soprano, Dame Nellie Melba, after one trip in the car with Benjamin at the wheel, promptly named it 'The Yellow Peril'.

9. Prior to its discovery, the joke inside the family was that Benjamin died 'worth 135 francs', the precise sum found in his possession. Details of the worth of the estate were never disclosed, but estimates put it between 10 and 60 million pounds.

10. Franz von Fürstenberg subsequently remarried and is the father of actress Betsy von Fürstenberg.

11. *Diana Cooper*; collected volumes of her autobiography. Michael Russell (Publisher) Ltd, 1979.

12. Montagu was killed four years later in an RAF exercise over England during World War II.

Chapter 8

1. *The Times*, 22 September and 5 October 1921.

2. In 1946, Guinness Mahon Representation Co. Inc. was set up in New York and, on arrival in the city with Alfhild, the 58-year-old banker, asked

by reporters if this was a 'second honeymoon', retorted, 'Nonsense! We're still on our first!'

3. As Alfred Bossom he had found a place in the anthology of Churchillian quips when, on hearing the unfamiliar surname pronounced from a Conservative Party platform, Winston muttered to his neighbour: 'Bossom . . . *Bossom*? Why, that's neither one thing nor the other.'

4. Terence Mullaly, art critic of the *Daily Telegraph*, in his foreword to the catalogue for the March 1979 exhibition at the Roy Miles Gallery, London.

5. Creator of the private eye 'Philip Marlowe' and author of *The Big Sleep*, *Farewell My Lovely*, *The Lady in the Lake*, etc.

6. Twelve of his letters to Helga are included in the posthumous collection of his correspondence, *Raymond Chandler Speaking*, edited by Dorothy Gardiner and Katherine Walker (Houghton Mifflin Co., Boston, 1962). Extracts from others are incorporated in Frank MacShane's *The Life of Raymond Chandler* (E. P. Dutton & Co., 1976).

7. MacShane, op. cit., p. 251.

8. Ibid., p. 252.

9. Ibid., p. 261.

10. *Dead-Man's Fall* (The Bodley Head, 1980).

11. *The Rise of a Merchant Bank*, by Ivy F. Jones.

Chapter 9

1. *The Times*, 24 August 1956.

2. The youngest son of the 4th Baron Ampthill, whose great-uncle, Alex, married Marjorie Guinness.

3. *The Times* and the *Sun*, 8 November 1978.

Chapter 10

1. *Guinness's Brewery in the Irish Economy, 1759–1876*, pp. 107–108.

2. *Daniel O'Connell*, by Denis Gwynn (Cork University Press, 1947), p. 122.

3. According to his granddaughter Joy Guinness in her biography *Mrs Howard Taylor: Her Web of Time* (Lutterworth Press, 1949).

4. *For Such a Time As*, by Lucy Guinness (Victory Press, Evangelical Publishers Ltd, Eastbourne).

5. Hodder & Stoughton, 1882.

6. *Creation Centred in Christ*: in library of Royal Astronomical Society, London; the British Library (4425.cc.1); and Library of Congress (NG 0595119/20).

7. Published in 1754 under the title, *Remarques historiques, chronologiques et astronomiques sur quelques endroits du livre de Daniel* (British Library, Shelfmark 8561 e.24).

8. Volumes all published by Hodder & Stoughton, London.

9. Marshall Brothers, London, 1907.

10. Fifty-eight members of the China Inland Mission lost their lives in the uprising.

11. Published by the China Inland Mission, 1930.

12. Vol. One: *Hudson Taylor in Early Years—The Growth of a Soul* (CIM, 1911); subsequent editions of this 500-page volume ran into 23,250 copies by 1925. Vol. Two: *Hudson Taylor and the China Inland Mission—The Growth of a Work of God* (CIM, 1918); subsequent reprints reached 23,000 copies by 1927.
13. Joy Guinness, op. cit., pp. 250–51.

Chapter 11

1. Sir Benjamin Lee was made a baronet in 1867; Sir Reginald Robert was knighted in 1907.
2. *The Life of Raymond Chandler*, p. 260.

Chapter 12

1. At the age of 24, he became the first man to reach an official speed of two miles a minute, at Saltburn.
2. No. 17 is now the embassy of the Irish Republic. Holmbury, an ugly grey stone edifice commanding a superb view of the Surrey Downs, now houses the Mullard Space Science Laboratory of University College, London. Glenmaroon has become a home for retarded Irish children.
3. *The Paris Embassy*, by Lady Cynthia Gladwyn (Collins, 1976), p. 139.
4. Constable, 1937.

Chapter 13

1. *Helen's Tower*, p. 141.
2. He appeared in the title role of his most famous play *Grumpy* 1,300 times in Australia, Canada, New York and London.
3. The hotel changed ownership in 1977.
4. *Chips: The Diaries of Sir Henry Channon*, edited by Robert Rhodes James (Weidenfeld & Nicolson, 1967), p. 4 of editor's Introduction.
5. Ibid., p. 42.
6. Harold Nicolson, *Diaries and Letters, 1930–39*, ed. Nigel Nicolson (Collins, 1966).
7. *The Channon Diaries*, p. 59.
8. Ibid., p. 81.
9. Ibid., pp. 122, 123.
10. Ibid.
11. Ibid., p. 126.
12. Ibid., p. 38.
13. Ibid., p. 114.
14. Ibid., p. 106.
15. Ibid., p. 147.
16. Ibid., p. 148.
17. Ibid., p. 147.
18. Ibid., pp. 147, 148.
19. Ibid., p. 140.
20. 'Little Willie', as he was derisively dubbed during World War I by

Allied cartoonists, had been put under house arrest after the defeat of the
Nazis. He was released after giving evidence for the prosecution at the
Nuremberg Trials and lived thereafter in seclusion in the family seat at
Hechingen, near Stuttgart.

Chapter 14

1. Duckworth, 1974.
2. Jan Marsh, *Daily Telegraph*, 14 March 1974.
3. *American Aristocracy: The Lives and Times of James Russell, Amy and Robert Lowell*, by C. David Heymann (Dodd, Mead & Co., New York, 1980).
4. Farrar, Straus & Giroux, New York, and Faber & Faber, London, 1973.
5. Heymann, op. cit., p. 490.
6. The first such union had occurred nearly a century earlier; the second in 1887.
7. *Harper's*.

Chapter 15

1. *My Life* (Thos. Nelson & Sons), p. 363.
2. *A Portrait of Dublin* (Batsford, 1967).

Chapter 16

1. This despite the revelation in 1979 by the US Food and Drug Administration that only two beers out of a list of 30 different brands on the American market were free of all traces of nitrosamines, suspected of being a cancer-causing agent. These were Coors, made in Colorado, and Guinness.

Chapter 17

1. Quotations from an article by Sally Brompton in the *Daily Mail*, 6 May 1978.
2. *Daily Mail*, 25 April 1968.

Appendix

1. *Irish Pedigrees* and *The Guinness Family* respectively.
2. *The Guinness Family*. A pedigree compiled by Henry Seymour Guinness and Brian Guinness, 1953, and available from Arthur Guinness Son & Co. Ltd.
3. Ibid., p. 20.

Index

COLLINS